The New Rules

INTERNET DATING, PLAYFAIRS
AND EROTIC POWER

Catherine Hakim

GIBSON SQUARE

First published by Gibson Square

info@gibsonsquare.com
www.gibsonsquare.com
Tel: +44 (0)20 7096 1100 (UK)
Tel: +1 646 216 9813 (USA)
Tel: +353 (0)1 657 1057 (Eire)

ISBN 9 7 8 1 9 0 6 1 4 2 7 0 4

The moral right of Catherine Hakim to be identified as the author of this work has been asserted in accordance with the Copyright, Designs and Patents Act 1988.

Contents

Foreword

Facebook, other social networking sites, internet dating websites – they have all changed the way we look at people, profiles, relationships. Websites for married dating are one element in the wider trend. If the pill made pre-marital sex among young people a lot easier, the internet facilitates playfairs among older married people.

I expected people on these websites to be more French in their attitudes, more Mediterranean, or at least European. And so it proved. As more people travel abroad on holiday or for business, English people are adopting more cosmopolitan lifestyles. There is a learning curve of course. Women are surprised by the freedom.

In the Anglo-Saxon world divorce is often the knee-jerk response to affairs, if discovered. This leads to serial monogamy. In France and many other Mediterranean countries, affairs are simply ignored: playfairs, these dalliances are too ephemeral and fugitive to count for much. Marriages are, as a consequence, longer-lasting in these countries.

I know too many people who got divorced, hastily, for all the wrong reasons. Typically, because one of them had a fling with someone they knew, or just a fling with a stranger on a business trip, and the other party bridles up in rage and walks out of the relationship. From the French perspective, this is insane. You choose your spouse for lots of good reasons, and invest years in developing a life together. How can one small night cancel out such a huge mountain of good experiences?

I have known Michael and Suzanne ever since we were all at university together. He is tall, dark and handsome, and immensely successful in the City. She is vivacious, attractive, warm, and has a good academic job. One day, she turns up in tears, enraged at coming across evidence that suggests her husband might be having an affair with someone he met in one of the cities where he stayed regularly on business trips. She wants to throw him out, get a divorce, her life is in ruins. After she has calmed down, I suggest the best way of dealing with it is simply to let it go. Affairs blow over, never last long, it will end of its own accord, I say. Again she is enraged. 'How can you make light of something so serious?' 'But how can you throw away a good marriage just when you have had a new baby?', I counter. Eventually, a bigger picture emerges. Suzanne pretty well lost interest in Michael after the baby was born. Her baby was so beautiful, smiling, calm and easy, perfect in every way. He was a loving child, and she basked in the unconditional adoration of an infant who knows only its mother. The baby was soft, sensual, tactile, even erotic. She had fallen in love in an entirely new way. She needed no-one else, and was lucky enough to have a full year's maternity leave to fully enjoy the new relationship. Suzanne began to see that she had unwittingly played a part in Michael's dalliance. 'Be nice to him, instead of nasty', I suggested. 'Let him share the baby with you. He will fall in love with it too, if you allow him in. He needs to feel welcome when he comes home, not an intruder on a private love affair.' Reluctantly, Suzanne agreed to try my strategy, and to ignore the evidence of his affair, which was equivocal anyway. To her surprise, Michael responded with visible delight, overjoyed at being offered his place, a role as father and husband again.

All went well for some years. Then Michael invited me to lunch at a swanky City restaurant. After chatting about nothing in particular for a while, he said he knew Suzanne was having an affair with a student, a boy of 21, a child, a nobody. The insult was intolerable. He would leave her, despite the adorable son and daughter. He was not wanted at home anyway, he now realised. It was only his money that mattered. 'Don't be silly', I said, 'she is not serious about the boy. She believes you had an affair with someone much younger years ago, and this is her tit-for-tat affair. Suzanne needs to prove to herself that she can do it just as well as you could, that she too is attractive and desirable. It is a way of rebalancing things psychologically, because she feels so dependent on you. She will soon get bored with the boy, in fact this has already started. The way to deal with it is to let it go.' 'How can you trivialise her infidelity', Michael insisted, 'after all I have done for my family'. 'That is the point', I respond. 'You are the rock on which the family rests. Suzanne knows this, which was why she was so distraught when she knew you were having an affair.' And so he calmed down, they stayed together, and are very happy they did so. Years later they do not really recall those emotionally turbulent times.

In contrast, my friend Amanda was determined to divorce her husband when he came home one day and confessed to a fling with a beautiful girl within their circle of friends. They were both young at the time, had no children, and she felt she wanted to start again with someone she could trust. The insult was too great to bear. She had married her first ever boyfriend and childhood sweetheart, so they had been together for ten years and not just the two years of marriage. Hours of persuasion, to think again, to not throw everything away for a one-off incident, had no effect. The divorce was speedy and uncontested. Amanda moved to another city, made a fresh start, dated loads of men, but has never remarried, and never had the children she so desperately wanted. She is attractive, well-dressed, intelligent, and professionally successful. But somehow she never shook off her bitterness over the infidelity, became far more cautious of men, developed a rigid and unbending self-righteousness that could be discouraging even for friends. She was unable to forgive and forget, which is crucial in sustaining any long-term relationship. Needless to say, her husband remarried within a few years, had a big family, and is very happy.

From my French perspective, Amanda's response to a single incident seems worse than excessive. Using a sledge-hammer to crack a nut destroyed everything. The unforgiving Puritan Anglo-Saxon response to affairs results in a much higher incidence of divorce, with all the misery and trauma that entails – for partners and for any children. Men find it much easier to remarry than women, especially if the wife retains responsibility for any children. I know lots of attractive divorced women who never remarried, as they assumed they would. The French perspective on affairs is more philosophical, more tolerant. They are not actively recommended, but they are not prohibited either. They are accepted as something that may happen in a long-term marriage, precisely because it is a long-term relationship, with patches of boredom or friction. As Suzanne's story shows, there is usually something that prompts an affair, even if it is not immediately obvious to outsiders, and is not necessarily a sign of problems in the relationship.

I am not sure where I picked up the relaxed French

approach to affairs. Maybe from reading too many novels by Colette. Certainly not from my French education. We were taught to admire Napoleon as the first true European. But the teachers had nothing to say about love, sex, marriage or affairs. But we became aware of the ubiquity of official mistresses as well as official wives in the French courts. Madame de Pompadour was the favourite, as she seemed so lively - and she had fabulous dresses! Mistresses and lovers were obviously a luxury, one of life's greatest pleasures, but maybe a necessity for kings and princes whose daily lives were controlled by protocol, formality and obligations. I have always been baffled by the sour and rigid English view of affairs. An existentialist, hedonistic, laissez-faire attitude seems to work better, in practice. None of us are perfect, so there is little point in demanding perfection from others. Another way of looking at such problems comes from an odd source. The message in the Ministry of War propaganda poster from the Second World War (that can still be bought from the Victoria and Albert Museum in London) is Keep calm and carry on – on a blood red background.

1

Introduction

Hello again! I was on this website three years ago, and met a wonderful lady, with many happy times together. Sadly, she is off to Australia now, so I am back again. I thought I would get her to write me a reference, so here she is: 'This is a crazy thing to do! But John is a lovely man, and I am off to Melbourne with my family, so I hope he meets someone who will take good care of him! John is kind and cuddly, funny and warm, considerate and sensitive – and he is very sexy too! We had great times together over the last three years. If he were to come to Melbourne, I would be tempted to lock him up and throw away the key! But he stays in England, so I hope he gets lucky again, and meets someone nice!' If that persuades you I am worth trying, write to GreatGuy.

A successful affair while married is one that makes both parties happier than they would otherwise be, but has no negative consequences for the two families, and does not of itself prompt any divorces – as illustrated by the experience of GreatGuy. It requires some skill and *savoire faire.*

Romantic affairs break the rules, yet have their own conventions. They are full of surprises, yet follow predictable paths. They occur throughout history and are found in all cultures (and apparently occur also among some birds and animals), but each culture provides a distinctive frame and style for affairs. Affairs and their consequences provide the central plots of countless novels. The sexual passions and dreams they provoke inspire poems and erotic paintings across the centuries. Despite the guidance of the *Kama Sutra*, and the unique testimony of the Taj Mahal, marital love and passion only rarely provide an equally rich source of the exalted feelings, transports of delight and misery that we commonly associate with the ideas of love and romance. Affairs are about excitement, being alive, seduction, flirtation, love, affection, sexual bliss, lust, caution, eroticism, fantasy, recreation, games, imagination, role-playing, risk, danger, adventure, exploration, reinventing yourself, re-discovering the world, friendship, tea and sympathy, the expression of individuality, and the determined refusal to grow older gracefully.

However this perspective – based on the experience of those who have affairs – is typically French and uncommon in Puritan cultures. In puritanical Anglo-Saxon countries, such as the United States and Britain, affairs are typically classified as taboo, illicit, and wrong. This puritanical classification is not universal. On the contrary, many cultures regard affairs (including casual sexual 'flings') as an exciting luxury, wonderful if you can afford them, in time and money, and have the seduction skills to initiate them. The kept mistress, the concubine, is an indicator of wealth and status, not something to be ashamed of, even if good manners require a degree of discretion. The alternatives are serial monogamy, as practiced in Java and North America, or polygamy, as practiced in parts of Africa and some Moslem societies, or frequenting brothels, prostitutes and courtesans in all their guises across the globe, including modern call girls and escort girls, and the male equivalents.

In the upper classes and aristocracy, marriages were generally arranged with close regard to property, finances, and social status, while the mistress and lover were chosen on other grounds. For kings, whose wives were chosen for political reasons from other countries, and who might well be younger or older, the official mistress was the chosen consort and confidante, usually from his own country and class, someone with whom he could relax and be a private person, separate from the public, role-playing job of monarch. The mistresses of the French kings often became famous national figures in their own right, patrons of the arts and culture, sometimes politically involved and influential, in much the same way as queens – as illustrated most famously by Madame de Pompadour. As is often remarked, the British admire ruling queens, whereas in France they celebrate the royal mistresses, who were French.

Affairs (like sex itself) get a negative press in Anglo-Saxon countries, where they are discussed in pejorative terms such as 'infidelity', 'adultery', 'cheating', and 'dishonesty'. It is an approach to relationships that turns marriage into a prison, by insisting that marriage entails absolute sexual fidelity. One consequence is high divorce rates, and serial monogamy across life. For over three decades, about half of all first marriages in the USA have ended in divorce.[1] Britain follows closely, with one-third of first marriages ending in divorce.

In the southern European view, marriage is a more flexible relationship – it is essentially about children, property and inheritance, so marriage is for life, pretty much; but where necessary both spouses find friends and lovers outside the marriage. It is divorce that is frowned on, and much less common. French and Italian marriages end in divorce less often than almost anywhere else in the Western world.[2] There is no assumption that spouses must fulfil all of each other's needs, all of the time, exclusively. Affairs and *petites aventures* outside marriage may be agreed, ignored or exceptional, but are generally conducted with great discretion, with consideration for the dignity of the spouse who must never be embarrassed in any way. In the hedonistic or libertine perspective, affairs are tolerated, with everyone turning a blind eye to them, so long as they are properly discreet. The French President Mitterand had a long-standing relationship with Anne Pingeot, a mistress who was effectively a second wife, and who brought up their daughter outside the glare of his formal Presidential duties. The French press only commented openly on the relationship after Mitterand ceased to be President, and after his death. A key factor is that French law, and the media, draw a sharp distinction between public and private lives.[3]

These contrasting perspectives are displayed in responses to recent national interview surveys. Extramarital affairs are pretty universally condemned as wrong by over 90% of Americans and over 80% of the British, consistently in all social groups, with the proportion slowly rising over time.[4] Even among the tolerant Dutch, public opinion also swung against affairs between 1970 and 1997, almost certainly due to fears about AIDS.[5] In Britain and the USA, around four in five men and women insist that sexual affairs harm a marriage. At the same time two in three British people reject the idea that sex is the most important part of any marriage or relationship, and two in five hold inconsistent views on the subject of sexual fidelity. In other words, around two in five men and women in Britain have vacillating or inconsistent views, and one in five men and women tolerate affairs.

Southern European attitudes are significantly more permissive. Less than half of Italians, two in five, regard affairs as unacceptable (although people are a bit more disapproving for wives than for husbands). Most Italians, men and women, explain and excuse affairs in various ways, seeing them as something that can happen to everyone, sooner or later, a private choice which has to be respected, perhaps not a good idea but unfortunately inevitable. A tiny minority of one in 25 (4%) even regard them as beneficial and desirable. The most highly educated, and younger people, are most tolerant of affairs. This permissive culture helps explain why affairs are not unusual in Italy: one in four men and one in eight women admit to one or more, with graduates and older people most likely to have indulged at some point. For women, the most common reasons given are falling in love, their partner's lack of affection towards them, a general dissatisfaction with life, or a tit-for-tat revenge affair. Italian men typically seek affairs to escape routine, for novelty, variety, change, excitement, the risk involved, and because they are not sexually satisfied at home; but one in five also fall in love.[6]

In Spain, half of all men with a spouse or partner admit to being unfaithful, and so do one-quarter of wives. One in ten couples know they have both had affairs. It appears that husbands generally know when their partners have been unfaithful, whereas only a minority of wives are aware of their partner's infidelity. One-quarter of Spaniards do not regard sexual fidelity as fundamentally important. Half point out that social conditions in modern society do not encourage fidelity, and few regard religion as the barrier it used to be. A four-fifths majority of Spaniards say the main prophylactic to infidelity is a good relationship with their partner, and for many it is only the fear of being found out that prevents them playing away from home. This laissez-faire attitude to sex is probably linked to greater openness about commercial sex in Spain. It is indicative that sex surveys ask about prostitution, whereas most countries are reluctant to address the topic. Over one in four of Spanish men have paid for sex at least once, or do so regularly, compared to only one in a hundred women. Around one in four regard people who sell sex as doing a job, just like any other.[7] The prurient attitude that dominates British attitudes is absent in Spain.

The French have even more permissive views on affairs and casual flings, which are taken for granted as something that happen throughout life, if you are lucky.[8] Surveys show that two in three of Frenchmen and half of French women believe that sexual attraction inevitably leads to intimacy; two-third of men and one-third of women agree that sex and love are separate; two-fifths of the French think love does not require complete sexual fidelity; and one-quarter even believe that transitory infidelities can strengthen love. So the French are five times more likely than the Italians to see flings and affairs as beneficial, overall. Perhaps most importantly, French people perceive their social environment as tolerant and permissive, so that they can rely on tacit (or even active) support for any affairs. Three in four of the French believe some or all of the close friends in whom they confide would favour extramarital flings and affairs: they would not seek to dissuade anyone. Surveys suggest that something like one-quarter of men and women are enjoying casual flings and affairs at any one time. Mossuz-Lavau's account of sexual lifestyles in France automatically has a chapter on affairs, noting that alongside those (possibly the majority) who choose fidelity there is a substantial minority that take *aventures* and *vagabondage* for granted, as the following story illustrates.

Michel, a factory worker, explains how a chance event overturned his assumption of fidelity in marriage. One beautiful spring Sunday he and his family were out walking round the local fair, his wife and son in front, he and the child's uncle behind. The uncle remarked to Michel that they were being followed by a pretty young woman with a child in a pushchair. After a while he concluded ruefully that she was following Michel, not himself. The family went into a bistro. Intrigued, Michel popped out to ask the girl with the pushchair if they knew each other from somewhere? No, she replied, but I would like to know you. She invited him to her home, close by. Give me half an hour, said Michel. He returned to the bistro, and soon found an excuse to absent himself for an hour or two. Leaving his family in the bistro, he found the girl's home, and had an intense and passionate sexual encounter. So much so, that he was determined to see the girl again. But she had already lost interest in him, being excited by change and novelty, and refused to see him again.[9]

Despite the moral condemnation of affairs in Puritanical countries, affairs still happen, possibly just as often as elsewhere.[10] Kinsey's surveys in the USA found that half of all men and one-quarter of women had extra-marital sex at least once in their lives. A later review of the evidence concluded that about half of adults had some extramarital experience in the 1970s, rising to 65% in the 1980s. These high figures are reinforced by an American study showing that interviewing people in depth doubled admissions of affairs, from 30% to 60%.[11] Surveys in Britain find one in fifty wives and one in twenty husbands of all ages admit having two or more sexual partners concurrently in the previous year. Of those with two or more sexual partners in the last five years, two-thirds of men and half of women have had a casual fling. Among people married for at least five years, one in ten men and one in twenty women admit having had an affair.[12] In both the USA and Britain, and across all age groups from 18 to 60 years, one in fifty women (2%) and one in twenty men (5%) had an affair within the last year.[13]

The peak ages for affairs in the United States, Britain and Finland are 45 for women and 55 for men, although there appears to be a small subgroup of people who have affairs throughout their lives. In all countries and cultures, highly educated people, those in more prosperous social strata, high income groups, and people living in cities have the most permissive views about affairs, with experiences to match. All surveys find that men report affairs at least twice as often as women.[14]

The puritanical hang-ups that distort and constrain sexual attitudes in Anglo-Saxon cultures are absent in many countries of the Far East, such as Japan.[15] Sex is regarded as a pleasure to be enjoyed fully, without guilt or shame, and courtship rituals are less fraught. Japanese pornography is consumed openly, by women as well as men, on the metro and in other public places. Traditionally in Japan reproductive and recreational sex were kept separate in the upper classes and aristocracy – marriages were arranged, but lovers could be chosen personally. Pillow books and diaries record the affairs conducted discreetly in princely courts and palaces around the country, and romantic liaisons were reflected in art and poetry traditions. Even today, it is conventional for politicians and wealthy men to have mistresses and enjoy the company of hostesses, geishas and courtesans. Hostess bars are perhaps better known than the equivalent bars offering toy boy companions for wealthy women, but both types exist. Here too, discretion and maintaining public face are of paramount importance, so that most Japanese publicly decry affairs, and deny that they ever happen. But the 'love hotels' of big cities and country spa inns are used by married people and their lovers as much as by courting single couples seeking privacy.

China has a very different sexual culture. Among men and women, sexual experience is limited almost exclusively to their spouse – just one partner. Reports of sexual activity tend to conform to social norms, discussion of alternative sexual positions is taboo, and divorce is traditionally abhorred. Yet even in this constrained and conformist sexual culture, affairs are accepted. Around half of all couples, in cities and in rural areas, regard affairs as understandable, especially when there is marital disharmony, or not meriting any interference. Around half of couples regard affairs as 'not glorious' or even reject them as 'sinful'. About one in ten marriages are celibate in the broad sense of sexual intercourse having ceased completely (for one year or more) or being rare (less than 12 times a year). One in ten husbands and one in twenty wives admit to having had at least one affair. Prostitution is a crime in China, and was effectively eliminated, so this has only recently become an additional (risky) option for men. The high level of tolerance for affairs (around 50%) suggests that their incidence may be much higher than is indicated by only 5% of wives and 12% of husbands admitting to any affair.[16]

Finally there is the even more permissive sexual culture of the Nordic countries. Studies of sexual lifestyles by Elina Haavio-Mannila and others routinely discuss 'parallel relationships' rather than affairs.[17] These include affairs between work colleagues lasting thirteen years as well as the more common pattern of flings during holidays and trips away, and lovers in other towns visited regularly on business trips. The underlying rules focus again on discretion, so that spouses are never embarrassed. But complicity and mutual tolerance between spouses and partners appear to be far more common than elsewhere in Europe, especially in the younger generations, to the point that someone who only has occasional sexual flings (during trips away, for example) is classified as fully monogamous. As early as the 1960s, one-quarter of Swedes thought occasional acts of infidelity should be overlooked by spouses, and one in ten thought affairs were acceptable, especially if they were concealed from the spouse. Almost half of Finnish men and almost one-third of Finnish women have had at least one significant parallel relationship (as well as any number of flings, which don't appear to be counted as significant). In Sweden, the proportions are two in five for men and one in five for women. Figures are even higher for people in Estonia and St Petersburg in Russia. The usual comment is that after the pill, and other reliable forms of contraception, broke the link between sex and pregnancy, there is no longer any practical need for monogamy and exclusivity in the 'contraceptive society'. Sexual fidelity becomes a personal choice rather than an imposition and an obligation. Many married people choose discreet parallel relationships instead. The advent of DNA testing reinforces the trend, as paternity can now be established where there is any doubt about who is the father of a child.

Globalisation now brings all these sexual cultures into closer view, so that we can no longer assume our own perspective is the only one going, that it is inevitable and 'natural'. Sexual cultures vary across the world, and even within Europe. In multi-cultural and multi-ethnic societies, we all have to learn to be tolerant of other cultures and ways of living.

The unfair, asymmetric affair

One good reason for the negative image of the extra-marital affair is that it often involves a successful and prosperous married man enjoying a relationship 'on the side' with an unmarried woman, who is typically younger, attractive, and poorer. Even if there is no disparity between the lovers in age, wealth and social status, the mere fact of the man being married while she is not makes the relationship unbalanced, asymmetrical, potentially unfair. He enjoys the emotional security, social support and physical comforts of marriage, while she does not. Almost invariably, the young woman's aim is to become his replacement wife, but the conventions of marriage and serial monogamy dictate that it is down to him to invite her to marry him and get divorced from his current wife. Such affairs often involve the young woman providing the venue for lovers' trysts in her own home, thus encouraging her to fantasise about a permanent relationship, and to display her domestic skills in order to encourage her lover to see her as a competent replacement wife. Sometimes, the man ends up enjoying two parallel homes with two parallel partners, and in some cases the *de facto* bigamy continues for decades.

The asymmetric affair is open to the criticism of male exploitation of younger women,[18] especially as the received wisdom is that men do not marry their mistresses, and those that do, thereby create a vacancy.[19] In the past, the mistress would be never-married; today, she is more likely to be divorced or separated. The opposite arrangement, with an older, wealthy, married woman attracting a younger, attractive, poorer unmarried lover, has been rare in most societies. It seems to be on the rise, as indicated by the notion of 'toy boy' lovers for older women, as illustrated by Madonna's long string of handsome younger lovers. These relationships seem to be just as tricky as those between married men and unmarried women, due to differences in wealth and status. Differences in age can matter because there are so many cultural and lifestyle differences between age groups. Occasionally, a *ménage à trois* works so smoothly that outsiders never notice it. The actress Tilda Swinton, star of *Orlando*, lives happily with her long-term partner, 68-year-old John Byrne, the father of her children, but is usually accompanied by her younger lover, 31-year-old artist Sandro Kopp, when she travels. Reportedly, all parties are happy with the arrangement. John Byrne has also had a younger lover for some time, 43-year-old Jeanine Davies, so it is perhaps a more balanced 'open marriage'.

It is often forgotten that the glamorous mistresses of the French kings were generally married women. If they were single when they first caught the king's eye, they would normally be married off to someone suitable fairly promptly.

A royal mistress who was repudiated for any reason thus had a good home to go to; she was never totally at the mercy of royal whims, and was provided for in her 'retirement'. In contrast, the pretty secretary who has an affair with her boss has no safety-net, and might even lose her job if and when the affair comes to an end, and her presence becomes embarrassing. Women's liberation and gender equality ideology have made the position of a younger and poorer mistress even *less* secure and attractive than it was in the past. Men can now pretend that because women and men meet as social equals, lovers should share the costs of an affair, and women should not seek to 'take advantage of' a married lover by expecting gifts or financial support.

Sarah Symonds' book *Having An Affair*, and her linked website *Pillow Talk*, give some notion of the misery caused by the asymmetrical affair, especially those where the never-married woman has fallen in love with a wealthy married man and is convinced that he will dump his wife and children in order to make a new life with her instead. The book describes the mistress' jealousy of the man's wife and the financial security and comfortable lifestyle she enjoys; her resentment at her married lover's freedom to enjoy the best of both worlds; the anxieties, frustration, despair, misery, and anger experienced by a woman in this situation. These feelings are usually concealed, because the unmarried mistress does everything she can to be an attractive, sexy, cheerful alternative partner at all times, in order to persuade her married lover that she is the more attractive option for him. If their lovers' trysts take place in her home, she will endeavour to present herself as a domestic goddess as well, serving elegant candlelit dinners in congenial surroundings as well as being the sexy mistress in beautiful lingerie. Symonds emphasises that there is no point in dating, marrying or being a mistress to a poor man, and she takes it for granted that there must be financial benefits for the mistress, in the shape of wonderful gifts, foreign travel, dining out at expensive restaurants, and periodic financial help for her basic expenses. In effect, she argues that compensating benefits are essential to balance out the inherent unfairness of an asymmetrical affair. The counterpart to the distressed and disappointed mistress is the distressed wife who discovers her husband has been 'playing away' despite the fact that he claims to love her, still.

This book should help wives understand why and how affairs start, and end. Here, the focus is on what might be called the symmetrical or 'balanced' affair, where both parties are married, and intend to stay married. Both parties have the usual comforts and security of a happy home life, and both have just as much to lose from any careless indiscretion. However there is no sharp dividing line between the two types of affair. Most people's first affair is with someone in their workplace, or someone they meet through their job – as illustrated by the married man who has an affair with his PA or a colleague. It is usually at a later stage that people move on to using websites where things are more evenly balanced.

Roadmap of the affair in the 21st century

It is said that sex, in one shape or another, constitutes over half the traffic on the internet. Our focus is ordinary hetero-sexual dating that is similar to singles dating except that it involves people already married or 'attached', apart from a few who are ex-married or cohabiting, as we shall see.

However these websites are not easily distinguished from the myriad of similar sites in an internet search. Married dating websites can be confused with the multitude of others specialising in purely sexual hook-ups, swinging, cyber-sex and cyber flirting, second life fantasies, and those catering to a wide variety of specialist sexual tastes and interests.

This book presents the accounts of men and women who decided, at some point in their life, to take a walk on the wild side. Names and identifying details have of course been changed to ensure anonymity, and some stories are 'composites' combining two or three very similar experiences into a single account. Any likeness in terms of names or personal circumstances to any individual is entirely accidental and unintentional. Most of the voices are of people using websites for married dating, but some offer accounts of affairs started through other avenues, including workplace meetings and adverts placed in the 'Personal' listings in newspapers. Some are first-timers; others are experienced libertines with a long history of affairs. Of course, every affair is unique. The aim here is to identify the highs and lows, common features, recurring patterns, salient turning points, unanticipated features of the websites and the people using them - a travel guide, or roadmap of the affair in the 21st century through the voices of players in this hidden parallel world.

There are dozens of guidebooks advising on the dos and don'ts of singles dating, on how to be successful with women, or how to be attractive to men.[20] One of the most famous is Ellen Fein and Sherrie Schneider's book *The Rules*, which advises women on how to capture the heart of a man who wants to marry you. There are also websites, especially in the USA, dedicated to dating and match-making for non-married people, and parallel websites offering reviews of website services, guidance on how to use them, and the dangers to avoid. By contrast, almost nothing is known about the impact of the new secretive world of married dating through the internet.

In some respects, it is no different from ordinary dating. Many men, in fact, assume it is exactly the same as singles dating. But as the following chapters show, there are fundamental differences between singles and married dating which can totally change the rules of the game. The rules for married dating and affairs are substantially different from those for singles dating, where the ultimate aim remains finding a permanent partner.

Some Europeans may question the need for this account. After all, the art of seduction and having affairs are so much part of continental European culture that all sophisticated and urbane men and women know how to proceed. It is no accident that the French have produced some of the most important novels about affairs, notably Colette's numerous stories. Novels and operas recount the amorous exploits of Don Juan. In *Les Liaisons Dangereuses*, Choderlos de Laclos demonstrates how even the most virtuous wife can finally be seduced by a libertine. Through the internet, Puritan Anglo-American culture is finally playing catch up with the seduction skills and experience of lovers in continental Europe.

On the other hand, new technology introduces one fundamental change into the traditional world of romance and affairs. In the past, seduction was limited to people within one's own social circle and neighbourhood. You were never anonymous, or an unknown entity, and the risks of exposure and, more importantly, repercussions in a Puritanical culture were high.

The internet changes this, allowing everyone to meet people well beyond their own social circle, far beyond their own neighbourhood or workplace community. Anyone can meet anyone, quite literally. It is this unpredictable social diversity that leads some people to regard internet dating as 'unsafe' or 'dangerous', because it involves moving outside your comfort zone. There is less social predictability, there are no fixed boundaries, no gatekeepers to exclude 'undesirables' since that is entirely a matter for each individual to decide. One complaint about singles dating websites and newspaper personal adverts is that they are used by married men pretending to be single and looking for a girlfriend, thus seducing single women for purely sexual purposes. In married dating this complaint is obviously not important. Nonetheless, on the internet, people can reinvent themselves, or be economical with the truth, more easily than in face-to-face situations. Anyone can pretend to be anybody.

Thus the internet has revolutionised dating and hook-ups. Even in cities, where there are plenty of opportunities for meeting people, thousands still use dating websites. Thousands of people see each other daily, on buses and trains, but never manage to break the ice and talk to each other, no matter how much they are mutually attracted at first sight. In areas where car travel dominates, meeting strangers can be even more difficult. Flirting in the workplace is now constrained by worries about sexual harassment in Anglo-American culture. Websites on the internet provide a new avenue for meeting like-minded people, whatever the common interest, from conventional aims like flat-sharing, friendship, casual dating to long-term partnerships. Agencies and websites specialise in hook-ups for country-lovers, pet-lovers, music-lovers, wine-lovers, vegans, people who are HIV-positive, the disabled, nudists, political activists, Jews, committed Christians, Moslems, Buddhists, Hindus and Sikhs. Some websites specialise in introducing potential brides from Russia, Thailand, and other Far Eastern countries. There are websites for 'gold-diggers' that facilitate hook-ups between wealthy men and young and beautiful women who expect to be paid a retainer for their time and friendship. In this revolution fit the websites that facilitate hook-ups between married men and married women.

Romance versus sex

So how does the art of seduction work in this context? For some people, romance suffices. Dates with someone special light up the week, especially if you can share an interest in music, opera, theatre, films, food and wine, sport, travel, or any other leisure activity not shared with a spouse. For men who visit other cities regularly on business, having a girlfriend to go out with in the evenings can be hugely attractive – dinner alone is never as pleasant as with a companion. Most people hope to meet someone they like well enough for physical intimacy to be in prospect.

Married-dating websites are sometimes confused with websites for purely sexual hook-ups (including casual sex), especially as some men and women use both simultaneously without differentiation. Websites that focus on purely sexual encounters often advertise their services with photos that seem to belong to a call-girl agency. The distinction between the two can be obscured by the language used: 'quality time' can mean very different things in diverse contexts. A taste for the 'finer things in life' can be equivocal. Websites concerned with purely sexual hook-ups seek to glamorise their activities so as to attract the widest possible interest from women, who are always in short supply. (Specialist websites for swingers are generally more straightforwardly about sex as they are aimed at couples acting together.) Some websites seem to straddle the space between sexual hook-ups and conventional romance-oriented dating, trying to have it both ways. Many men do not notice any confusion or ambiguity, because sex remains the central objective for them, whichever route they take, whatever the packaging.

Websites for exclusively sexual hook-ups attract vast numbers of married men looking for extra sex, more varied sex, or more arcane varieties of sex games. They are also used by single men and women who simply want to enjoy more sex than they are getting already without any obligation to maintain an ongoing social relationship with sexual partners. The emphasis in these websites is on sexual performance and variety. It is common for the first meeting to lead fairly directly and swiftly to a sexual encounter if the parties find each other acceptable – there is little or no social element in meetings. People on these websites feel free to specify particular sexual tastes and interests. Users of these singles websites who switch over to ordinary dating websites for married people (where the sex ratio is more favourable for men), can be extraordinarily blunt in their demands for sexual encounters.

Realising the fantasy

All affairs involve some element of imagination, fantasy, creating something that did not exist, exploring new avenues. The focus here is on fantasies made real, people who actually meet and develop affairs in real life – social, emotional, sexual, and whatever else appeals.

Inevitably, there are overlaps with virtual dating, cyber-sex and virtual affairs on the internet. Second Life and other websites allow people to invent avatars who lead an imaginary life in virtual reality. Quite often, the avatars have affairs. In some cases these virtual reality relationships become real enough to impinge on real-life relationships and lives. Inevitably, some of the people who decide to subscribe to dating websites discover that they are content with the fantasy, the secret friend, the confidante, the lover who is unattainable because there is no practical possibility of ever meeting. Starting in the United States, there are global websites specialising in virtual reality affairs, and books by Monica Whitty and others explore the experiences of the players, cyber-flirting and cyber-affairs. The most obvious problem here is that people can completely re-invent themselves, to the point where there is little or no correspondence between the website persona and mundane reality – as players discover if they ever make the mistake of meeting off-line.

The outer edge

We look at genuine affairs in real life, but of a fairly mundane variety – involving what some call 'vanilla' sex and 'normal' social relationships. At the other extreme from imaginary virtual affairs, there are a host of clubs, websites and magazines facilitating every conceivable variety of sexual adventure and relationship. Occasionally, players from these other 'scenes' stray onto the websites for married dating. A few insist on remaining on them, contrary to expectation, for reasons of their own – possibly seeking new recruits to their scene. In the following chapters we see how these visitors from the outer edge impinge on the dating and mating process.

The diverse sexual activities covered by the 'swingers' label are well described in Mark Brandon's book *Swinging*, but essentially the focus is on sex in and for itself. Married couples normally participate together with other couples, but single men and women sometimes join larger group sex house parties. Some swingers use married dating websites to attract partners for sexual threesomes in their own home, or for swinging house parties. For swinging couples (or individuals) the focus is on 'no-strings' recreational sex with like-minded couples – the idea being that both partners get sexual variety, and because it is all in the open, no-one gets jealous or hurt.

Kinky sex, including fetishwear and BDSM (bondage, domination, sadism and masochism) are the other main sexual communities that overlap slightly with married dating, at the margins. Mostly, players patronise specialist clubs with public displays, where styles of clothing are important.[21] Small numbers of people on married dating websites have tastes leaning in that direction, without being so pronounced or definite that they move over to specialist websites and clubs. There are hints in some profile descriptions or in attached photos. For example Grenadier's profile consists only of the following enigmatic description: 'Sensitive but strong, kind but firm'. Another man posts a fairly routine profile description, but then attaches a bondage photo of a naked woman. Possibly, he just likes the erotic photo.

Magazines such as *Forum* advertise many other specialist sexual interests, but these are sufficiently rarified not to turn up on married dating websites. For the most part, married dating websites attract people who seek conventional romance with sex. But people do stray in from adjacent areas, and may not advertise their predilections very clearly, often because they are not too definite about them.

2

Puritans and Sex

People live longer, so marriages last much longer, long past the stage when spouses were in love, romantic and still excited by the novelty of each other. In pre-industrial Britain, marriages only lasted about 20 years, on average, due to the early death of husband or wife. Today marriages can last 40 to 60 years, unless they end in divorce, in which case they last 11 years on average. Good marriages often develop into companionable friendships, become platonic relationships, predictable and secure, but without the wild hedonism of the early days. At the same time, the sexual revolution of the 1960s made sex a major leisure activity, free and available. Easy access to reliable modern contraception means recreational sex is now divorced from pregnancy, and has grown exponentially. The commercial end of recreational sex has become a major industry, with massive growth in pornography and prostitution in many forms, including sex tourism, and latterly the driving force of the spreading internet. The private side of recreational sex has also become a big industry, with articles lauding a good sex life as a personal right in magazines, marital sex counselling, sex therapists, sex toys, lingerie, bubble baths and all the other accoutrements of an active sex life. There is a new ideological discourse of sex for all, sexual 'rights', a social movement that is almost a religion.

As a result people are enjoying more frequent sexual activity than ever in the past. National surveys of sexual lifestyles in Britain found that in the short space of ten years between 1991 and 2001 there were sharp increases on all measures of sexual activity, for men and women, especially among young people aged 16-24 years.[22] For example, the proportion of women who had ten or more partners in their lifetime doubled to one in five, although this was still below the one in three men reporting ten or more sexual partners by 2001. The number of women with concurrent partners in the last year also doubled, with a smaller increase among men. The proportion of men who paid for sex in the past five years also doubled, showing that commercial sex expanded at the same time as private forms. The obsession with sex leads young men (and some young women) to feel obliged to maximise their sexual philandering before marriage. In his book on internet dating, *Millions of Women are Waiting to Meet You*, as he contemplates marriage at the age of 39, Sean Thomas anxiously wonders whether he has had enough sexual partners before settling down to monogamy. He works out that he has slept with about 60 women, or 70 if prostitutes are included. He decides his score is average for his generation, as he knows men who had slept with 'hundreds of women' and others (the happiest men, he notes) who had only slept with their wife. Even Casanova only managed 130 flings in his lifetime.[23] No wonder married people feel a pang of jealousy when they consider the promiscuous lives of the youngest generation.

Couples counsellors, especially marriage counsellors in

Puritan Anglo-Saxon countries, rarely suggest promiscuity and affairs as one possible solution to sexual boredom, sexual difficulties and celibacy within long-term relationships. For example, Esther Perel admits that sexual desire and erotic playfulness can drop out of a relationship after a few years, especially after the second child is born and the social dynamics of the household become child-centred. She quotes experts who define a 'sexless marriage' as one in which couples have sex less than eleven times a year, and observes that some 15%-20% of couples in the USA fit this pattern, one in five marriages.[24] She notes that even animals frequently refuse to mate in captivity, yet cheerfully advises couples to spend years in expensive therapy in order to re-create and reconstruct an erotic life together. However she admits that awareness of one's partner's attraction to others, and the jealousy it stimulates, can be beneficial and stimulating for any relationship, forcing couples to see each other in sexual terms again instead of as comfortable friends and companionable home-sharers.

Another American therapist, Mira Kirshenbaum, is more realistic about extramarital affairs. In her book *When Good People Have Affairs*, she points out that affairs can help a marriage, but it is essential that they remain private and never intrude on the spouse. Kirshenbaum claims that half of all married men and one-third of married women in modern societies will have an affair or a fling, at some point in their life. She lists seventeen situations that can prompt an affair, but she never addresses celibate marriage as the most common single root cause underlying the more visible triggers and immediate excuses. She recognises that marriages may be perfectly happy except for particular needs that are not met by the marriage, including sex.

In Britain, Relate counsellors (the largest charity active in the area) often deal with the emotional upheavals caused by affairs and their aftermath. Yet Julia Cole's *After the Affair* fails to admit that a wife's pregnancy or a small baby at home are the most common triggers for a first affair, because the husband feels neglected or rejected, sexually and emotionally.[25] The Relate classification of types of affair (with advice on how to avoid them) sidesteps celibacy as a common problem among couples married or living together for any length of time.

The hidden agenda of books by therapists and counsellors is to enforce exclusive monogamy. Serial monogamy is permitted, but parallel relationships are not. Counsellors form a kind of emotional and intellectual police to enforce proper behaviour. This underlying perspective is hidden behind language that frames affairs as deviant escapism, fantasies without merit, attractive only to people who are not properly adult, who have failed to deal with issues from their childhood and adolescence, who use sex like a drug, who are actually miserable and conflicted and feel guilty.

This killjoy attitude is exposed most clearly in Frances Cohen Praver's *Daring Wives*, another book by a counsellor that claims a feminist concern to empower women and give them agency. Praver guides her clients back onto the straight and narrow road of exclusive monogamy, by replacing lovers with, *inter alia*, singing lessons, a postgraduate degree course or, yet again, expensive couples therapy 'for as long as it takes' to re-establish sexual relations in the marriage. This insistence on recreational sex exclusively within marriage is a bit like therapists advising that couples must learn to like going to the cinema together, must learn to enjoy the same types of film, and must never watch films with someone else instead.

The new morality

Sex has become a major leisure activity of the 21st century in the Western world, accessible to everyone, married or not, rich and poor. The invention of the contraceptive pill and other forms of reliable contraception in the 1960s opened up a new playground of recreational sex. We now have increasing diversity in sexual activity and everything associated with it – pornography and erotica, music, films, commercial services, and all the advisory stuff on how to do it, be adventurous, and get the most out of it.[26] The internet is hugely expanding and causing the coalescence of groups and communities with particular sexual interests and tastes, transforming fringe and rare practices into the commonplace. Transvestites, transsexuals, and cross-dressing normalise gender-bending, and European Union discrimination laws legitimise variations in gender identity and sexual preference.

Particularly in puritanical countries, sexual cultures and social conventions are still struggling to catch up with this new diversity in the sexual playground. Pleasure and procreation provide the two underlying anchors of sexual morality. Cultures that underline the pleasure principle are relaxed about any resulting offspring. Casual sex, even between strangers, is acceptable, unremarkable, and there is some emphasis on seduction skills and sexual skills. Western culture tends to conflate sexuality with procreation, so morality confined sexuality to marriage to ensure that offspring are adequately cared for.[27] The pleasurable and playful aspects of sex were downplayed, ignored, even denied in the past by the 'sex-negativity' of Christian morality.[28] All this was turned upside down by the contraceptive revolution, which allows pleasurable, recreational sex to grow exponentially, uninhibited by concerns about pregnancy and child-rearing. However, our ideas about sexual morality have not yet been revised and updated to fit the new reality.

Sex is not of itself a moral issue any more than is eating a good meal. The fact that we eat most meals at home with spouses and partners does not preclude eating out in restaurants, to sample different cuisines and ambiances, with friends or colleagues. Affluence increases the options available for eating out, and there is likewise increasing diversity and variation in sexual activities.[29] The main constraints are cost and time. Similar market factors appear to be dominant in the growing sexual playground. Opportunities are defined largely by your sex appeal, and the time and money you have available. It is not surprising that there is far more emphasis today on physical appearance and stylish dress, for men as well as women. Techniques for looking good are available, largely because there is increased demand for looking good, at all ages. Cosmetics, hairdressers, wigs, tanning beds, cosmetic surgery, cosmetic dentistry, diets, gyms, deodorants and perfumes, advice manuals by the ton on how to dress and how to be seductive – all these raise expectations and aspirations for sex appeal and attractiveness. Among young people, the competition can be relentless, for men as well as women .

Given the liveliness of feminist debate, it might have offered a modern sexual morality appropriate to the 21st century, to replace the old double standard that imposed greater restrictions on female sexuality than on male sexuality. In practice, Anglo-Saxon feminism never liberated itself from the Puritan morality that downplays or rejects all forms of pleasure as sinful, with sexuality treated as particularly problematic. Antagonism to men is displayed in feminist discussions of sex, sexuality and all things related. Marriage, prostitution, heterosexuality, marginal sexual tastes and activities, abortion and adultery have all been attacked. Marriage is presented as slavery; prostitution is an extreme form of the same sexual slavery and female subordination to men. Paradoxically, Anglo-Saxon feminism has tended to reinforce the idea of a split between 'good' and 'bad' women, monogamous and promiscuous women, madonna and whore – an idea that has been used for centuries by men to control women and confine them to their homes.

Sex, sexuality and gender are all turned into problems by feminists, treated as contested ideas employed to subjugate and control women. Each year, thousands of young women (and tiny numbers of young men) take gender studies courses that portray conventional heterosexuality as a cultural and patriarchal imposition and the family as a prison for women. Textbooks present women as victims of male violence, sexual harassment and economic subordination, with prostitution as the ultimate exploitation of vulnerable and impotent women by men. Academic books on sexuality and gender today are more likely to present them as 'contested' ideas and sites of exploitation than as a normal source of pleasure and identity. There is no recognition that heterosexuality continues to be chosen by 95% to 98% of people. In contrast, French feminism confidently rejects the idea that sex and sexuality are the foundation of men's oppression of women, is relaxed about prostitution in all its forms, asserts the importance of eroticism and fantasy in life, regards women as perfectly capable of defending themselves from men where necessary, and insists on the importance of feminine and masculine sexual identities and seduction skills. In sum, French feminists reject Anglo-Saxon victim feminism in all its guises.[30]

Discarding the sexual double-standard entails dropping the idea of 'good' and 'bad' women. Given the upsurge in sexual activity, prejudices against promiscuity also seem outdated.

It is not clear that these classifications were realistic anyway. Laura Maria Agustin shows that selling sex is, as a matter of observable fact, one of many jobs women (and men) take up, in conjunction with other work, or as a temporary measure, whenever they need to make a lot of money rather quickly. Migrants find it especially attractive because there are no entry barriers, and it is better paid work than domestic service. Women drift in and out of selling sex, especially when they are young and have the sex appeal that guarantees high earnings. Western social values that denigrate the exchange of money for sex are a carry-over from the Puritan and patriarchal values that sought to restrict sex to marriage and constrain women's freedom. Friedrich Engels once argued that the difference between the bourgeois wife and a courtesan was that the wife sold her body on a long-term contract while the courtesan sold hers on a piecework or short-term contract basis. High divorce rates make lifelong marriage uncertain and reduce the distinction even further.[31] There are many examples of women who drifted in and out of selling sex, or being a kept mistress, in their youth before achieving great fame in other work – such as Jean Rhys, author of the novel *Wide Sargasso Sea*, and Edith Piaf, the French chanteuse famous for the song *Non, Je ne regrette rien*. Punitive attitudes towards male and female promiscuity and prostitution appear to be even more outdated and inappropriate in the 21st century. Despite the growing affluence, people slide in and out of commercial sex, promiscuity and monogamous relationships in the course of their lives. There are no fixed boundaries, morally or biologically.

Overall, French sexual culture seems best adapted to the new world created by the internet, given its long tradition of courtly love and celebration of eroticism and sexuality, within and outside marriage. In contrast to Anglo-Saxon feminists, French feminists celebrate sexuality, especially heterosexuality. In *The Second Sex*, Simone de Beauvoir noted that femininity is a performance as much as a physical reality, but she did not belittle the performance. The feminist writer Luce Irigaray insisted that 'What we need for our future civilisation, for human maturity, is a sexed culture'.[32] The French state attaches sufficient importance to the quality of sex that it pays for all new mothers to have a course of *re-education perineale* (pelvic exercises), so they can resume sexual relations (and regain their figure) six weeks after childbirth.[33] French sex surveys reveal the highest rates of orgasm during sex, and the highest rates of sexual satisfaction, well above levels in the United States or Finland.[34] Sex outside marriage is not forbidden, but men and women prize seduction skills. Affairs happen when there is mutual attraction and circumstances permit. The conventionality of affairs is displayed in the concept of *le cinq a sept*, the magical space between 5 and 7pm when men see their mistresses. The only general rule is that one should never choose lovers within the immediate circle of family, friends and neighbours, as this would be socially disruptive. In Anglo-Saxon countries, this tends to be Happy Hour in bars and pubs.

French affairs are about seduction, eroticism, pleasure, the celebration of masculinity and femininity, playtime, time out, adventure. Many affairs are short flings. Some become long-term committed relationships. But discretion is always essential. The rules of the sexual playground are the same as in all civilised relationships – good manners, consideration for others, plus some ability to negotiate the tricky situations thrown up by social and cultural diversity in modern cultures. There is greater emphasis on social skills, self-control, emotional intelligence, and cultural sensitivity. The opportunities for meeting anyone at all are greater now, and so are the hazards, but sophisticated cosmopolitans can make it work.

The emphasis on sex as a leisure activity in consumer society allows people in celibate marriages today to see their situation as something that can and should be remedied instead of something to put up with stoically, as in the past. Websites appear to make it easy, and provide mass access to finding your own mistress or lover, something that used to be a luxury of kings and millionaires. The following chapters reveal the reality behind the glamorous fantasy, the experiences of men and women who take a walk on the wild side. Many get lucky. Some go away empty-handed. We explore the reasons for contrasting outcomes. Married dating has features in common with singles dating, but there are certain crucial differences which trip up some people.

3

What Married People Find in Affairs

'I lost interest in sex after my daughter was born' says Julia. 'Actually, I lost interest after my first child was born, my son. I was tired all the time, but also so engrossed in him – he seemed magical, utterly adorable, perfect, so smiley. I was vaguely aware that my husband felt rather left out, neglected. He was not the focus of my attention any more. So after a while, I made an effort, and anyway I wanted another child, and was hoping for a girl the second time. But now I have two, a boy and a girl, the family seems complete. So there doesn't seem much point in sex any more? I could say I am tired at the end of the day, looking after these two. But really, it's that I have lost interest in sex. I keep reading articles about how important it is to maintain a good sex life in marriage. But, really, I don't need it! It's for him, isn't it? Just for him.'

Celibate marriages

For women, sex is a part of marriage, especially at the beginning, but the arrival of children can be the catalyst for a fundamental change of focus. Looking after small babies offers a different, but engrossing sensual and emotional relationship which may supplant the sexual relationship with their husband. This transformation never happens to men. For most men, marriage means unlimited, enthusiastic sex with someone they fancy. The absence of sex is felt keenly as a breach of promise, and a personal rejection. 'Where did my sex kitten go?' screams Simon Jones in an article in the *Sunday Times*, as he complains about his first wife, then his second wife turning into a lactating mother.[35] Celibate marriages are the most common cause of affairs today. We can include in this category relationships where sex has become so rare and exceptional an event that one partner (typically the husband, but sometimes the wife) feels that it is sexless in practice, and resents being the one who always wants more. The routes into celibacy are numerous. It can happen to anyone, even the most outwardly 'perfect' and attractive couples.

Daniel was a classically handsome man, tall, with dark hair and blue eyes, an elegant manner and great smile. He had never had any difficulty attracting women, and he always got on well with them. Diana remembers being persuaded to meet him by the photo, with his smile that lit up the day. Daniel made full use of it at work, persuading staff to do what he wanted, even the impossible and unreasonable sometimes. He had started out as an accountant, but was already climbing the corporate ladder through senior management on and up to Finance Director, on his way – eventually, hopefully – to Chief Executive somewhere. His home life, in an affluent suburb in west London, was also charmed. He had married a lovely girl, who now worked part-time in a local company, while bringing up their three children, who were all lively, good-looking and doing well at school. The only negative point, and it mattered to him, was that the sexual side of the relationship had almost vanished. He had discussed the problem with his wife, but she saw it as relatively unimportant within the bigger picture. As she pointed out 'We have a wonderful home, wonderful children, a wonderful life and a wonderful relationship, so why spoil everything just for this minor matter of sex?' It was not that she refused, absolutely, but it always seemed to be a favour to him, making him feel like a beggar. He wanted more, so joined a dating website for partnered people.

Time constraints were always a problem, given the ridiculously long hours he worked, but Daniel was determined. After meeting several women over lunch in the City, he persuaded Diana to meet him at a discreet hotel one afternoon on a rare day off work, after he had been talking to head-hunters. 'It did not go well', she recalls. 'We had agreed to meet in the hotel bar, which was deserted and cold, but he was not there. He arrived very late, drank only water, and seemed stressed out from his meetings – or possibly by the hotel tryst itself? After he sorted out the room and key, we went up. The room was grand, but too cold to be comfortable or cosy. I wore sexy lingerie, but he seemed uninterested. He was hopeless in bed, just not into it for some reason, and fussing with condoms did not help. He apologised for being out of practice, promised it would be better next time – but honestly there was no incentive to see him again! Also, he offended me by his behaviour on leaving. He insisted on a cloak-and-dagger style exit, with me leaving by a different hotel main exit from him, so as to be absolutely sure he was not seen with me, even though the hotel was in an obscure back street. While he was determined to meet a lover, he was even more determined to keep it absolutely secret, and not jeopardise his perfect family life and perfect career in any way at all.'

Successful wives

While a virtually sexless marriage is the underlying cause, there is often an additional trigger prompting an affair. For Paul, it was his wife's success in business, which was all the more astonishing because she had dropped her job as a PA secretary to become a full-time mother for fifteen years after their first child was born. For their entire married life, Paul had been the main or sole breadwinner. Without realising it, this became important to him, to his sense of his role in the family. He enjoyed his professional job hugely, was good at it, and had risen to a team-leading managerial position. But his identity as family breadwinner was a separate, important role for him at home, whatever happened at work.

After years of being at home full-time, his wife decided to start a catering business, and to everyone's astonishment, it grew rapidly. Soon she was employing staff, needed an accountant, was out all day and evenings as well, and was making more money than Paul did. She hid this from him, so as not to upset him, he thought. But it became obvious the day she decided to buy a luxurious holiday home in the south of Spain, paying cash. What upset Paul was that his wife treated her income as her own private money, to do with it as she liked, whereas his earnings were family money. Further, she did not consult him at all on the Spanish house purchase, telling him what she had decided to do, rather than asking for his opinion and advice. Paul found his wife's new financial autonomy and independence unsettling, even insulting, coming on top of the absence of sex. He started taking long walks early every morning with his dog, and took comfort in the fact that the dog would not eat from any hand but his. In time, he joined a dating website for married people. He claimed it was for the sex, but he really wanted someone to see him, admire him, and like him in the way his wife once did, years ago.

Greedy jobs and neglected wives

A celibate marriage can be the result of a husband's total dedication to climbing the career ladder, whether the corporate ladder or by developing his own business, leaving no time for a normal family life let alone for any sex life. Wives feel neglected by husbands who leave home at 6 in the morning and do not return until after 8pm. Business trips entail dawn departures and whole weeks away from home. Business entertainment means dinners out at expensive restaurants, so that he only returns after midnight. Most of the time, wives are not included in the dinners, and would be bored anyway. Wives who have a job of their own, or children to look after, are not free to join their husbands for business trips, which can often be arranged, and re-arranged, at short notice, not necessarily in attractive locations. For some, the benefits of a luxurious lifestyle offer compensation for the solitude and the slide into celibacy. Some wives find a boyfriend or lover. One small group of women on married dating websites are these well-off, even wealthy wives who need a boyfriend to entertain them during the day and/or a lover for the physical intimacy lacking at home. Typically, if a husband finds out, he will do the same, for vengeance, 'to even the score'. Tit-for-tat affairs are not uncommon among couples who seem to have a glamorous 'perfect' marriage.

Stuart had worked his way all the way up the corporate ladder from a working class background and an active role in the trade union movement. He had once met Arthur Scargill, and for a time considered aiming for a career as trade union boss himself, but decided management was the easier route. He had been married several times, each new wife appropriate to his rising status as well as more attractive than the last. His current wife was a sculptor whose work was effectively subsidised by his income, as the pieces rarely sold, and were costly to produce. But he liked her, a lot, and he liked the artwork too. Then one day he came home early from a business trip to hear his wife laughing, in a particular way, over a drink with a young craftsman who helped to make her sculptures, and who left the house almost immediately. Initially, she denied that anything was happening. Eventually, she pointed out that his devotion to his management job for years and years had left her lonely, and feeling neglected. Her young assistant provided company, friendship, affection. Stuart privately concluded that an affair of some sort had been going on for a while – he did not want to know the details – and he insisted it should end. He decided to retire early and spend more time at home, instead of going for one last promotion up the corporate ladder, to a Chief Executive job he had been aiming for. However his restless energy won out, and he set up a small business he could run from home. This also provided the cover he needed to have an affair himself, to get even with his wife. He joined a website, dated several attractive women for a while, but in the end never got into bed with any of them. After years of celibacy, the urge was too weak. He needed to prove to himself that he could do it, if he wanted, but flirting over a drink or dinner, and stolen kisses with other women were enough to soothe his ego, especially as he was certain he could have taken things further if he had wanted to.

Roger also started out from a working class background, but he got an excellent degree from a top university, enabling him to join a small family firm as a specialist engineer. Promoted quickly to senior management, he stayed with the firm until over 60, playing a big role in the firm's expansion into a huge enterprise with foreign subsidiaries. His dedication to the firm's development was exceptional: he routinely worked 12-15 hour days, sometimes longer when travelling around the country on business. Unwilling to retire, he transferred to a less demanding Director role which left him plenty of free time. Part of the reason for continuing work was the empty shell of his marriage, which discouraged him from spending time at home.

His wife had given up work early on to be a full-time mother to their two children. Many years before, he had discovered she was having an affair with a neighbour who was a househusband caring for his children while his wife worked long hours as the main breadwinner. The two first met at the school gates, delivering and collecting their respective children. Then they started spending part of the day together, both of them feeling lonely and isolated as full-time homemakers. In time, the relationship developed. When Roger discovered the affair, he was enraged, was determined to leave his wife and get a divorce. In practice, he and his wife agreed to stay together for the sake of their young children, and to split up only later on, after the children left home. But by the time the children had gone, his wife had become ill with multiple sclerosis and he found it impossible to abandon her. So he started to live something of a bachelor's life, looking for a girlfriend to see during the large amounts of unaccustomed spare time he now had.

Having worked non-stop all his life, Roger found he had little idea how to spend leisure time, almost needing to be re-educated. After so many years of celibacy, sex was never going to be the top priority in a relationship, although he still wanted 'a full relationship'. He met Adele in a city bar one evening, and they started meeting regularly. A single mother who was perpetually short of money, he was able to help her financially. Adele was a somewhat bohemian, lively and attractive woman over 15 years younger than him – he never discovered exactly how old she was. She cheered him up immensely, introducing him to new entertainments, clubs and bars in the city. As he summarised the relationship, 'we were using each other', but the relationship worked well, for a long time. Then one day Adele moved to California, suddenly, leaving large debts behind, and he never heard from her again. Despite the somewhat instrumental character of their relationship, he always missed her, missed the fun, the breezy cheekiness and cheerfulness, even her lies. She had exposed a big gap in his life, and he needed a new girl-friend. So he turned to married dating websites.

Bad luck

Celibacy can be the result of singular bad luck, accidents and illnesses that prevent normal sexual functioning, or destroy libido for good.

Max had married his wife because she had the most fantastic legs, and body, he had ever seen and could not resist pursuing her. Tall and elegant, she invariably stood out at parties and in offices. His work as a consultant took him all over the world for long stretches of time, and she always went with him, doing whatever jobs she was able to pick up in each city. They became very close, partly because they remained childless for a long time, due to their constant moves and never feeling they were settled anywhere, and partly because their itinerant lifestyle made it hard to keep friends for any length of time. Finally, they decided to return to Britain and start a family, even though it meant curtailing his consultancy work to some extent. After sorting out where to live, and their new home, his wife also sought medical advice regarding a small problem that had been troubling her for a little while.

Unfortunately, his 37-year-old wife was diagnosed with advanced endometriosis, a cancer-like disease that produces growths in the stomach, with no known cause or cure. She required a hysterectomy and other surgery, which eliminated a significant part of her bowels and left her unable to have children. Physically, she became a shadow of her former bouncy self. She was also obliged to take considerable amounts of medication permanently. Max did everything he possibly could to make life easier for her, but they both knew the disease could return to do more damage, and she was cautious about trying to resume a normal life again. She spent a lot of time at home, was reluctant to get a new job, or even drive a car. Max cared greatly for her, but something in the relationship had broken permanently, had been spoilt.

Hospital consultants had advised them they would both need counselling to come to terms with the new situation. After a year of complete celibacy, he came to the view that the situation was probably permanent, and he needed to do something about meeting his sexual needs elsewhere.

More often, however, it is men who fail to get medical attention in time. Andrew brushed aside his periodic heart palpitations until the day a colleague at work was rushed to hospital after collapsing with a heart attack which killed him. This finally prompted Andrew to see a doctor. After several appointments with specialists, he was on complex medication for heart problems, including Warfarin, a rat poison. Unfortunately, one side effect is erectile dysfunction, and in Andrew's case there was a complete loss of libido as well as impotence. Frances, his wife, took it well, reassured him that it didn't matter, remained cheerful. One year later, Frances started to feel differently about celibacy as a permanent feature of her life. Andrew's libido had vanished, but hers was unchanged. In due course, she started exploring the dating websites.

In some cases, a temporary illness can still produce a permanent change in relationships. Alistair had married a slightly older woman, who had always been more zany and unconventional than he was, one of her key attractions for him. But difficulties in her job led to a particularly bad patch of depression, with hysterical outbursts and just being generally difficult and unpredictable to live with. As he put it 'she was not herself for a while' and sex was the first thing that vanished, and never restarted again. There was no question of a split, given the children, but the end of their sex life drove him to seek alternatives to cope with his own sexual needs. Once Alistair got into the habit of meeting other women for sex, he carried on long after his wife recovered. Because of the somewhat chaotic nature of their life together, with two homes, it had always been easy to conceal his affairs, so she never became aware of anything having changed – and emotionally, they were just as close as before anyway, after she returned to her usual self.

Delayed adolescence

Many good marriages develop into comfortable companion-ships after a time, to the point where sexual passion seems almost inappropriate between good friends. Married dating websites, however, have many users under 40, which is rather young for companionable celibacy to have set in. Here early marriage turns out to be at the root of the need for an affair. The large number of articles on sexual gratification and sexual technique in magazines these days, suggest everyone has an active sex life. It is easy to forget that some people, young as well as old, still have narrow sexual experience, sometimes limited to their spouse alone. Sheer curiosity drives some of them to have an affair, or at least one fling with someone else, at some point in their life.

Alan had grown up poor. Home life during his childhood had always been a bit of a struggle for him and his mother, who was widowed very young by an accident, and later remarried largely to provide for her family. Fortunately, Alan was very clever at school, winning scholarships that ensured him a good education and secure employment as a professional. But he needed to marry and leave home as soon as he was able, as he never got on well with his stepfather. He married a very religious girl he met at university who, like him, wanted a stable and secure family life. He chose well, and they were happy together. But she was his first and only real girlfriend, first and only lover, as he was for her. As a teenager, money had been too tight for girlfriends to be much of an option, and he had needed to do exceptionally well at school and university to earn the scholarships. For many years, the exclusive nature of their sexual relationship created a strong bond between him and his wife. But in his early 40s, Alan started to regret his narrow sexual experience as a young man, and to wonder what it might be like to have sex with another woman.

His fantasies were driven in part by sex becoming a lesser and lesser part of his marriage, while religion played an increasing role in his wife's life. Despite the fact that she worked only part-time, she was always too busy 'to spend quality time with me', as he put it. If he invited her to retire to the bedroom, she would insist on first washing the dishes and putting the laundry in the washing machine. He began to feel that he always came second, or third, on her list of priorities. Gradually, he became aware of opportunities that had probably been there all along, but were now obvious to him. At a work-related conference in Germany, he realised that several women were attracted to him, flirted with him, and were inclined to seduce him, if they could. For the first time, he was tempted to give it a go, to enjoy the carefree adolescence he had never had. Finally, he joined a website, and met several women he found attractive, in one case stunningly so.

*

Edward had also never had any lovers before he met a beautiful girl he pursued determinedly for months until she finally agreed to marry him. With a convent school education, his wife had regarded sex as being reserved for marriage, whereas in his case it was simply that he had never met anyone who took his fancy in propitious circumstances. They married early, in their 20s. After 30 years of marriage, it had become a platonic relationship, focused on their four children and several grandchildren. His wife had made it plain she was no longer interested in sex, and she concentrated on her successful professional career, which took her abroad, lecturing on her books at conferences around the world. However, Edward's libido was as strong and urgent as ever, and he detested masturbation, having been raised to think of it as a perversion and immoral. After putting up with years of celibacy, he decided he really had to do something about his problem.

Edward joined a website, but given his age and world-weary appearance, he had no success; all his approaches were rejected, politely, under one pretext or another. With the same determination that characterised all his activities, he finally persuaded one woman, Parvati, to meet him, and to his astonishment she was even nicer and prettier than her profile suggested. But still, he could not make the emotional leap into physical intimacy. For over a year, he dated and courted his girlfriend, as he would have when a young man, with lunches and dinners in elegant restaurants, gifts of jewellery and perfume. He would have liked to spend whole days with her, but that was never a practical option. In time, he came to think of Parvati as being part of his life, so that sex became emotionally possible, finally, even for him.

Celebrating success

Angela arranged to meet Stephen in the bar of one of the most glamorous hotels in London. At lunchtime, it was deserted, but the restaurant staff still courteously guided her to her blind date. He turned out to be an extremely attractive and smartly dressed man who was pondering the extensive champagne list. He invited her to choose one. Astounded to see the prices, all in the hundreds of pounds per bottle, she chose one of the cheapest. He accepted her choice, but implied she could have chosen anything she fancied. It emerged that Stephen was in a celebratory mood, and the date was a treat for himself. He had set up his company many years ago, with the intention of running an ethical business that delivered its promises. At the time, that was a novel, even crazy idea, as everyone believed success required the lowest prices and a cut-throat approach to doing business. But his business had grown, and was now one of the biggest and best known in its field, having absorbed several smaller companies along the way. That evening, Stephen was attending a trade association annual dinner with several senior staff in his company. There would be a prize-giving, and he had understood a hint from someone suggesting that his firm would be a major winner – which was why he had invited along quite a few of his senior colleagues, to enjoy their collective success and recognition together.

After a glass of champagne, they moved to lunch in the dining room overlooking Hyde Park. Stephen was charming, in good spirits, and entertaining company. He clearly liked Angela, and they got on exceptionally well. Lunch went on well into the afternoon. Towards the end, he enquired whether she might like to join him in his hotel room for an hour or so? Reassured by his frankness, and the absence of pressure, she agreed, despite her rule never ever to go to bed with anyone on a first date. Stephen was as wonderful in bed as in the bar, and it was a glorious extension of a brilliant lunch date. He told her that in his car on the drive down to London he had fantasised about how the blind date would turn out, and his wildest aspiration was to meet a woman with whom he wanted to spend the afternoon in bed.

Afterwards, he phoned Angela and texted her, first to thank her again for a wonderful day, and then from his dinner to tell her that his company did indeed win the prize, and all his staff were hugely pleased. She never heard from him again. The date was a one-off celebration, not the start of a new habit.

Opportunity knocks

Attending international conferences, trade meetings, business events of all kinds can be the catalyst for all sorts of reflections on your sexual life, or lack of it, and they also provide the opportunity to do something about it. Away from home, alone in a nice room with a huge bed (queen size beds having become the norm even for single rooms in international hotels), it is easy to fantasise about sharing it with a lover. For speakers and other active participants, such events provide a public confirmation of career success and their achievements which becomes a massive testosterone high. This alone drives flirting and mating activities in the bars, corridors, and social events of the evenings.

Gordon had risen through the ranks of medical research in hospitals until he finally got to be Professor and head of his own research team. The next time he attended a conference, he was an invited keynote speaker in a prime slot, was introduced as Professor in his field, and attracted a lot of admiring attention. For the rest of the day, he felt restless, energised, sexualized. He dared not attempt anything with the women at the conference, however sexy and admiring they were, because it was too close to home, they were all members of his professional community. If anything went wrong it might backfire on him later on. So he went out trawling round other hotel bars in the city, fired up with testosterone, and eventually picked up a young single woman who was in the city on business. He would have seduced her into coming back to his hotel room, except that they went to hers in the end. Psychologically, this one-night fling was the event that broke the pattern, changed his mindset, taught him he could do it. It renewed his self-image as a sexual being, a man who could still attract women, as he did in his student days. It was not that his marriage had become entirely platonic, but sex had dwindled into such a rare event it was non-existent, in practice. On his return home, he was determined to do something to rectify the situation.

Is this all there is?

It is often called the mid-life crisis, but it can happen at any age, and it rarely comes as a crisis. On the contrary, it is the absence of any turmoil or upheavals or *excitement* that is the problem. At a certain point, life has settled down into a fixed pattern: you have reached a plateau in your career, with few or no new challenges to test you in different and new ways; home life has become routinised, predictable as well as comfortable and contented; arguments about holidays have been resolved into an agreed pattern of entertainments. Stability can be reassuring, but also boring. At some point, you wake up and wonder 'Is this all there is? Is this it?' and it feels as if something has died.

Some have an affair just for the excitement, to recapture their youth, when their life was full of promise, when they felt that 'The future's so bright I gotta wear shades'. Some have an affair as a reward for their career success, a reward for all the long years of self-denial and self-control. They take time off work to finally reap some benefit from all those hours of unpaid overtime and weekend working to meet deadlines. Some have an affair to give themselves a new challenge, to test themselves. Can I still do it? Do I still have what it takes to attract a partner? Some have an affair because it is something new and different; it breaks the monotonous predictability of their life as it has turned out. Some have an affair to prove that they have reached that point in their career where they can do it – they can afford the costs, they can get away with the absence from their office, no-one can reprimand them. The affair becomes an entertaining new badge of success, of achievement. Virtually all want to see the glory of their lifetime achievements reflected in the admiration and shining eyes of a lover who is impressed by it all when hearing it for the first time. Whatever the emotional logic that leads to the affair, a lover's admiration is crucial, for most men. Hence any lover must have a modicum of intelligence and education, to fully appreciate what their wife takes for granted by this time.

These existential anxieties can affect women in the same way as men. For other women, the mid-life crisis plays out differently, and happens soon after her children have left home – whether for school, or boarding school, or university, or to get married themselves. The greater a woman's investment in her children, the more likely it is that their departure triggers a period of reflection, self-doubt, even depression. 'Has my purpose in life effectively come to an end?' – slightly different questions and reactions from those of men. But here too, one solution will be the life-affirming affair that strengthens your sense of self and boosts your ego. For women also, a principal need is to prove their sexual attractiveness, that they are more than the job they do, or more than a good mother.

The extra dimension

For those in creative and artistic professions, the extra dimension of an affair is an emotional necessity, even beyond the question of a marriage that is celibate or not. A stable and contented home life and a supportive partner are essential for creative people to be able to focus their energies on their work. But they need stimulus as well, and affairs are one way of getting it, especially if there is diversity in the sequence of lovers – in their personalities, social backgrounds, cultures, and interests.

Jake is a successful musician, partly because he married a woman who is supportive of him and his work, partly because he had never had children to distract him, and partly because of his dedication and talent. With a flat in central London and a big house in the country, he and his wife often spend time apart, and the solitude is important to him when he is writing or composing new material. It also gives him the space for the series of affairs that he regards as necessary to him, almost a work prop. Tall, with thick blond hair worn shoulder-length, scruffy jeans and a leather jacket, Jake looks like the classic artist or pop star. He cultivates this appearance because it works so well with the women among the many admirers he attracts. In the country, he finds it easy to invite women discreetly to his home there. In the city, he is more cautious because there are many people who might recognise him somewhere and make an unfortunate comment among friends later on, or offer a suitably embroidered story to the gossip columns. The dating websites proved a boon, once he discovered them, because he can use them when he has the time, filter out unsuitable women, and meet a far greater diversity of women than he encounters within his usual circle. It is this feature of websites that proves the most valuable to him – the opportunity to meet women with very different lives and interests and personalities, which provides a constant source of novelty, even inspiration at times, relatively risk-free, and at a relatively low cost.

Unhappy marriages

There are unmet needs in virtually all marriages. Spouses and long-term partners are rarely sufficient unto each other, and need other friends and family, hobbies and sports, activities and entertainments for a full life. The need for more sex, or different kinds of sex, outside marriage does not necessarily indicate a poor marriage. Most celibate marriages are contented, work well. However a small fraction of people who join married dating websites seem to be in really unhappy marriages. It is the rarity of such people that proves the point about most users being happy at home.

Graham offered a photo that showed a handsome man with the most dazzling smile, and generally sounded like a great catch, with many interests. He explained his presence on the website as due to 'a dead marriage', which Sheila took to mean a celibate marriage. They met for lunch in a City restaurant so popular that it was really noisy, an odd choice for a first date. Graham insisted she order the wine, although he had claimed to be a connoisseur of good wine in his profile. But as lunch progressed, they got on really well, with many common interests. Eventually, Graham started talking about his various marriages, which became a fascinating catalogue of disasters. He seemed to have chosen the wrong woman for the wrong reason repeatedly, with difficult divorces every time. He appeared to live apart from his current wife to a large extent, explaining that her two daughters had destroyed their relationship. His step-daughters had never accepted Graham as part of the family, because they had never come to terms with their own father's sudden exit, years ago, to live with a new woman. Sheila came to the conclusion that Graham probably needed a new wife rather than an affair, and was unlikely to be much fun.

Gemma knew married dating websites were not the ideal place to look, but it was the best she could do, and it was free. Having left her thuggish husband, she desperately needed a benefactor to support her, financially and otherwise. She was happy to offer sex, and whatever else was wanted, but she definitely needed a regular monthly income. She saw no prospects of being able to get a reasonable job to support herself independently, as she had not worked for many years. Perhaps she was too blunt (or straightforward) in setting out her needs, but finding the right man proved more difficult than she expected. Most men rejected her proposal.

Craig was a young, self-confident, determined and ambitious man who had successfully courted and married a beautiful blonde Sharon Stone look-alike. As a Catholic with traditional views about family life, he had first made sure his future wife would be happy to give up her career to be a full-time mother. She proved to be a brilliant mother to their two children, who were beautiful, good-natured and never cried, and she became a perfectionist homemaker. The only problem was that she also pretty much ceased to be his lover. The longer they were married, the more punctilious she became about every domestic detail. No matter how much Craig did to help at home, his wife complained bitterly about his inadequate and faulty contributions. Given the long hours he worked at his job, he finally started to feel a deep sense of grievance, but his traditional values and the two perfect children who adored him tied him irrevocably to his family. By the time he had resolved to use a married dating website, contrary to his strong family values, Craig had become an angry and conflicted person. Despite his many attractions, he found it difficult to get a second date with any of the numerous women he met.

'Pull' factors

Books and media feature stories on affairs, and advertisements for dating websites for married people, are sometimes accused of encouraging people to have an affair. In reality, they only appeal to people who already have an interest in that direction. People who are blissfully happy in their home lives simply do not notice adverts for such services, or pass over them heedlessly. People who notice them are already looking that direction, however haphazardly or subconsciously. Dating website advertisements can be the immediate trigger for someone to subscribe and start looking for a lover. But neither the books nor the websites are ever the root cause of an affair. They are just the tools used by people who have already embarked on that idea, mentally and emotionally. Affairs are never driven exclusively by opportunity. The thousands of married people who attend trade fairs, conferences, and business meetings every year, staying alone in attractive hotel rooms, do not automatically fall into bed with each other, even when they meet someone they find devastatingly attractive. Opportunity is a 'pull' factor. But there is invariably a 'push' factor as well, somewhere in the background. Paul Newman, one of the most handsome and successful actors of his generation, when asked why he never had affairs, famously replied "Why go out to eat burgers when you can have steak at home?"

Accounts of married men and women who have affairs show that a few are indeed hoping for an escape route out of an unsatisfactory marriage, but the majority are complementing a stable marriage with the additional excitement and novelty of an affair or brief fling.[36] Additional sex to compensate for a relatively sexless or celibate marriage is one common incentive, and typically prompts a series of affairs. Most married people who have affairs are more highly sexed than the average, and have the resources to attract a constant stream of partners. A few have finally decided that a sexless marriage has become intolerable, and are looking for an alternative partner for a fresh start.

Most women find it very difficult to admit, to themselves or to anyone else, that their relationship at home is not perfect, and that the lack of sex has something to do with it. It generally takes women years to come round to the idea of using a dating website or having a sexual affair. For men, it seems to be easier, either because men are more comfortable about saying they want (or "need") more sex, or else because men are more open to taking risks. Many men on the websites boast about their strong libido, their need for energetic sex, their inability to be confined by a celibate marriage, or even their need for more sex than is offered by a normal marriage.

A sexless or low-sex marriage appears to be the most common root cause for the types of affairs represented here: successful 'safety valve' affairs in marriages that are, overall, contented and working reasonably well. The people in unhappy or difficult marriages that end up in therapy and counselling are rarely found here. They do not make attractive lovers, because they have problems they need to deal with on their own, and many people regard them as risky as well. People in unhappy marriages may decide they want to change partners, or want an excuse to break up their existing marriage, and no-one wants to be part of that mess. People who are unhappy at home are more likely to be moody or angry than cheerful and relaxed.

Celibate marriages are far more common than we realise, because sex surveys do not bother to provide the relevant statistics. Surveys report the number of sexual partners, but rarely specify whether these include or exclude spouses. Married men and women who report only one sexual partner may be referring to their lover rather than their spouse.[36a] So celibacy extends well beyond the numbers reporting total celibacy, which are surprisingly high, especially after the age of 40 or 45. Even a marriage that is not totally celibate may be sex-starved, as far as one partner sees it.

Naturally, celibacy is common among young people under 25 years who have not yet made their sexual debut. But it is equally common among people aged 45 and over. The 1990 survey of sexual lifestyles in Britain found one in ten women aged 45-59 had no sex at all in the previous five years, and one in five had been celibate for over a year. Proportions are consistently lower for men in this age group. The lower someone's socio-economic status, the higher the incidence of celibacy, but also the higher the incidence of promiscuity: some people have numerous sexual partners while others have none at all. Men generally report many more sexual partners than women, but the numbers of sexual partners increases dramatically in younger age groups. Across all ages, one in twenty married men reported two or more partners in the last year, compared to only one or two per hundred married women. Three or more sexual partners in the last year are reported by 1.2 per cent of married men and 0.2 per cent of married women. These figures imply men are five or six times more promiscuous than women, at all ages. The general pattern is for men in the higher professional and managerial occupations to have started their sex lives later, but to have had more partners overall, while people in the lower socio-economic groups start earlier but have fewer partners in total. However sex surveys reveal a tiny minority of highly libidinous people, who start their sexual careers before age 16, and are more promiscuous at all ages – roughly one in twenty men and one in fifty women fit this pattern of a sexually active lifestyle throughout life.[37]

The British sex survey also demonstrates that the frequency of sex is determined primarily by the length of a couple's relationship, not by age. At all ages up to 60, people had sex around ten times a month in the first two years of a relationship, on average, with a sharp decline thereafter, to an average of twice a month after 6 years together.[38] Surveys everywhere find a faster decline in sexual interest after the first two years among women than men. Familiarity often breeds boredom. Novelty is sexually exciting.

In the United States, about one in five marriages are sexually inactive, defined as the spouses not having sex in the past month. These couples are more likely to report young preschool children at home, ill health of one partner, and a lack of shared activities, but they do not report arguments over sex.[39]

In Italy, a survey of people aged 18 to 80 found one in ten men and one-quarter of women saying they are not sexually active (with no sex at all in the past year); they were generally unhappy about this, especially in the older groups. Among married and cohabiting couples, around one in ten report being sexually inactive, and the same proportion say their sex life is not satisfactory. Once again, there is a sharp difference between spouses. One in ten wives say they are not sexually active (with no sex at all in the past year), twice as many as the husbands – which suggests that at least one in ten husbands have lovers outside the marriage. The most common reason couples give for declining libido is boredom with their habitual partner.[40]

In Spain, surveys suggest around one in ten couples are in practice celibate as they never have sex (none of the men admitted this, but 4 per cent of the wives did) or else they have sex only a few times a year (almost one in ten of all couples).

However celibacy is concentrated among couples aged 50 and over, one-quarter of whom never or rarely had sex in the past year.[41]

Sexless marriages are just extreme examples of couples with different levels of sex drive. All the recent sex surveys reveal a large difference between men's and women's sex drives – a sex deficit. The received wisdom on men always wanting more sex than their wives emerges not as a stereotype or prejudice but as fact. The gap in sexual desire between men and women is observed in every country and culture where sex surveys have been carried out, and it shows up in all age groups over 30 or 35 years. There seems to be no sex difference in sexual capacity or sexual enjoyment, only in sex drive, which is stronger among men.[42] In addition, men and women continue to have very different attitudes to sexual activity.[43]

The stronger male sex drive is manifested everywhere, on virtually every indicator of sexual attitudes and behaviour ever devised. In Australia, one-quarter of men said the ideal frequency of sex would be daily, three times as many as women wanting daily sex.[43a] Men are at least two or three times more likely to engage in, or seek, every sexual activity, and they are two to three times more likely than women to want yet more sex than they are getting. Men are far more likely to use commercial sex services, more likely to have affairs, more likely to use erotic entertainment of every sort: books, videos, telephone sex, erotic shows, and also private erotic fantasy (which costs nothing). Men masturbate more often, even when married. They express greater interest in trying a variety of sexual activities, and have tried more types. Men report three times more lifetime sexual partners than women. Perhaps most important, men are three times more likely to engage in erotic fantasies, and to do it frequently, whether they have a sex partner or not. Overall, the sex surveys suggest that men with strong sex drives enjoy auto-eroticism, commercial sex and ordinary partnered sex as complementary practices, rather than as mutually exclusive alternatives.

The large difference in libido is not due to women's sexuality being culturally repressed, as it has been in the past. It is just as obvious in Scandinavia, after decades of gender equality policies and sexual liberation, as in more traditional cultures. In Finland, for example, men are twice as likely to find porn sexually arousing; are three times more likely to have affairs, are five times more likely to regard having several parallel sexual relationships as the ideal, report twice as many sexual partners over their lifetime, almost invariably orgasm during sex compared to a minority of women, and are ten times more likely than women to have offered someone money for sex. Among people living in couples, only half of men report lack of sexual desire as a problem in the past year, compared to three-quarters of women. Across all age groups from the age of 30 onwards, four in ten Finnish men want more sex than they are getting in their current relationship, compared to only one in six women: 40% versus 16%.[44] Reports on Scandinavian sex surveys emphasise every minute decline in sex differences between surveys, but the reality is that they remain just as large as everywhere else.

In short, the majority of couples experience an imbalance in sexual desire and interest after the age of 30 or 35, and a sense of sexual boredom that can begin soon after their first few years together. However, universally, the sex deficit affects more men than women.

Celibacy and incompatible sex drives may be the most common root causes of affairs, but usually there is some trigger prompting the decision to take action. There are people, especially men, for whom a friend's enthusiastic comments on a married dating website, or a magazine article about people having affairs, is a sufficient catalyst. However, there is usually something else that pushes someone to take the initiative. Milestone birthdays – 30, 40, 50 and 60 – affect almost everyone psychologically, prompting reflections on passing youth and vigour, achievements and losses. One of the strongest themes in website profiles is the desire to recapture one's youth, and the associated thrills of desire and passion. Or the catalyst is something more punchy – a row at home or at work. Intimations of mortality can be important, anything that reminds you that your best years will soon be gone. For some men, a 'mid-life crisis' is prompted by a friend's heart attack or their own illness, which makes them feel they will not remain young, or alive, forever. For mothers, it can be the youngest child finally leaving home, opening up the possibility of a new, hedonistic life as an unencumbered woman again. Triggers and catalysts can be trivially small events, or major milestones in life, but they all have a big emotional impact.

There are various routes into an affair, numerous causes of sexless and sex-starved marriages. However sexual deprivation is more commonly a male problem, and men feel the impact of any triggers and catalysts more strongly than do women.[44a] What is common to almost everyone taking this road is a desire for intimacy and connection with others as well as sexual release. Another common element is a social environment that tolerates affairs – friends and colleagues who will be sympathetic, even helpful.[44b] In their absence, the new dating websites can provide an alternative source of support.

4

Impacts

The Puritan Anglo-Saxon view of the unfair affair is so negative that all impacts are said to be noxious. Affairs endanger marriage, and exploit the single women that married men prey upon. When affairs prompt a divorce, everyone in the family suffers from the consequences, at least in the short term. We deal here with quite different types of liaison, between people who are both married, both committed to their marriages, who are discreet enough to avoid social and emotional catastrophe. In this different, special situation, the impacts can potentially be almost entirely positive. The main impact of a good affair is that people become more contented in their marriages, and with life in general, as any sexual or other needs not fully satisfied in their primary relationship are satisfied elsewhere. Most affairs have a variety of other impacts as well. Affairs are exciting, add a new buzz to life.

After meeting Sonia for the first time, Walter wrote to her to say 'There will be smile on my face and a new spring in my step the next time I come to London'. He had always viewed his business trips to London with dread, as he felt lonely and out-of-place there. With someone to see in the evenings, who knew places to go to and things to do, his trips became something to look forward to, instead of resent. He found he was happier in his job as a result. The main disadvantage of the job was transformed into an advantage, and he stopped grumbling about business trips.

Men who have devoted their entire adult life to working hard to climb up the corporate ladder can find that an affair forces them to stand back from their workaholic lives, take a break, decide to spend a bit more time and money on themselves, devote more time to leisure and entertainment instead of working all hours. An affair can be part of a work-life re-balancing process. It helps people to appreciate what they have already achieved, and re-consider what their new life goals should be.

For some reason, reaching 50 had not bothered Nikolas in the way it unsettled his friends. But his 55th birthday felt like a milestone. His 60th birthday was now in sight, and he had always intended to retire then, while he was young enough to change tack, start something different from his workaholic career as a company director. His children were all safely embarked on rewarding professional careers, albeit still living rent-free in various London flats he had bought as long-term investments, with no signs of imminent marriages.

An unsettling discussion with his eldest son one evening gave him a new perspective on the pattern of his own life – marriage at 21 to a lovely girl he met at university, three children by the time he was thirty, and a lifetime of twelve-hour workdays that left little time for leisure activities that were not business-related in some way. His sons did not want to emulate this pattern. Nikolas started thinking about what he wanted to be doing after 60, and this prompted wider reflection on what he was missing now. Finally, he did two things to change his life. First, he bought a sailing yacht which he kept moored on the Dalmatian coast in the Mediterranean. He learnt to sail the boat and started taking proper summer holidays on it. Second, he joined a dating website for married people and set about finding a mistress who was attractive and elegant, intelligent, sensual and fun. He needed a companion to force him to take time out from work, revive the dominant male in him, be the catalyst for redirecting some of his energies away from business to all the other interests he had dropped long ago, especially the arts. He fantasised about taking his mistress with him on sailing trips in the Mediterranean, until the practical difficulties became too obvious. Nikolas was clear that he had to start restructuring his life before he reached 60 and retired. He was also convinced that his wife could never be a force for change in his life because they had been leading separate lives for many years already, being an efficient partnership rather than a close couple.

Contrary to many subscribers' expectations and advertising blurbs, dating websites cannot guarantee a perfect match and a happy outcome for everyone. They only provide an opportunity to search for and potentially meet like-minded partners. It is up to each user to find, court, and win a lover. At some point, almost everyone loses sight of their own role in the search process, and complains about the website 'not delivering', or starts behaving discourteously towards other users. Almost everyone will have unhappy experiences of one sort or another at some stage – even if it is only being gently rejected by someone you really fancy. At these times, going home to a family that always welcomes you, even if they sometimes take you for granted, is a boon for a damaged ego.

Arguably it is far more than a boon, it is a central feature of these affairs: you are never ever dependent on the other person for human warmth, happiness, acceptance, friendship. There is always the comfort and dependability of your own home and family, your own bed, your hobbies, friends and neighbours. The familiarity of your existing family life provides a secure anchor throughout the ups and downs of dating a string of strangers whom you may or may not get on with or like, who may or may not be as courteous and considerate as you expect and are yourself.

This is probably one reason why dating married people is far more ruthless than singles dating, even more ruthless than internet dating for singles. It is easier to bounce back from a disappointing or upsetting encounter when you have a nice home life to return to at the end of every day. In fact, one of the impacts of an affair, or attempts to start an affair, can be a new appreciation of your spouse who is always there, always warm and welcoming. Many people come to realise that their spouse is more of a gem than they appreciated, and compares favourably with the newcomers they have met.

Even when an affair progresses smoothly and enjoyably, without misunderstandings and mishaps, there can still be a bounce back to heightened appreciation of family life and your spouse. Most people are aware that meetings with a lover are a holiday from reality, a glorious romance kept perfect by meetings that are always too short and too infrequent to become humdrum. Holidays and trips abroad can be exciting. But it is always good to come home afterwards.

The value of sex

Most affairs involve sex, at some point, even if they are rarely about sex exclusively. Short 'flings' are about the excitement of seducing a stranger quickly as much as about sex, since the quality of the sex cannot be guaranteed, and can often be poor with a complete stranger. Longer term affairs are usually about a lot more than just sex. Some women continue with affairs even though the sex is less satisfying than sex with their husband, who knows how to please them.[45] However sex is an important element.

Sex is a 'Use it or lose it' pleasure. People who have been celibate for a long period gradually lose the urge, their libido and sexual desire atrophy, sometimes permanently. For those who have lost interest in sex, affairs and short-term flings make no sense at all, seem to be complete madness. Affairs can only be worth the effort, and make any sense at all to people for whom sex and sensuality still matter, remain a permanent need, just like food, water and exercise. Being without a lover is a kind of starvation. The majority of people on the dating websites for married people are in relationships where sexual activity of any sort has faded out completely, or has become a rare event, allowed only on 'high days and holidays' or as a special favour. The marriage has developed into companionable friendship, or an efficient partnership, and ceases to have romantic or sexual tones. Universally, the impact of the affair is to solve this sexual mismatch between partners who are otherwise committed to staying together – sometimes for the children's sake, sometimes because 'marriage is about family and property', sometimes because one spouse is ill and cannot be abandoned, but sometimes because a platonic relationship can be satisfactory, in its own way. In a real sense, the good affair, one that is properly managed and kept in the shadows, has no impact at all, or no visible impact on the primary relationships, the marriages of those involved. It is a safety valve, allowing one partner to express the sexuality that no longer finds expression at home.

In his book *Millions of Women are Waiting to Meet You*, Sean Thomas describes a sex holiday he took with a friend in Bangkok. In common with a lot of young single men in London, living alone, with marriage delayed until their 30s (age 39 in his own case), Thomas never had enough sex, even when he had a girlfriend. In Bangkok, he found a girl he liked in one of the Patpong hostess bars, and invited her to stay with him in his hotel room for the two weeks of his holiday. For the first time in his life, he had as much sex as he wanted and needed. The impact was dramatic. He experienced a new feeling of calm, complete relaxation, being at ease with the world for the first time since puberty. He says 'I felt relaxed at last. It felt like a car alarm had just stopped blaring; an alarm that had been blaring so long, I was starting to forget it was there in the background. What I experienced was close to serenity, a unique period of blissful liberation from the insistent and tedious demands of my libido…. The final absence of desire.' He later adds that '…the urgency, persistence and overwhelmingness of male sexual desire is not fun'. In his late 30s, Thomas realised just how much of his private life was dominated by the raging sexual needs that had never been completely met. Obviously, he thought the cost of the holiday, and the girl's time, were well worthwhile. People for whom sex is relatively unimportant, or who have a satisfying sexual relationship, can discuss these sex holidays purely in terms of morals. But for men (and some women) with a strong libido, they can provide a welcome avenue for sexual expression, and a release.

In their paper 'Money, Sex and Happiness', two economists, David Blanchflower and Andrew Oswald, estimate the value of a good sex life at $50,000 a year at 2004 prices – so well over that figure today. They analysed the National Opinion Research Centre's General Social Survey which provided data for about 16,000 Americans, men and women, to identify what caused people to be happy with their lives. They found the average American was having sex two to three times a month. Those under the age of 40 had sex once a week, on average, about four times a month. Women over 40 reported having sex once a month, on average, while men over 40 reported an average of two to three times a month. Blanchflower and Oswald speculate that the reason for the discrepancy in the over-40s group could be due to male exaggeration, to men having younger partners, or to seeing prostitutes. Affairs might be another explanation. The study estimated that increasing the frequency of sexual intercourse from once a month to at least once a week provided as much happiness as putting an extra $50,000 in the bank each year. For comparison, a lasting marriage offered about $100,000 worth of happiness a year. Celibacy and very low levels of sexual activity were effectively the same thing as regards their impact on happiness. (This effectively justifies classifying marriages as sexless when the frequency of sex declines to less than once a month.) One-third of those aged 40 and over reported leading a celibate life, but the proportion would be over half if the group with very low frequency is added. The effect of sex on happiness is stronger for those with higher education. The study was criticised for saying nothing about the quality of the sexual activity. However even sex surveys have been unable to assess quality other than by frequency of orgasm, which is not a very helpful indicator, as orgasm is almost guaranteed for men and rarer for women, whatever their sexual lifestyle.[46] Assessed on the basis of frequency alone, Blanchflower and Oswald show that regular sex (once a week) can offer roughly half as much happiness again as a stable marriage. That is a very substantial addition indeed.

The majority of couples will experience an imbalance in sexual desire beyond the age of 30 and after the initial 'honeymoon' phase is over. In all cultures, and at all ages, most men have stronger sex drives than most women. So we might expect that the value of a regular sex life is rather greater for men than women. In purely sexual terms, affairs seem to be more valuable for men, so they will be more disposed to spend money on them.

Sexual harassment in the workplace

People can also become more relaxed and pleasant colleagues at work. After the equal opportunities revolution of the 1970s allowed women to take up occupations and professions previously dominated by men, there was an inevitable rise in sexual harassment in the workplace. Men and women are now far more likely than before to meet and interact in the workplace, to attend work-related training sessions or social events together, to travel together on business. Opportunities for social interaction between men and women have increased hugely in the workplace, and with it, opportunities for what is labelled 'sexual harassment' by some or regarded as 'flirting' by others. In continental Europe, especially France and Italy, it is more often taken for granted that sexual flirting, and sexual propositions of all kinds, will happen between colleagues and indeed between adults everywhere. Since you can always graciously decline any advances, these are not a problem, and should be seen as flattering compliments. French women, in particular, point out that occasional unwanted attention is the inevitable price we pay for wanted sexual attention.[47]

Users of dating websites find that their sexual interests are diverted away from colleagues in the workplace to the website instead. So there is a consequential reduction in sexual harassment, and possibly also flirting, in workplaces. One of the main reasons for using websites is that they allow people to transfer their search for partners outside their own social circle and work networks. Most commonly, someone's first affair is with a work colleague, broadly defined. When this goes sour, or ends, the disadvantages of getting involved with work colleagues become clear, and people switch to using a website instead. This also helps to explain the disproportionate numbers of men who are freelancers, self-employed, or owners of their own business on the websites. They may have few or no colleagues, and would not dare alienate a client by flirtatious advances. So this group seeks out the dating websites much earlier and more quickly than do employees.

People who have been having affairs on and off for many years, possibly throughout their married lives, often become rather blasé and cynical about relationships generally. Libertines, as we might call them, can become very skilled at conducting their affairs: maintaining secrecy, courting prospects appropriately and successfully, getting what they want. But this can be at the price of becoming cold, hard, selfish, instrumental and unfeeling towards lovers. For this reason, some website users actively avoid those who openly advertise their skills and experience in this field. Clumsy innocence and amateurism can be more attractive than the cynical and calculating self-centredness of a Don Juan.

One of the hazards of any affair is that what may have started out as an essentially sexual and contained adventure can turn into a habit, then into a need for being with that particular person, regularly or even all the time. Men find it more difficult than do women to admit they have fallen in love, and the strong emotions stirred up by an affair can take ages to settle down.

Howard made the classic mistake in his first affair, and seduced his secretary, a divorced mother of two who really needed to find a second husband. Helen was fifteen years younger than him, with lovely long blond hair and a wonderful smile. They worked well together, and she openly admired him. Howard had taken her out to lunch for a more relaxed social chat soon after she came to work for him. After a while, he invited her for a drink after work, once, twice, then regularly. Six months after Helen arrived in his office, they had become lovers, using her home which was not far from the office. The affair lasted three years, growing into a second parallel marriage for him. When he stayed for dinner with Helen and her two daughters, he became aware that they both hated him and resented his intrusion into the family. He took Helen out in the evenings to plays and shows he was interested in, telling his wife he went with old work colleagues. As they met almost every day at the office, it was easy to organise their dates, and to make last minute alterations, as she knew his timetable and diary better than he did.

The affair ended one summer when Howard was away for

thrcc wccks on holiday with his family and Helen had a brief
'fling' (as she described it) with a single man of her own age
while he was away. Howard was aware she really wanted and
needed to get married again, and he was clear that he would
never leave his own family. Generously and courteously, he
withdrew, insisting that Helen should continue seeing her new
man. To his dismay, they were married within two months, and
Helen left England to live in Hong Kong with her new
husband. Howard had no difficulty replacing Helen with a
new secretary, but the huge void in his emotional life was
harder to deal with. Finally, he found a counsellor and booked
a series of appointments with him to try and make sense of
how very upset he was at Helen marrying someone else, so
quickly!

He ended up seeing the counsellor for almost a year, a fairly
costly exercise in time and money that sort of replaced his
dates with Helen. After a while, he reluctantly came to the
conclusion that he had been in love with Helen all along. The
hole in his life was bigger and deeper than he thought
possible. He also came to realise that he had become addicted
to her admiration, her compliance with his every mood or
request, her constant desire to please him. As he said later 'I
was adored!' and her adoration was addictive. At one point, he
tried to erase the memories by registering with a dating
website for married people, so he might start a new affair to
distract himself. This did not work, as it felt artificial. In a way,
he needed a period of mourning after his affair with Helen
ended, especially as he had yet to deal with his resentment and
anger at her accepting a new partner so swiftly. In time, he
finally admitted that Helen had always been hoping that
Howard would leave his wife to live with her instead, and
marry her. She had done her best to persuade him she was the

nicer partner, the better housewife, the more adoring lover. Allowing the affair to continue for three years had been a mistake, implying a long-term commitment that he never intended to deliver. A long time later he admitted that he had set out to enjoy a sexual adventure, to get sexual variety in addition to his excellent sexual relationship with his wife, but that he had taken advantage of Helen, allowing her to hope that he might marry her, so she continued seeing him. Perhaps the two daughters who hated him had seen things clearly after all.

For many people, an affair offers a massive boost to their ego, making them much happier in consequence. This is especially true for women, who are more likely to have spent years at home looking after children and domestic concerns. Men are more likely to have achieved promotion and success in their careers, and the tangible rewards of good earnings, to boost their egos. Even so, for men and women alike, whatever their achievements in their jobs or businesses, the admiration of another person is invariably flattering. Being seen and liked enough for someone to seek you as a lover is always going to boost your self-esteem, and cheers up anyone. As a result, people having an affair are generally nicer at home in consequence, so their families benefit as well, indirectly.

An affair allows everyone, man or woman, to see themselves, and be seen, as an individual and a sexual person again, instead of as one part of a larger family unit. No matter how much you are loved at home, and admired by colleagues at work, a happy affair gives something different, something extra. Some people say it allows them to recapture the period when they were young and single, with their whole life before them, with far fewer responsibilities and constraints. Others regard this as a fantasy, unlikely to be achieved even with a younger partner. But almost all regard an affair as offering some 'fun and time out' from their normal life, a mini-holiday of sorts, a space to be yourself as you want to be, or to be a different person from your day-to-day persona. Precisely because it is a space apart, an affair allows re-invention, creativity, innovation, and playfulness. For women, it is a space where they can look their best, be their most charming, recapture the temptress of their youth. For men, it can be an escape from the fixed personalities and roles they have developed at work and at home.

Wives who have had the opportunity to see their husband's mistress sometimes express astonishment that she was not a great beauty, as they automatically assumed, was even ordinary-looking. While it is true that very attractive women are more likely to be courted by men, and find it easier to attract a lover, affairs typically involve rather more than arm-candy. A woman who is full of life and great fun to be with, someone who is fantastic in bed, an imaginative and playful lover and playmate, someone who makes the time to simply sit and listen, someone whose conversation is lively and interesting and makes a total change from routine work-related chats, the total admiration of someone who does not take your achievements and income for granted, someone who knows a lot about something you are interested in but had no time to pursue – all these things can be enormously attractive, even addictive, in a lover. Short-term affairs and flings are usually about physical attraction and sex primarily, but not exclusively. Longer term affairs almost invariably involve a lot more than just physical attraction and sex. Affairs are a very special kind of social relationship, which seeks to avoid the dull and less pleasant parts of relationships.

Artificial, but nonetheless entertaining escapism.

For pretty well everyone using the dating websites for married people, their ability to enjoy an affair is tied strongly to their awareness that both parties are in a similar situation, are on an equal footing, so that neither is exploiting the other, or enjoying the benefits at the expense of the other, as in the case of the traditional affair between a married man and younger single woman who really wants marriage rather than an affair.

5

The Pitch

Desirable detached property now available, constructed 1950s, excellently maintained, with no subsidence or bulges, seeks cultured articulate M, interested in long tenancy. Viewing essential.

Assertive, strong, yet caring & laid-back guy, 45, professional, city banker, loves theatre, arts, good food, countryside, seeks unassertive F, any age, to share glass of wine, romance and more.

Brown-eyed girl, F, 27, attractive, sporty, generous and loyal, bit of a social animal, loves beauty, tranquillity, exploring, music and reading, would like to meet M, 25-35, capable of laughing at himself and making me laugh.

Everyone enjoys flipping through the personal ads in newspapers at times, to wonder whether they might reveal an attractive catch, to speculate about the people behind the brief blurbs, to laugh at the witty ones. Some married men used these to meet women well before the specialist websites were started. There are entire pages of personal ads in national and local newspapers, and in magazines. Other pages offer advertisements for escort girls, call girls, rent boys, telephone sex and related services, as well as lap dancing clubs, striptease, burlesque and the like. Even in the Catholic countries of southern Europe, national newspapers carry advertisements for sexual services spelt out in graphic detail. The one exception (still) is married dating, which is ideally suited for the internet.

Similar to singles dating, one of the most important decisions married people make in writing a website profile is the username, call name, or profile name that heads up the description. This name is used to identify messages sent to another user, so it is the first thing they ever see, and can colour their reception of your message. Newcomers often misunderstand this item, and insert their real name, or else choose a name carelessly in the rush to write their profile description.

The short profile name may seem unimportant. Until you think of how much we are subtly influenced by people's names (and voices) in everyday life. Max and Jake sound more decisive and strong than men called Bobbles and Tiddles. Marilyn Monroe creates a different image from Norma Jean, and James Bond feels different from Raskolnikov or Rothko. Some people duck this problem by using a word-label, but this too requires thought. LostWithoutYou and Spyder might work better than UncleBob; CarpeDiem and DreamLover probably get a better reaction than MikeTheBike or Gotcha! The worst profile names are a meaningless collection of letters and numbers, such as Asdfasd60 or Brhu3, which lack the flavour of romance married people are looking for.

The self-descriptions in these profiles matter. Of course looks are important – but they are ultimately a matter of personal taste. The best ones say what the person does or does not like. If high heels, long fingernails and basques are a turn-on, they will say so, making clear whether they are merely desirable or essential features. Everyone likes to have a laugh and believes they have a good sense of humour (GSOH) – but what counts as funny is again a matter of taste. Humour can be a slippery thing, and can backfire in initial messages to a complete stranger as there is always the possibility of misunderstandings. Humour is expressed in profiles, sometimes.

> Tom Cat. I am ugly, boring, and have no sense of humour. But I love life, and am especially good at cleaning shoes with 3-inch heels. I dare you.

Arguably, the GSOH label in these profiles has nothing to do with humour and wit. 'GSOH' functions as a substitute for good manners and a knowledge of social etiquette, a substitute that serves well in the informal social gatherings and unstructured venues that characterise singles dating. Any embarrassment or lack of *savoire faire* can be glossed over and excused by joking about the social clumsiness. Adding GSOH to a profile is often a statement that someone prefers a relaxed, cheerful, easy-going style of socialising; 'no rules' informality over formality, and meeting in a pub or bar over meeting in a restaurant.

Colin described himself, appropriately, as 'a gentleman' in his profile. Educated at public school, he played cricket in a team based around his bank job, and wore conservative suits with colourful ties. But he was the funniest man Nuala had ever dated, recounting story after story of his cricket team's wild exploits and his own misdeeds that had her crying with laughter. It only struck her afterwards that he had never claimed to have a GSOH, and had sounded like such an old fogey, or rather a young fogey, that she had initially been uncertain about agreeing to meet him.

On a dating website for people who are attached, it seems obvious that users are married. It is those who are *not* married that need to explain themselves and why they have chosen this website in preference to a singles dating website. It matters hugely to the married people looking for romance. Newly separated people can cite a fairly self-explanatory reason – they are 'between things'. But the long-term divorced and single need to explain their choice, yet often fail to do so. Some pretend to be married in order to avoid questions. Divorced men often write that they are continuing to look for the right woman, but in the meantime, are dating married women. Some non-married people are definite about not wanting any permanent relationship – the time for the compromises of marriage has long gone. A woman of 49 in senior management explains in her profile:

> I am a busy, fully employed woman who enjoys her work totally, but finds it leaves very little time for 'normal' relationships. To be honest I have been single now for so long I believe I am slightly selfish! I want to do what I want, when I want, and with whom I want, without having to check first with a regular partner if that's OK. I have a very active social life … Being a tad selfish I do not intend to give up anything I already have – and I don't see why I should. But I do miss having a lover in my life. I just don't want one man permanently in it 24/7!

Politeness and courtesy are as a rule displayed in all behaviour on a website, and not only claimed as an attribute. Actions speak louder than words. Nonetheless, an astonishing proportion of men claim that they 'know how to treat a lady' in their profile, but are rude, domineering or insensitive in initial correspondence.

Married-dating website rules will vary regarding explicit mention of sex. 'Let's see where it goes…' is more common than a shopping list of sexual tastes and turnons. Many websites generally caution users not to discuss sexual tastes at an early stage, and some prohibit it. (All dating websites have the usual codes of conduct that forbid racist and other defamatory or abusive language.)

General advice offered to internet daters on how to write a profile can be counter-productive. Guidelines are developed primarily for singles dating, a situation that differs from married dating and affairs. The only general rule that applies to both situations is the beauty-money trade-off. Typically, women are chosen on the basis of physical characteristics and beauty. The most multi-purpose attractive feature for men is money and status, but a good physique and skills in the bedroom can be important on dating websites for married people. Profiles for women always describe their physical features and attractions, while those of the men focus on affluence and generosity. In married dating, leisure interests are somewhat peripheral, as few people spend weekends together – and so are details of family life.

Under the guise of 'advice', some websites pressurise new subscribers into conformity with their unwritten rules. For example they reject women's profiles that are 'too short' and insist on greater length. They suggest that people should say something about how they dress, what music they like, their ideal date, and so on. As this imposes a uniformity which works against expressions of individuality – which is what married daters really want, as this helps them to identify kindred souls, personalities and attractive styles – so married daters seem to ignore it where they can. TomCat's profile above says nothing useful, but reveals everything.

As anywhere on the internet, liars cannot be ruled out on married-dating websites, no matter what guidelines are offered. But liars are quickly found out. There seems to be no point in pretending to be anything other than what you are. A 'boring' person is simply someone with different interests to you: sport rather than politics, for example. Country people like walks in the country and cosy inns. City people are more likely to focus on trendy bars and fashionable restaurants. Intellectuals focus on people's tastes in reading or the arts, as this will always be a topic of conversation. Sporty people like to meet similarly fit partners. People who are interested in current affairs and politics generally prefer people who are well-informed.

As the object of married dating is very specific, profiles reflect this and the successful ones do not try to appeal to everyone, to create a 'mass market' product. Guidelines sometimes push people in this direction, fruitlessly, as few have time to date dozens of people at a time. The writer may be in the minority, but that is not important if it ensures they meet one person they like and can easily get on with rather than ten near-misses. As straightforwardness seems to work best, people will say they like McDonalds, are a wine connoisseur, prefer the Arctic Monkeys to Bach, jazz to country, cycling to football. Most of the 'lies' in profiles consist of people exaggerating their positive features, or understating their age.

Given the higher social status of married daters, spelling, grammar and punctuation matter terribly. This is regularly quoted as a turn-off by many people. As one woman put it in her profile: 'If you don't know the difference between there, their and they're I don't think you are for me.' One of the most common spelling errors is the use of discrete for discreet. One of the most common turn-offs is the use of text-speak and spelling in website profiles and introductory messages, where abbreviations are inappropriate, and suggest illiteracy. Interestingly, the focus on writing style puts science graduates and IT specialists at a disadvantage on the dating websites. Their profiles rarely sparkle, but blunt honesty can still make them winners.

The advice the best profiles seem to use is 'Be your best self'. No-one likes a miserable person, someone who constantly complains about the hardships of their life. The old adage is still true on the internet: 'Laugh, and the world laughs with you. Cry, and you cry alone'. This advice is frequently offered to singles who are looking for a potentially permanent partner, but it applies equally to married people seeking a lover.

All the advice on appearance and manners offered to single women and men seeking a partner is equally valid for married adventurers. If anything, it is twice as important for married people, especially those who are contented at home. You get lazy at home. You slop around in comfortable old clothes, and no-one objects. You stop saying 'please' when asking for favours, and 'thank you' every time someone makes an effort to please you. You may not be getting your hair trimmed as regularly as you need to, to look smart all the time. Women who are full-time homemakers are especially likely to stop bothering with make-up, pretty clothes, perfume and sexy lingerie. People who have been married a long time stop seeing each other with the sharpness of new acquaintances, who notice the stain on the tie, the hole in the sweater, the unpolished shoes. An appearance, and manners, that have become 'normal' at home and do not excite comment in your family, or from your spouse, is inadequate for the dating scene. Yes, you know how to dress up when going out to a party. But do you take the same care every day, every week, all the time? The new lover will be looking for someone who is committed to looking good.

Those who are successful at married dating sort themselves out well before they launch their profile on any website or in the personal ads. If overweight, they will eat less and lose weight beforehand. Being fat is the single most common reason men give for rejecting a woman, even if she is otherwise attractive. Men ditch the habit of wearing shirts until the cuffs and collar are frayed, and invest in some fresh new ones, and get more colourful ties. Women who work in an office, start acquiring a few things that are more cheerful, even sexy and pick a perfume that really suits them.

Jekyll and Hyde

Profiles paint a picture, however sketchily, and posting a self-portrait on the internet requires courage. They tend to come across as positive and cheerful, even witty, but given the covert nature of married dating this has its own risks. Many people then ruin this positive start by exposing their nervous anxieties and hesitance in their bumbling first steps and over-cautious initial contacts.

Jonathan's profile said he was a lawyer in central London, and indicated an interest in wine, a witty self-deprecating tone, plus unspecified cultural interests. A brief but suggestive profile. He sent numerous approaches to several women, with no response at all. He sent a second message, then a third, to one woman in particular, Liza, whose profile caught his attention, partly because it was concise and clear. On the third attempt, she replied, noting that this was actually the first and only message she had received from him! Jonathan realised he had been doing something wrong at the start, which explained the lack of response to his approaches.

Cheered up by Liza's reply, he launched into some silly nonsense flirtation with her. She responded in kind, playing his game, on his wavelength, a meeting of minds. After a while she suggested lunch, he agreed, and they found a mutually convenient date and venue. Then Jonathan started to worry that he actually knew nothing concrete about her, so he asked for a phone chat. Liza remembers that the man on the phone seemed to be a different person entirely: anxious, nervous, a control freak who insisted on going though a series of irrelevant interview-style questions. She reminded him that she could tell him anything at all over the phone – he had no way of checking the truth! So the interview was pointless.

Jonathan went away to think about this. He eventually rang back to say he wanted to meet her anyway. By this time, a new date had to be found, which was several weeks ahead, due to Liza's imminent business trip to The Hague. Jonathan decided to pull out, after all. Several days later he was back, agreeing to the new date after all. By now, Liza was weary of his prevarications, anxieties, and accusations of dishonesty over her reluctance to answer every question in detail, before meeting. The witty and relaxed tone of their early correspondence (and his profile) had been replaced by an unrecognisably domineering and suspicious persona on the phone. Possibly, the profile displayed his normal self. But with so little to go on, and distracted by other enthusiastic approaches, Liza gave up on him, saying 'Life is too short to spend it reassuring ditherers.'

Photos

People consider photos provide reassurance. But photos can reveal, conceal, and lie. In the worst cases, women post photos of Playboy-types, scantily-dressed, with the face cut off or obscured. When the woman who turns up for the date is obviously a different person, attractive but fat, the man in question can legitimately be angry at such extreme deception. Similarly a man who describes himself as being 53 with black hair (with the appropriate photo), but who turns out to be now 65 with a head of thick white hair, or else bald, is being a little economical with the truth, rather than just remembering (and still feeling) the way he used to be.

But below this level of clear (self)deception is a sea of half-truths and creative self-presentation. Photos capture a still-life fraction of someone's appearance. They can be misleading in both directions – showing someone as more attractive, or less attractive, than they 'really' are. Photos taken at parties, or on holiday, after several glasses of wine, can make anyone look dissolute and crumpled. Sarah recalls one man who supplied three different photos of himself, in a suit, on holiday, in close-up. She thought he looked like three completely different people, his appearance changed so much between photos. Alison found that photos of men were so vague as to be almost useless. Several times, she had failed to recognise someone from his photo when they met for the first time.

Young single people on blind dates routinely say they failed totally to recognise each other from their photos – so age is not the key factor here. However it is generally women who change their appearance most dramatically with different hair styles (or lengths), different make-up and clothes. Some users even invest in professional portraits with a professional make-up artist.

Reading profiles

Intentionally deceptive photos and profiles are rare on married-dating websites. Most people struggle to write a profile that describes them well, with some polishing to present themselves in the best light possible. People tend to see themselves as they were ten years ago – identities take a while to catch up with reality. So it is commonplace for people to shave up to ten years off their age, as this reflects how they feel, and think they behave, and look. They can be right. Women claim to be blond, because that has been their identity all their life, even if their hair recently turned grey-white, so they are now 'arctic blonde'. Profile self-descriptions are true, more or less, and tell you how people perceive themselves, even when they are reporting what 'my friends say about me'. Occasionally, website profiles go much further in reinventing a persona, either with outright lies or a degree of self-delusion.

Neil's profile suggested he would be a real catch. His headline said he was seeking a spirited, inquisitive Princess. He continued by saying he wanted someone '... who is broad-minded, and seeks romance, intimacy, while being pampered as she enjoyed once before! If you seek someone adventurous, mischievous, who will make you laugh, kind and sensitive, thoughtful, perceptive, gentle and affectionate … Are you seeking a tall, sincere, intelligent mate who will make you feel like a Princess and will rekindle your fire while… If you have a great sense of fun and adventurous spirit, please get in touch…'. Neil's initial approach to Sophie repeated some of his profile, and was full of flattery and flowery language. After her cautious response, they got chatting and Neil invited her to have lunch with him next time he was in London on business. It was a blind date, but they had both described what they would be wearing on the day, so it would be easy to identify each other in the bar of the restaurant.

The bar was effectively empty when Sophie arrived, so she saw Neil immediately, with his blue and white striped shirt, and went up to say hello. Even after she introduced herself, he looked at her as if he was baffled as to why she was there. For the next half-hour, he continued to behave like a scared rabbit in car headlamps, ill at ease, staring at her fixedly, stiff and unsmiling. Neil's approach to conversation was to drill away at her with questions on the details of her family life and children, her job, and why she was on the website. He had already met several women in his local area, but rejected them all as not meeting his high standards – or so he said. Sophie decided she had no desire to succeed herself, and was relieved when Neil concluded that the date was not working out, so there was no point in continuing with lunch. They each went their way.

Sophie thought that Neil seemed half mad, not completely of this world. There was no link whatever between the personality of the man in the profile and the man she met, although the physical description matched up. In particular, he seemed extraordinarily ill at ease socially, and with women especially. Her reaction was reinforced by an email Neil sent her over two months later: 'Perhaps can we talk again, now the sharks have stopped circling?' Possibly, the message was intended for a subsequent victim of his attentions? If so, it was extraordinarily clumsy of him to send it to Sophie instead, two months after he should have deleted her email address.

Men who work in a man's world and rarely have dealings with women, and less educated men, often use flowery and romantic language when describing their ideal date, and when writing to women. The exaggerated language of 'princess' and 'pampering' used in Neil's profile often indicates someone who is not completely at ease with women, so has to resort to strained language and behaviour. A similar flowery style appears also to be used initially by many Asian men.

Rural or urban residence can subtly colour assumptions and expectations in affairs and profiles, altering what counts as 'successful' or 'glamorous'. Cosmopolitans can talk to anyone with ease, on almost any subject. People who have travelled extensively around the world, work in multi-national companies with colleagues from many cultures, or speak several languages, are generally more comfortable with meeting people from different cultures, religions, ethnic groups and social backgrounds. People who have lived in a particular region or town all their lives are generally more rooted in their own culture and its traditions; they may or may not be open to meeting people with different backgrounds. Residents of big cities, especially multi-cultural, multi-ethnic cities like London and New York, are more likely to be cosmopolitans than those living in small towns and rural areas.

When men embroider reality, it is typically to exaggerate their income and job status. The self-employed electrician becomes a manager 'running my own business', which is technically correct. When women avoid the cold truth, it is typically to exaggerate their physical attractions, which they know matter to men. 'Curvy' and 'cuddly' have become standard website euphemisms for women who are fat.

Amanda's profile said she had a doctorate, a professional job, and was a tall leggy blonde. She readily offered a photo, which made her look like someone in a *Penthouse* or *Playboy* spread, but with the head obscured. She got dates quite easily, but never more than once. When Neville met her, he could not believe her cheek. She had left school at 16, worked briefly in Woolworth's as a sales assistant, but had been unemployed (and unemployable) most of her adult life. Amanda said she was married, but Neville thought it possible that too was a fabrication. She was a short, fat brunette who openly admitted her photo was taken from a porn website or something like it. She was also slightly mad, or 'eccentric' as the English like to put it. Her clothes were bought in Oxfam and other charity shops, or in jumble sales, and she prided herself on choosing 'artistic' clothing, which meant that she looked like a scarecrow, in a fantastic collection of ill-matching zany skirt, blouse and jacket. Neville was pleased that he had travelled outside his usual part of London to meet her in a suburban area he never visited. The date was amusing, after the first shock, but did not last long.

Profiles that seem too good to be true are sometimes just that. But very brief, reticent profiles can indicate someone who is not absolutely sure they want to be on the dating website, so they are proceeding cautiously. They may be revised into longer versions after a while. Sometimes, brevity is due to someone having only just registered on the website, so the profile is a provisional version that will be expanded in due course. In other cases, reticence indicates someone who is successful or well-known in their field, so they are cautious of being identifiable if they write too much. Such people only reveal their identity, if at all, in face-to-face meetings, when they are sure that their date comes from a completely different field of work and can be trusted.

Married-dating websites that require everyone to give precise answers to a series of Key Facts about themselves, then leave people free to describe their personality and aims however they wish, seem to work best. Knowing someone weighs 70 kilos or 100 kilos is more helpful than labels such as 'athletic' or 'cuddly', especially as men and women differ so much physically. Statements of occupation, education and income (in broad bands) seem more helpful than leaving people to guess whether someone has a degree or not.

The Key Facts section of married-dating profiles is frequently used to filter out people who are too close to the user's own world. To be sure of avoiding meeting anyone they might know, they filter out people who live in the same neighbourhood, work in the same field, are a member of the same ethnic minority group, or belong to the same religious community. Whereas in singles dating people generally prefer to meet partners similar to themselves, married players are careful to avoid anyone too close to their own community.

Sex affairs versus love affairs

At the extremes married affairs are mainly about sex or mainly about romance. But the distinction can be fuzzy in between. Men find it easier to ask for (and offer) sex than love and affection. But the kind of self-validation they seek in an affair can go well beyond sex, even if sex is the concrete proof of their acceptance by someone attractive enough to matter. Some people even prefer a sexless liaison because it is proof that they are liked 'for themselves', their essential spirit rather than their toned body or sexual prowess. Sometimes a liaison that starts out as a purely sexual affair (as one or both parties see it) can develop into a love affair, on one or both sides. Sex, or the anticipation of sex, plays a part in most affairs, but romance can be an equally potent draw for married dating.

Married-dating websites advise users not to talk about sex in detail in profiles and before meeting someone, as this can be a turn-off, regarded as crude or insensitive. In any case, most people seek a flexible mix of romance and sex, or friendship and sex. Some profiles, or the initial approach, are more clear-cut in their focus on sexual encounters (often casual sex with many partners) or on a longer-term relationship with one person. Younger men and women are more likely to be focused on sex, pure and simple. Older people are more likely to seek 'romance', meaning flirtation, romantic trysts, respect and affection as the wrapping for sex. The focus on sex or romance is often left implicit in profiles and first approaches. Occasionally the script is set out clearly.

Justin's profile was similar to countless others of his age, but his opening approach to women was distinctive:

Hi, I hope you don't mind this short email. By way of a brief introduction, I'm a 42 year old company director, well travelled, intelligent, articulate, and if you like…
…walking in the misty rain (with appropriate clothing) on an autumn day followed by lunch near a roaring fire in a good pub…spontaneous days off to go to the coast

for a long walk, followed by tea in a nice old-fashioned coffee shop giggling at the 'knowing' glances' from two old women sitting at the window table… getting dressed up in cocktail dress for drinks at the Hilton… being happy to sit in silence without any discomfort and talk without speaking…then I would love to hear from you!

Similarly, James' profile offered the usual description of an 'attractive, friendly, well-educated, companionable, intelligent, successful City-based professional, 36, who hoped to meet a discrete female who enjoys laughter, friendship, evenings of fine wine, fine food, and fine conversation. An incurable romantic, who offers fun, warmth and tenderness.' After a couple of short messages introducing himself, and saying he was 'not entirely sure what I seek', he then set out a more definite agenda:

Since this site is all about being honest, then I shall be too… I am seeking someone who wants fun and lots of it. I like sex and am very good at it, and seek someone the same – I don't settle for second best outside the bedroom and won't settle for second best in the bedroom either. I seek someone who wants both to receive and give pleasure, someone who seeks oodles and oodles of hot passionate, intense, intimate, adventurous, wild, romantic sex, someone who will take her time during long, protracted, increasingly intense foreplay, someone who wants to be fucked hard, regularly, intensely by a man who stays hard for a long time, cums heavily and repeats often, someone who knows what they want in bed and won't be shy in asking for it, even demanding it, someone who wants more than boring missionary sex, someone who will experiment, try new things, and be adventurous, someone intelligent and confident enough to articulate her fantasies and desires, someone at ease with their body and needs and longing to be used, treated, pleasured, fucked, enjoyed, and sexually cherished accordingly.... But I am also seeking a special friend, someone I will enjoy spending time with out of bed, someone fun, someone with different and refreshing perspectives on life...

Married people who write out their scripts at length for strangers are probably similar to people who enjoy 'cyber-sex', purely imaginary on-line sexual relationships that can be conducted between people who never meet, and may even live thousands of miles apart. They are an exception. Most subscribers want to meet someone for real, even if affairs start in the mind, in erotic fantasies that have been developed and refined over years.

Escapism and erotic fantasy

A recurring theme in profiles is escape from the routine of life, the need for fun and excitement, as well as filling the sexual gap in their main relationship.

I have reached the time in my life where it is self-indulgence time! I want to make you feel very special. I love the finer things in life, and wish to share them with someone who would enjoy them with me. Life is too short, so let's enjoy exciting times together.

I'm considered to be very successful in business, but…I have taken the decision that the time has come for me to live life to the absolute full again.

I want the fun, excitement, passion and laughter that goes with the company of someone also looking for some good times.

I long for someone with whom to have a relationship with real passion, mental and physical. To reach out and touch a cheek. To kiss and feel that electric tingle on the lips.

For me, this is about recapturing some of that youthful vitality but with the maturity and experience which age rewards us with (?!)

I am happily married and I love my wife very much, but I'm looking for the rush, that feeling you get spending time with a special friend, someone to spend quality time with.

I am looking to meet someone who wants to escape from reality once in a while and briefly enter a world of intimacy and passion.

Over and over again, the affair is defined as a separate space and time, a private parallel world, where people can be set free from their everyday life with its duties and responsibilities, roles and persona. The potential for escape into a fantasy world made real is the big draw for some people. For others it is the idea of renewal, of reinventing themselves, or becoming the young person they used to be. Some never bother to actually meet anyone, in case the fantasy is spoilt by too much reality. Others want the real thing, but reality has to match up to the fantasy of the perfect lover that they have imagined over the years. Mills and Boon novels are a good indicator of the romantic scripts that tempt many women, with a successful and sexy male who can make everything happen. Many end up being impossible to please, and this is ruefully admitted in some profiles.

A Spanish survey found that the great majority of men but only half of women have sexual fantasies, and the great majority would like to implement them. Among men and women, around half the fantasies concerned their current partner, and around half concerned strangers (unknown people) or friends and work colleagues who were not sexual partners.[48] Similarly, an Italian survey of sexual lifestyles[49] found that erotic fantasies are far more common among men than among women, one-third of whom never have them. Erotic fantasies are typical of graduates and other highly educated people, and people in the highest socio-economic groups, but are rare in the poorest classes. Graduates and people in the highest income group are most likely to have affairs – one-third did so – being driven by a need for novelty and change, stimulus, risk and excitement even more than the paucity of sex at home.

Affairs are clearly linked to a strong erotic imagination. This is one reason why married men have affairs. Erotic imagination is much stronger among men. An American survey found that people who score high on autoeroticism (a combination of frequent sexual fantasies, use of erotica, and masturbation) are also highly sexually active with one or several partners, and engage in the most varied sexual activities. Women generally score low on autoeroticism. Two in five of men are highly autoerotic, compared to less than one in ten women. Half of all women never engage in any private erotic fantasies and activity, compared to one in seven men.[50]

Sex appeal and erotic power

One recurring issue in profiles and initial correspondence is the relative importance of physical appearance, especially for men. A few men claim they like all types of women, or that looks are less important than personality. Others excuse their 'shallowness' but insist on seeing photos at the start.

In fact, women's sexual attractiveness and their erotic power, often seem to be the only feature of any importance in married dating, even when men say they also value intelligence and a proper education. Women have two contrasting views on this, as illustrated by Laura and Melanie:

Men *say* they want to meet an intelligent woman, they *think* they do, but it's not really like that. No matter how clever they are, they still want a sexual partner who is compliant, who is bright enough to admire them, but will always defer to his superiority. The more successful the guy is, especially if he has been running his own business for a while, the more he *has* to be the boss – he *needs* to feel he is in control of things. They think they make the rules. In practice he wants a docile doormat, just the same as everyone else. Even the Rhodes scholar, the guy with the PhD, they are all the same!... In this game, men can't run the show. Or rather, they can, so long as they put up with a woman with no spirit and an IQ of 80 ... When they are confronted with a woman with some spirit, and an IQ over 120, an intellectual equal, someone who might *challenge* them, then suddenly they don't like it! Suddenly she's 'argumentative', or 'difficult', or 'intellectual'. All the old stuff they talked about, women hiding their intelligence from men – well it's the same here. When a woman plays dumb, the guy can write whatever he wants onto the blank slate of your persona, all his fantasies are written onto you. Men hardly ever see women.

A different view is offered by Melanie, who thinks that intelligence is actually a woman's greatest asset, in all relationships:

Men always think they want to meet beautiful, or at least very attractive and sexy women – although what that means varies so much of course. In practice, it is quite often intelligence that seduces them. Being with someone who picks up on all their moods, can talk intelligently about whatever topics they are interested in, is well-informed, but is also amusing, flirty, sexually responsive – that can be hugely attractive. Of course, it is important to be well presented, well groomed, nice clothes, and not fat. But it is personality that seduces, most of the time. That is the reason photos are useless – they tell you nothing about what someone is like to spend time with. And that's true for men as well as women. …I think of it as being like a geisha, or a famous Ginza hostess, someone whose attraction lies mainly outside the bedroom. Or like Shakespeare's view of Cleopatra, 'Age could not wither her, nor custom dull her infinite variety'.

*

Some degree of intelligence and/or education seems to be essential for married women to be found attractive companions to men who are clever enough to be senior professionals and managers, or business owners, whatever his education level. But the bottom line – for all men – seems to be that women must be sexually attractive as well, and that means slim (or at least not fat), shapely, moderately fit, and sufficiently well-groomed and well dressed to be presentable 'arm candy'. Men are often rejected if they look old and tired, but women seem to be invariably rejected for being fat, looking old and tired, or generally unattractive. Sexual attractiveness acquires such importance on these websites that it can be called women's erotic power in contrast with men's economic power.

Long and short

Profiles can be short and to the point, even reticent, or else loquacious and chatty, as a few examples illustrate.

Cavalier. Fun, early fifties, educated and own business. Looking for discreet afternoon excitement with intelligent and adventurous woman of similar age. Former athlete, 6ft, slim, fit, and discrete. In loving but sexless marriage.

Pussycat. Sexy woman in need of passion. Not looking to find 'the one' as I'm already married to him! I want to feel glamorous, so I make the effort. Looking for a gentleman who is confident in himself and in the bedroom. Central London only, and weekends away are impossible.

Rama. Hi there. I am a 40 year old, affluent, cultured, suave, well-read, well-travelled and sophisticated man of Indian origin. I am 5'8', very broad shouldered, am considered exceptionally attractive with sparkly eyes and a wicked smile. I have a wicked sense of humour and know reams of romantic poetry by heart … a lethal combination I am told. I have done many things in life, from racing motorcycles, to teaching poetry, to running a charity, reviewing music and working for Mother Teresa. I do some of these things to tame my very wild, hedonistic and unpredictable nature. I love all good things in life – nature, theatre, poetry, sensuality, wine, hedonism, etc. Travel to…(European city)…once every 6-8 weeks, mainly to give lectures, and often think company would be nice. I am an accomplished writer; an intelligent muse would be most welcome. I am a larger than life character, have a big 'psychological' presence, and even seem to occupy a disproportionate amount of space in a room. I am sexually voracious and quite skilled in the sensual arts. Above all, I am possibly one of the most well-read and intelligent people you will ever meet. I do not mean to sound either arrogant or totally 'insight-less' – I was born blessed with these gifts, and I do not mention them to take credit, but simply to encapsulate my 'essence' in a few sentences. I am in a relationship that I don't want to damage. I have two children, who are…. My kids are the still point of my turning universe, and I would never do anything that would or could harm my relationship with them. Hence discretion is absolutely vital for me. As is the other person's attractiveness, emotional maturity and intellectual independence. I am based in London, can easily travel. My problem in life is not having enough time, but any time spent together will be memorable, and quality will outshine quantity. Do reply if this is of interest.

Joy. I am uniquely me – intelligent, independent, insatiable about knowledge, touched with a little devilment, slightly quirky in my outlook on life, quick to smile, slow to anger, never to give up on a friend. I like to travel. OK, that's a vast understatement. I love to explore the world. This fascination keeps me constantly on the move to exciting places worldwide. I really enjoy seeing new places, cultures and having new experiences. I suffer fools, but not too well. I believe that life is not measured by the number of breaths we take, but by the number of moments that take our breath away. I colour outside the lines. I consider myself very easy-going, low-maintenance and spontaneous. I'm a paradoxical mix of left-brain stability and right-brain abstraction. My life is full … Yet, I am missing my mate. I want the spark of love and lust to be found with that someone special… He'll be a strong, caring person who isn't afraid to take charge of a situation … He'll have the soul of a gypsy, the heart of a romantic, an open spirit, an active mind, and a quick sexy smile. … In short, I want someone who lives passionately, loves faithfully, and travels well!

Most people on the websites opt for the middling length profile, and include key details about preferred location and timetable for any meetings.

Carmen. Fun-loving, intelligent, flirtatious and sensual without being overt, independent, strong-minded, and naturally submissive though never passive! Also have an increasingly high libido which needs satisfying – must be an age thing (39). However fun isn't about sex alone (though it's a good start), so I love being out and about in London, and I enjoy.... I'm half south-American, half-English, with olive skin, slim but curvy, long brown wavy hair and a fabulous smile! Ideally, I'd like to meet someone taller than me, naturally assertive, with a strong physique, for afternoon trysts.

Macho man (who states he is seeking casual encounters only). I'm your typical energetic, passionate, fit, fun-loving, creative, workaholic male, who despite having a full career, wants to make time for pleasure and romance. I'm athletic, and have been told my toned body is very sexy. I'm in a stable, long-term relationship, but it's got to the stage where we're friends more than lovers. I miss the intensity of an exciting physical relationship and the thrill of the chase, which probably makes me selfish, but I reckon life's worth living, and I am sure there are people out there who feel the same way. I'm strong, sexy, attentive, and a little wild at times. I pride myself on being discreet and a perfect gentleman when necessary. If you have what it takes to excite me, I'll dedicate myself to your every desire.

Calypso man. Married 1952 model, good condition for year, low mileage, careful owner, little rust, tidy bodywork, well maintained, long MOT, full service history, looking for similar, any age from mature young to young mature, for some TLC and friendship, love and cuddles. Have recently finished a 6-month relationship, looking for something longer-lasting with some soul and chemistry. Graduate, ex-City, now self-employed … South London Photo available on request.

Posting a self-portrait on a dating website requires a degree of self-knowledge as well as an element of reinvention, to see yourself as you might appear, on a good day, outside your routine environment. Returning to the dating and mating market requires courage or massive self-confidence. This may help explain why there is a preponderance of successful men in top jobs on the websites. They may have the time and the money, plus the imagination to know what is possible, but equally important, they have the confidence to carry it off, play the game, seduce and entertain.

6

Courtship and Shopping

Attached but seeking romance? Join XXXX to meet like-minded women ...

YYYY is the quality extramarital dating service for thoughtful attached men and women ...

ZZZZ allows you to search our database for suitable women, and contact them to arrange dates... It is a genuine married dating resource and not an escort service of any kind ...

VVVV delivers a dating arena for adults seeking extramarital relations... Because members have limited free time, there is an emphasis on intimate encounters ... the emphasis is on quality over quantity ...

Through TTTT you will be able to have quality sexual relations with people who are interested in upgrading their sexual lifestyle ...

In the past, marriages would be arranged by matchmakers, or were gently prompted by coming out parties, clubs or neighbourhood dances that ensured that marriageable young people met the right sort of potential partner. Your family, neighbours and friends were crucial to the entire process, and predetermined who was considered a suitable partner. In the 20th century, the self-service regime became dominant. Young and old singles frequented bars, clubs, and evening spots, joined sports clubs and special interest clubs, attended evening classes of all kinds; and dressed up glamorously for weddings and office parties, all with a view to meeting and attracting potential partners.

By the 21st century, the Do-It-Yourself (DIY) approach to mating has expanded so much it has become a new business. A new 'meet-market' industry has developed to facilitate introductions: internet-dating websites, speed-dating events in clubs and bars, singles-only evenings in bars and restaurants, plus commercial agencies specialising in introductions for marriage (usually) or dating generally. In big multi-cultural cities like London, the agencies and websites between them cater to a diversified market, facilitating link-ups for heterosexuals, homosexuals, music-lovers, wine-lovers, Christians, Jews, Moslems, Hindus, Buddhists, lovers of the countryside, socialists and radicals.

The shift has had important consequences for married women who have affairs. The big advantage of dating websites and agencies specialising in married people is that both parties are in the same boat and on an equal footing. Both sides have a lot to lose, so both will be concerned about ensuring discretion and confidentiality. This overcomes the unfairness of the traditional affair involving a married man and a single woman who feels exploited.

Dating websites for married people look similar to those for singles. They use the same software packages, so the process appears identical. The functional similarity is misleading, however. Singles dating services, and marriage introduction services generally, have roughly equal numbers of women and men subscribers given that women are more concerned with getting married and having children, preferably earlier rather than later, given that women's fertility declines rapidly after age 30. Men and women both pay membership subscriptions, typically identical fees, confirming the level playing field.

In contrast, services for married daters require men to pay to join, whereas women normally join for free. Male subscribers invariably outnumber women. Dating websites rarely offer information on user sex ratios. One report for a website specialising in sexual encounters (open to singles as well as married people) claims that it attracts 180,000 male subscribers but only 13,000 women, a sex ratio of 14 to 1. An estimate for a married dating website that specialises in more rounded affairs, is that men outnumber women 10 to 1. (There are dating websites for married people that claim to have roughly balanced numbers of men and women, but this is widely viewed as implausible.)

Men who are sharp and street-wise quickly realise that the odds are stacked in favour of women, and adjust their expectations and efforts accordingly. Many men, especially younger men who have fairly recently experienced the male advantage in singles dating and marriage markets, do not adjust their perspective and continue to behave as if they have the upper hand. In Europe at least, it is men who propose, who have decision-making power in link-ups. But in married dating, it is the women's choice. This is such an astonishing reversal of the usual power relations between the sexes that many women take a long time to understand it and take advantage of it. Few men ever really accept it.

Marketing to men

The websites for married people have an interest in looking as similar as possible to the singles dating websites that people may have already encountered, because they reassure men that they are in the driving seat, are in control, as usual. Beyond this, the software packages that define and shape the services vary a lot. What they have in common is the suggestion that a man can readily pick up a mail-order mistress, chosen to his exact specification, gift-wrapped and delivered to his door, free of charge. Pay your subscription for instant gratification.

Some websites are styled like a busy bar. The focus is on people who are currently on-line, available to chat to now. Only these people can be listed, and are easily contacted, by email messages or MSN chatting. Bar-style websites permit and promote a here-and-now style of interaction and attitude: grab a partner while you can, it is every man for himself, and don't waste much time on any one person – if she doesn't respond positively and quickly, move on to the next prospect. Bar-style websites/packages encourage casual encounters, short-term link-ups and a superficial approach to selecting a partner for an affair. It is doubtful that profiles are read properly – the focus is on photos, just as in singles dating. Despite the illicit character of married dating websites, many men and women post their photo openly on their profile, and the photo is shown in all listings of members, along with their age and geographical region, the two key selection factors. Users can also keep their photo hidden, but supply the necessary password selectively to people they approach – like a Carnival-goer removing their mask.

Other websites are styled like a mail-order catalogue. This encourages, even forces, a more considered, thoughtful approach to selecting partners. The website allows users to list all profiles, sort through them, and send approaches by email, which can be stored for future reference. The assumption is that responses may take some time, so users need folders to keep track of their correspondence. Profiles can be sifted and listed on the basis of a dozen or more selection criteria, such as:

- everyone who joined in the last month,

- everyone in a particular location or region,

- people who match certain criteria of height, physique, age, hair colour, race, religion, educational level, smoker/ non-smoker, teetotal versus drinker, etc.

This type of website invites users to supply more specific information on themselves, sometimes including occupation and income, although these two items are rarely offered as search criteria. You might expect sophisticated search criteria to allow negative criteria (eg exclude anyone in the real estate industry) as well as positive criteria (eg include non-smokers), but this seems rare.

All websites have someone to manage the site, deal with queries, and sort out problems. Some website managers actively interfere in the vetting and censoring of profiles – for example to insist on longer, more detailed descriptions, suggesting appropriate topics to cover in a profile, or by censoring language. They normally exclude or censor profiles offering telephone numbers, and other means of bypassing the website subscription requirements by supplying alternative contact methods. A particular concern here is to exclude call-girls using the site to post their telephone numbers and details. Websites vary a good deal in the sexual explicitness of the photos permitted. Some allow photos of people posing naked (usually with heads cut off or obscured) and exuberantly sexual poses. These photos may be posted openly on the profile, so they are immediately visible to anyone looking through listings of (on-line) users or in response to searches, or supplied selectively with a password.

Listings sometimes give the impression of being in an on-line brothel, with photos of (semi) naked men and women in provocative poses and sexy lingerie. This atmosphere is reinforced by profiles that set out sexual preferences, interests and abilities, such as 'I like a big cock', 'I aim to please a lady', 'I can keep going for a long time', 'I am a good lover', 'I am sensitive to a lady's needs', 'I like a woman who knows what she wants, and is not afraid to ask for it'.

Since websites are profit-making enterprises, and it is men who are the paying customers, the websites market themselves to men principally. Overall, the websites seek to give the impression that users can get whatever they want, because they have a large number of subscribers, in all areas of the country, and in all age groups. The message conveyed is that if men pay their subscription they will find an instant mistress, meeting their exact specification, delivered to them, quickly and easily. They will even have a good selection to choose from, and the choice will be theirs alone.

Women are seen as necessary to the business, even

essential, but are ultimately treated as second class citizens. Male customers who have met website managers report them as referring to female users in derogatory ways, as in the comment 'we have plenty of new stock' to refer to new women subscribers. The priority given to women who are new on the websites seems to be due to the fact that they are least likely to be aware of the user sex ratios that give women the upper hand. Newcomers are more likely to be nervous, shy, docile, grateful for any male interest, less choosy.

Whatever the style of the website, searches are time-consuming. Email correspondence or MSN chatting to potential partners is even more time-consuming. Results are not guaranteed. One step up from doing your own search of the website listings for suitable and attractive partners is the personalised service that some managers offer. The fees charged are generally substantially higher than monthly sub-scription fees – a tenfold increase or more. The service appeals to men (very rarely, to women) who have little spare time, money to spare, and dislike the idea of endless cyber chat which may finally get them nowhere. It tends to be used by men over 55 (who are most likely to find their age working against them), by people who are very anxious and nervous about the whole project and prefer to be guided through it, and by people who are accustomed to subcontracting functions to specialists in their own businesses.

The main advantage of the personalised service is that you progress immediately to dates with around half a dozen people, supposedly chosen specially to fit your preferences. Given the shortage of women on these websites, it seems doubtful that the selection process is very refined or tailor-made. But if people believe that it is, they expect to like, and get on with, the women they meet, and they do! There is probably an element of the self-fulfilling prophecy at work here. But the personalised service is faster and easier, by far, and almost always produces a satisfied customer. In contrast, a large proportion of website users do not succeed, having not met anyone they liked who also wanted to see them again. Given how the odds are stacked against them, the men need to charm to attract a partner among the women they meet. Some men are too self-confident and pushy, and fail miserably at this.

Some ordinary website users achieve the same speed as in the personalised service (at much lower cost) simply by moving quickly to fixing dates, by-passing the correspondence stage that can be so misleading as to be pointless anyway. This strategy entails a greater outlay (in time and money) on dates, instead of time spent in front of a screen chatting on-line. In general, moving quickly to a date suits people who have money but are short of time. Spending lots of time on correspondence first suits people with plenty of spare time but little cash.

The illusion of plenty

Sean Thomas' book *Millions of Women are Waiting to Meet You* offers a fascinating insight into the attitudes and perspective of young men using dating websites. The book title says it all: websites give the impression of huge meet markets for dating, sex, marriage and any other type of link-up. Thomas really did think he had the choice of millions of women, many of them exceptionally attractive-sounding. The reality was that no-one responded to his initial approaches. No-one at all. Slowly and painfully he discovered that his 'pull' factor was far lower than he imagined.

A recent study[51] shows that young people have become dramatically more narcissistic over the past thirty years, by an increase of one-third. Narcissists have inflated self-estimation, imagine themselves to be more clever, attractive, powerful and compelling than is the case. By 2006, the average American student has become as narcissistic as movie stars and famous pop musicians, and women have become just as 'me, me, me' in their attitudes as men. Such high self-esteem helps to explain young people's exaggerated expectations of instant success on dating websites.

Many believe that it makes sense to join the websites with the largest number of users, because these give you the greatest choice of potential partners. The elitist view is that it is preferable to join a website, or club, that is selective in its membership, and is therefore smaller. As one of the Marx brothers once said, 'I wouldn't want to join any club that would have me as a member'. Selective websites reduce search costs, by ensuring that all members reach a certain standard – of education, social status, wealth, culture or whatever. In a race to the bottom, most dating websites opt for the 'size matters' policy, and seek to maximise the number of users. The apparent size of their clientele is inflated by a lot of things, some partly accidental. These accidents seem to happen most often on married dating websites.

The profiles of people who have stopped paying subscriptions are usually retained, on the reasonable grounds that these customers may return eventually and want to re-use the same profile, and because it gives current users an indication of the variety of people who subscribe. However there is no tag attached to these 'ghost' profiles to show they are currently non-active. Some 'ghost' profiles belong to people who never fully joined. Websites invite newcomers to look around for free, even post a profile. Later on, they ask for fees when someone wants to respond to messages, or send messages. At this point, many women drop out, leaving their profile still on the site. Many websites, in fact, do not allow users to delete their profiles and correspondence records when they decide to withdraw completely; they must send a request to the website manager. Some forget to do this; some make errors sending the message so it is never received; and some send the request correctly, but the website manager leaves the profile in place anyway.

Constance made the mistake of using her real name when she first registered with a dating website, misunderstanding the procedure, like many newcomers. When she realised her error, she sent a request for her profile to be deleted, and assumed this was done. In any event, she quit the website soon after, as she met someone she liked. To her horror, her new boyfriend told her six months later that both her original profile using her real name, and the second one under another name, were still listed on the website. He had done one final search shortly before his subscription was due to expire. Constance then sent a strongly worded email insisting that the website manager delete both her profiles permanently. Of course, someone who has left a website is in a poor position for checking that their profile has been deleted, as requested.

As women do not have to pay, or pay very little to join a married-dating website, some try to maximise their chances of success by posting several profiles, each describing a different person, or emphasising a different aspect of their personality and interests – for example a blond version and a brunette version. Sometimes just for fun, or to see how it affects responses, women post several totally fabricated profiles – for example, one saying they are poor and uneducated but beautiful, another claiming to be a highly paid high flying banker in the City looking for purely sexual encounters, and a third saying they are a novice who is not sure what they are doing here. In addition to these speculative profiles, every website will have working girls: call girls and escort girls, amateur and professional, who think they might find customers among the men on these sites, especially those looking for 'no strings' casual sex, who may be happy to pay for it if they fail with ordinary subscribers. These women have every incentive to post multiple profiles with diverse descriptions to attract the widest range of interest, especially as they are regularly deleted from the websites following complaints from any male customer.

On top of all that, website managers invent profiles for women, to create the impression that the site is successful and attracting a lot of users. (These are usually described as being for 'testing purposes'.) Finally, some men are persuaded to subscribe for one year, on the grounds that this is the more cost-effective option, which gives them plenty of time, so they do not feel rushed. If they meet someone they like early on, they may stop logging on, but their profile remains listed for the full year, and possibly beyond that. Some websites code users according to how recently they logged on. Where this facility is available, it quickly becomes apparent that many users listed have not logged on for weeks, for months, or even years. In practice, they have 'gone away'. Occasionally, someone modifies their profile to say explicitly 'gone away' or 'not currently looking'.

Given this background, it is not surprising that most men have few responses to their opening approaches. Sean Thomas describes the illusion of choice in relation to singles dating in his book. The illusion is even greater for married dating websites. One estimate is that up to one-third of profiles are ghosts or other inactive users who will never respond to any approach; around one-third of users are too rude or lazy to send a polite response to an initial approach that does not interest them; so you can only expect a response of some sort from the remaining one-third. The general practice appears to be to send out at least 6-10 initial approaches in the hope of getting 2-4 replies. In the end, Sean Thomas met the lovely girl he married through a dating website, so his story ended happily. But his book suggests that his internet dating experiences taught him a few salutary lessons along the way that may have turned him into a more agreeable and appreciative partner.

Excluding the ghosts

Because men invariably outnumber women, it is usually the man who makes the first approach. To help out, many websites offer the option of a non-message approach: sending someone a 'wink' or a 'virtual kiss', or making someone a 'favourite'. These allow the man to wordlessly say I exist, I am on this website, I am interested in you. Some 'winks' include a brief quote from the man's profile. This puts the onus on the recipient to check out the sender's profile, and write the first message if she likes what she reads about him, or sees in any photo.

The wink and virtual kiss are used extensively by some men, to contact dozens of women in a shotgun approach, so some women routinely ignore them. Women's profiles sometimes include the statement that 'all virtual kisses are deleted on sight, so please do not waste your time that way'. Men's profiles sometimes include bitter comments on this practice, such as the man who complains about women who '… don't know, or are too far up your own backside, to realise the value of a virtual kiss and insist on a page of poetic prose without promising the same in return, or to realise that the men worth having are those who have a busy and interesting life'.

The next step up is a minimalist impersonal opening message. These can be very minimal indeed, such as 'Hi there!' or 'Try me!' More common is 'I liked your profile. Take a look at mine, and get in touch if you like what you see'. A sex-focused man tried 'How do you feel about anal?' as an opener. Here too, the man leaves the woman to write the real opening message, if she wants. Men defend these minimalist openers as recognising that, in practice, it is women's choice on these websites, so all they can do is point out their availability, and hope to stimulate some interest. Some men defend these unimaginative approaches with the argument 'Minimum effort, maximum return'. They point out their strategy has to be to eliminate the 'ghost women' first of all.

Given the fact that real users are in contented marriages, most invest some effort in their opening approach, writing at least a couple of sentences and sometimes up to a page of self-introduction, saying where they live, how long they have been on the site, previous experiences of affairs, plus something about what they found attractive in your profile. Just like job applications, where it is crucial to show you know what the firm actually does, they realise it is important to show you have read the person's profile properly, so the message is tailor-made in some way, rather than reading like a round robbin to several people.

Just as in job applications, the prime purpose of their opening approach is to stimulate enough interest that they get taken seriously, start a conversation, leading to a first date. The greatest compliment of all is the idea that they chose someone above all others, for specific reasons.

On singles websites, exchanging photos is an essential first step, and younger people often treat it as necessary on married websites as well. However lots of married people do not bother, largely because photos can be so misleading. Someone can send a picture from ten years ago, in part because they have lopped ten years off their stated age. Men often send 'landscape' photos that show a man in a suit in the distance. It tells you nothing except that he has a head, two arms and two legs – or did have, at some point. Photos are central to singles websites. The need for secrecy and discretion on married dating websites means there is far less emphasis on photos. Many people refuse to offer them, or supply one only after switching to private email addresses. On one website, several men claimed the password protection for hidden photos was not secure, so refused to supply any photos via the website. For many people, the offer of a date is conditional on never being asked for a photo, even after meeting, because photo files can be retained and pose a risk of being found out.

Previous encounters

At a rough estimate, at least half of the people who start using a dating website for married people have had one affair already, or a one-night fling, typically with someone they met at work, or through their work activities and business trips. The other half are people responding to adverts for such websites which give them the idea that an affair is easy, just like using the internet to go shopping, and that they can obtain loads of no-strings sex at no cost whatever, with minimal effort.

The first group, with prior affairs, is very different from the group of nervous, or brash, novices. They know that they are capable of going down this road and they already have some notion of the psychological and financial costs involved and know how to handle them. Some men therefore advertise the fact of having had previous affairs in their profiles, because some women refuse to meet novices with no prior experience. Novices often want to proceed slowly, getting to know someone before they take the final step of getting intimate. There is the possibility that the guy will give up and walk away from it all at the last minute. Women are much less likely to advertise any prior experience, and actually less likely to have any. Many married men actively seek out married women who are novices because they are less demanding, more docile, more amenable to whatever style of affair he prefers, whether focused primarily on sexual encounters or a more rounded girlfriend relationship.

What kind of affair someone had previously is usually a

good indication of what they seek now. The first affair exhibits all the needs and desires that someone seeks to fulfil in an affair, or else provides the template and pattern for later affairs. Someone's first affair can tell a lot about what style of relationship they automatically reach for. People do not invariably choose the same as before; they may seek something positively different if the first affair was unsatisfactory in some way. But the first affair establishes a pattern of behaviour and expectations that may well be repeated in subsequent affairs, simply because people are creatures of habit. Promiscuous adventurers seek a fantastic zipless fuck. The romantic hopes for the emotional trip of romance and falling in love again – sometimes, even a potential new wife. Some seek the aesthetic pleasures of arm candy, while others want good company for regular nights out when in town on business. For many, the aspiration is some magical combination of all of these things. So the first affair becomes a concrete model of 'what to expect', of roles and type of dates and a point of reference for both sides.

The New Rules

In their book on rules for singles dating, Ellen Fein and Sherrie Schneider advise women to let men do all the chasing, always, always, always. Even in the context of dating websites, they advise women to post a good profile and photo, then sit back and wait for men to contact them and offer dates. They argue that if a man cannot be bothered to make an effort to pursue you, offer dates, and make all the arrangements, he is not truly interested. This may well be good advice for women in the context of singles dating, where the ultimate aim is to find a husband, a lifetime partner and a father for any children you hope to have. *The Rules* are about 'capturing the heart of Mr Right' – not about finding a lover for private playtimes.

The rules for married dating and affairs are completely different, primarily because the normal power play is reversed. In effect, married women on these sites are put in the power position that French women assume is theirs. Men seeking guilt-free no-strings sex far outnumber women on the websites (and in real life), so it's ladies' choice here. All women on married websites receive numerous approaches; younger and attractive-sounding women are inundated at times. So it is easy to sit back and respond to offers. In fact, women (are more likely to) get exactly what they want when they become active users instead – searching through profiles and sending opening messages to the men who sound or look attractive. Men so rarely receive approaches from women that they are usually grateful for the attention, and well-disposed towards the sender. In Puritanical countries, mating markets where women have the upper hand are so rare that it is easy to overlook them.

Peter is an immensely successful commercial lawyer, and now also a judge, who made a small fortune by the time he was 62. He lives in a beautiful historical country house with his lively wife, and travels into central London to sit as judge in important commercial disputes. A creature of habit, he always stays in the same hotel, with views over the Thames. After several years of this routine, he began to welcome the idea of a sexy girlfriend to entertain him during his weekday hotel stays. He signed onto a dating website.

The first woman he met was Maya, a stunning black girl in

hcr 30s, hair piled up on top of her head, high heels, and a sexy dress. All heads turned to look at her as she walked into the restaurant, and was guided over to Peter's table. She was stunning. Her profile never mentioned that she was black, but frankly it did not matter. They had a cheerful and flirty lunch, sitting in the sunshine, by the window. Peter could not believe his good luck, and felt ten feet tall. Towards the end of lunch, they started to discuss practical arrangements for meeting again. Maya explained that she already had one regular boyfriend, but she could easily see Peter as well, whenever he wanted, there would be no conflicts of time as Peter was only in London in the middle of the week. She mentioned her normal monthly fee for unlimited time with him, at his convenience, to do whatever he wanted, stay in or go out. As Peter put it later 'I just laughed'. His idea was that paying for the odd lunch or dinner would be generous enough.

Six lunch dates later, Peter began to realise that Maya's terms were not ridiculous after all. Peter had no difficulty in fixing first dates, as he always offered lunch in a nice restaurant. But none of them were interested in dating an unattractive bald man of 62 who thought that joining him for a walk by the Thames after he had finished his day's work was a romantic offer. Things never progressed beyond that first date.

An important feature of dating websites is that they are open to all – all religions, nationalities, social classes, educational levels, ages, races and ethnic groups. You can never be sure who you might be meeting, especially if they do not identify themselves fully. This openness is one of the great advantages of the internet. It also means that good manners and diplomacy are extremely important, as there is always room for misunderstandings and crossed wires at any stage of communication. Behaviour that is standard practice for one person may be regarded as rude by another user. Successful married users make no assumptions. In particular, they do not assume that everyone else lives exactly the same way as they do, with the same norms and expectations.

For Patrick, the diversity of website users was the biggest draw. As a writer and journalist, he was comfortable meeting people from all walks of life, and was skilled at putting them at ease so he could get the best information from them. Dates with women from the website were always exciting, as he never knew who would turn up – someone similar to or rather different from the profile description. Overall, descriptions were reasonably fair, although some women were either far more attractive, or less attractive, than their profiles implied. But then, he was equally aware that some of his dates had been visibly disappointed with him in the flesh.

Websites for married affairs do have some bona-fide subscribers who are single: divorced, separated or never-married. Most of them are seeking a regular girlfriend/boyfriend/lover without the prospect of marriage as a potential final destination. Singles see marriage as the implicit goal on all singles-dating websites, especially for people who prefer to have a regular or long-term lover rather than a series of romantic encounters with a new partner every time. At least some of them are commitment-phobes who want all the benefits of a long-term secure sexual relationship without any of the social and emotional obligations that typically accompany it. Commitment-phobes are not exclusively young, carefree addicts of freedom and autonomy. Philip Roth's novel *The Dying Animal* (made into Isabel Coixet's film *Elegy*) depicts an ageing professor who is unable to commit to a young and beautiful woman, an ex-student who has fallen in love with him, despite the fact that he is already old enough for his friends to start dying.

Some married website users actively seek out unattached users who offer more flexibility, are free to meet lovers without constraints, and can provide the venue for sexual trysts, since they live alone. Others avoid them, seeing them as selfish and self-centred people, lacking in generosity of spirit, who are changed by many years spent living alone, or by the scars of acrimonious divorces. The profiles of this group usually state that they are not seeking marriage or a permanent partner, but are treating the website as if it were an ordinary singles dating website, which means they prefer dates in the evenings and at weekends. They are also relatively unconcerned with discretion and maintaining secrecy – the two things that typically matter a lot to other users.

She's mine, all mine! Exclusivity and jealousy

Married people with jobs generally find it hard to spare time for an affair, and have to work hard to create free time. Those with no job or part-time jobs have far more time to play with. Women who are full-time homemakers can have just as many restrictions on their time as women with jobs if they have children at home to care for. Others are ladies of leisure with real time sovereignty. This, plus the disproportionate numbers of men on the websites, means nonetheless that women can have the option of seeing several men in any year, especially as there may be long gaps between dates due to work deadlines, foreign travel and holidays.

Some men also seek to have two or three lovers, and even say so explicitly in their profiles, but they generally have a harder time with this. Men who do have spare time usually advertise this factor clearly in their profiles. Firemen, policemen and army staff take early retirement in their late 40s or early 50s, which gives them plenty of free time even if they pick up a part-time job. This, combined with the physical fitness that goes with these jobs can make them a popular choice for an affair. Some men underline all this by posting a photo of themselves in their fireman's outfit or policeman's uniform, which have a particular appeal to some women.

Overall, women are more likely to have control over their time, and more free time, than do men on the dating websites for married people. The imbalance in numbers is exacerbated by an imbalance in time freedom. This can prompt jealousy and anxiety about exclusivity, typically among married men, in sharp contrast to the normal situation among dating singles.

The reality is that men simply do not know, cannot ever know, whether a mistress sees anyone else as well. In any case, such jealousy is counter-productive. As La Rochefoucauld said, there is more self-love than love in jealousy. Married men who like to be in control demand exclusivity in their affairs, arguing that anything else is 'exploitation' by the women they are interested in. Other men simply ignore the question, assuming that their married girlfriend sees them only.

Caroline got on extremely well with her boyfriend Simon except for his jealousy, which became paranoid over time. He was extremely busy with his job, working long hours, and could only make time to see her once a month on average. Although he kept in touch when they were apart, he started to wonder whether Caroline ever saw other men from the website. His subscription had lapsed after three months, so he was unable to check whether she had been online recently. In any case, Simon kept reminding himself that women could subscribe for free, so Caroline did not need to retain her original profile – she might have a new one! He started asking Caroline whether she still used the website. She laughed, and said not. But Simon was not sure he believed her. He kept throwing out suspicious comments about her opportunities to see other men in the long gaps between their dates. Caroline ignored them, but he became more obsessed with the idea anyway. After many months of pointless accusations, Caroline finally decided to dump him. Simon's jealousy was souring their affair.

In contrast, Tatiana dated two men simultaneously for a while. One year, she met two men she liked and gelled with, pretty well at the same time. Both of them were busy with their jobs, and travelled a lot, so she saw them infrequently. John had a marketing post with an international firm. Raymond ran his own company selling software and IT services to international conglomerates. They were very different men, but she liked them both.

Tatiana noticed that it was only Raymond who was obsessively concerned with her being 'Mine, all mine!' as he put it. He was used to being in complete control of his business, and felt that it was his close attention to detail at every stage that had earned his firm such a high reputation.

The contrast in his relationship with Tatiana was uncomfortable for him. Unlike his wife and his secretary, he had no idea where Tatiana was most days, and he could not insist on her being available to see him when he wanted, or even available to take his phone calls when he wanted. Raymond knew he was a control freak, always had been, which was why he had never liked being an employee. While seeing Tatiana gave him great pleasure, and forced him to take short breaks from work for the first time in years, he was constantly fretting at his inability to be in control of the situation – and of her. Tatiana disliked the idea that anyone would even think of trying to control her. Tatiana noticed she had no such problems of control and exclusivity with John, who was simply delighted to see her whenever he could spare the time. That relationship proved to be the one that endured.

For women, married dating websites provide an enormous opportunity. As they really do create open and transparent mating markets, people quickly establish their relative ranking, or what is currently called 'pull factor', in terms of social desirability, physical attractiveness and sex appeal. This can be much higher, or lower, than they initially imagine.

After years stuck at home being a good mother, Holly had little sexual self-confidence. The website made a big difference. 'It boosted my self-confidence enormously! I discovered that men still find me attractive – and it was men of all ages, not just older men, who are always going to be pleased to date a younger woman. I got approaches from men as young as 21 and 25 – Yes! – all the way up to 65. And virtually all the men I met wanted to see me again – for sex.

Now, I know men are not choosy about who they sleep with, but most of these guys seemed genuinely keen! It was great to have the choice. I really did have a lot of choice.'

For men, the experience can be quite the opposite, and this is especially upsetting for men who are successful in their careers, used to winning, and regard themselves as alpha males. As Conrad puts it 'I found the whole experience very dispiriting. Most of my messages got no response at all, and I sent out quite a few approaches! Most of the married women I fancied meeting, from their profile descriptions, excluded me because they wanted to meet successful men aged 40 to 50 and at least six foot tall. Some of the women who approached me themselves appeared to be working girls who charge money for sex.'

Women get cheered up enormously by discovering their sex appeal, and hence their relatively high power in negotiations about an affair, while large numbers of men discover that success at work does not automatically translate into romantic and sexual desirability, unless they are prepared to be generous with time, attention and/or money, and are sexually very competent as well.

No single website provides a microcosm of the whole world, but several websites taken together offer an excellent picture of meeting markets, as they cover the entire country and all age groups. In this playground, married men think they can fix the rules, as usual. Married women don't argue, they just walk away.

Website experiences are hard to read. Civilised people invariably conceal their rejections of an interested partner behind gradual fade-outs, stories of being unexpectedly busy at work or family crises. You rarely discover what led someone to reject you – though the three most common turn-offs are being an obese woman, a stingy man, or coming over as an exceptionally 'needy' person. Even people who give a reason for rejection will courteously mention just one technical or practical impediment, whereas there may have been several other factors which are more important and more personal. All the users know for sure is their success rates for initial approaches and for first dates, and whether anyone wants to continue seeing them.

7

The Actual Dates

Patricia approached dates with a relaxed, sunny attitude that was rare, and hugely successful. Before each date, she reminded herself of an actress she had seen in a play years before. The actress played the role of a beautiful woman, around whom all the action turned. She walked tall, smiled a lot, was serene, graceful, charming, elegant in her person and in her manners with everyone. Afterwards, looking again at the photo of the actress on the programme, Patricia realised she was actually average in looks; but she played a beautiful woman, and that was what you saw. So Patricia acted the beautiful woman when she went on dates. No matter what happened, or who she met, she tried to remain a serene, charming, elegant and well-mannered beautiful woman. Most of the men she met found her attractive. Rejections were rare. In her view, there was no point in meeting someone unless you presented your 'best self'.

The French word for an affair is *une aventure*, and that is how successful married people approach dating for an affair. First dates, further dates after that, should all be seen as an adventure. Nothing ventured, nothing gained. There are no certainties, there will be many misunderstandings, many disappointments, but every date teaches them something about what they are looking for to spice up their marriage.

The risk of a poor match may be reduced, but is never eliminated through a website. Extremely positive on-line liaisons are not necessarily a good indicator of what happens when you meet someone. To a large extent, the two activities are separate.

Soon after joining a website, Scott thought he had found a soul-mate in Anna. They hit it off immediately, with a similar style of flirtatious banter and sexy jokes. The only problem was, she lived in another city. After several weeks' correspondence, Scott took the day off work to travel to Anna's city to have lunch with her. Like many men, he reasoned that if they really were well-matched, he would be prepared to travel to see her. She chose the restaurant, and the meet-up was smooth. Unfortunately, they found they had absolutely no rapport at all when they were finally together. Somehow, the witty repartee of the on-line chats had vanished. Neither of them felt the other person was what they had been expecting, had fantasised about for weeks. The lunch fell completely flat. He summarised the mood as 'there was nothing there'.

Misleading profiles can give a poor start to first dates, but this is rarely the only factor. David and Fiona chatted on-line for weeks before they finally met for a drink. Early on, she provided a photo, so he knew he found her attractive. He also found her lively, amusing, well-informed on almost every subject that came up. So he was astonished that the first date was a disaster. Fiona was really fat, something that had not been obvious from her head and shoulders photo, and was not mentioned in her profile. Just as important, she was so ploddingly dull. He did not recognise her as the livewire he met on-line. He figured that her job in the media had allowed her to bone up on topics quickly before she replied to him on-line, so that she always seemed well-informed, in their correspondence. Whatever the reason, she found it hard to hold a conversation with him. In the end, they did not even get as far as a second drink, and the date ended quickly.

Time and time again, men select women on physical attraction and youth only, then find it impossible to hold a reasonable conversation with the young woman of modest intelligence and limited education that they meet. Similarly, women meet men who sound lively and interesting during on-line chats, but turn out to look and behave old and tired, are fat and unfit rather than 'in good shape'. Men who claim they 'know how to treat a lady' turn out to be clumsy and rude. Physical attractiveness can be enough for those seeking purely sexual encounters, but they are rarely enough for the more rounded relationship, which involves conversation, that most married daters look for.

Internet dating guidebooks for singles often recommend a slow step-by-step approach: chat on the website, chat on the phone, exchange photos, switch to private email addresses for further chatting before finally meeting briefly for a coffee first, then possibly a full date later if all goes well. There is no evidence that this time-consuming procedure guarantees to eliminate undesirable people. What works for singles dating does not necessarily make sense for married people who are not seeking a long-term partner. Most people on married dating websites move quickly to meeting anyone that sounds attractive. This approach is typical of busy and confident people, who have little time to waste. Sexual attraction is clearly important, but you can only judge this by meeting someone. Also, married people have less time to spend online, and may not be able to do this at home in the evenings and at weekends.

The type of initial date can indicate whether someone is interested in seduction and romance, or is just shopping for a convenient sexual partner. Men generally focus on sex as the central interest, while women variously seek good sex or a boyfriend. Married people seeking sex, pure and simple, often regard meeting for coffee, or a drink, as sufficient to establish whether the other party is sexually attractive enough to be worth proceeding with. They are not interested in wasting time on 'getting to know you' conversations, and stay focused on the 'where and when' practicalities of a sexual encounter. People who are interested in a more rounded relationship are more inclined towards a longer initial date, such as meeting for lunch or dinner.

You may get on well with someone socially, on a date in a public place, but things may not work out at all well when you finally get intimate. Women usually focus on the former. Men are often more concerned with sex. Many men try to insist on intimacy on a second date, or even the first, talking about the need to check 'sexual chemistry' and 'sexual compatibility'. Women often feel this is 'rushing things', as they will not make up their minds for certain about someone without at least two dates. Men's impatience is usually misplaced, since couples who get on well for two dates often move on to physical intimacy by the third date anyway. However the relative emphasis on sex versus a more rounded relationship can be a stumbling block in the first few dates.

Dalton agreed to meet Margaret in a garden centre coffee shop. She sounded attractive, and he had no time for on-line chatting. Both in their late forties, they got on easily. But on meeting, her appearance astonished him. She was dressed like an ageing hippie, with a long full skirt, silver ankle chains, long loose hair and big silver hoop ear-rings. He invited her to lunch at a nice hotel with a good restaurant on the river nearby. For some reason, she seemed resistant to the idea, but agreed. As lunch went on, Margaret seemed increasingly restless, finally saying they were 'running out of time'. It emerged that she had allocated exactly two hours to her mid-day date with him, and expected this to include a worthwhile session in a hotel bedroom. From her point of view, lunch was a waste of time. She was registered on several websites, including those specialising in purely sexual encounters, and was prepared to sleep with anyone available, but with a preference for 'men with a big cock'. Dalton had thought he was interested in a casual encounter, with sex looming large, but discovered that the blunt reality of it simply did not appeal. In practice, he did not like being regarded purely as a sex machine.

Pamela liked the look of Matthew from his photo, and agreed to meet him, despite the fact that he worked in IT, which she regarded as a 'geek' field. They got on well, he went out of his way to be charming and courteous, and clearly found her sexy. They had several dates over a month or two, including a visit to an exhibition, and a ride on the London Eye, before Matthew got round to suggesting she might come back to his hotel room next time, after lunch in a rather nice restaurant. It was a freezing cold but sunny winter's day, and Pamela was wearing a warm winter coat. When they got to the hotel room, she found that Matthew had left all the windows wide open, 'for fresh air'. Politely, he agreed to pull them almost shut for her, but the room remained an ice box. The sex turned out to be perfunctory. Feeling cold even under the bedcovers, Pamela was happy to get back into her warm clothes and winter coat and leave as soon as she could. After some desultory further email chatting, they never got round to fixing another date.

Tom disliked email chatting and texting, and had no time for it anyway. So he always moved quickly to fixing dates, to meet women for real, before deciding whether he wanted to see more of them. When he met Cassandra, he saw a lot more than he expected. They met for dinner on the outskirts of the City of London, in an informal tapas bar-restaurant, which provided an excellent venue for many of his first dates. Coming straight from work, Cassie was dressed in a severe business suit that was totally unsexy, but she was still visibly attractive with long curly blond hair, blue eyes and a great smile. An American with an international bank, she had not been in London long, and was curious about everything. Tom guessed she was probably earning substantially more than he did, but that did not seem to worry her, and she clearly found him attractive. After several glasses of wine and small dishes, she pulled out her mobile phone, and started showing him intimate photos of her naked body and genitalia on the phone. She was clearly trying to get him excited, and wanted to move to a sexual encounter as soon as possible. Tom had always thought of himself as open-minded and easy-going, but he found himself reacting with shock to Cassie's explicitly sexual approach to him. Partly, he disliked being viewed as a sex object. Mostly, he felt it had to be him who made a move on a woman, he needed to be in control of events, especially anything sexual. (Most married men do.)

Some women are unwilling to discuss sex, especially before meeting a man, because they regard it as vulgar and unfeminine. For a lot of women good sex involves the man taking the lead, so that they have little experience of taking a more active role. They know that men generally prefer this. Men and women who are reluctant to discuss sex, and are generally reticent, can still be enthusiastic partners when things progress that far.

George's first date was with a stunning brunette, mid-30s, fantastic figure, everything she said in her profile. He was crazy about her, but although they had a good time when they met for a drink after work one evening, she was non-committal about meeting him again. He tried to fix another date, repeatedly, but each time she was evasive, never finally agreeing to anything. Eventually he gave up, and started approaching other women again, conscious that his website subscription would shortly expire. His second date was with Zoe, a woman 4-5 years older than himself. She suggested a rather smart and busy Italian restaurant in the City, so he was surprised when she turned up in a pretty dress and a big smile rather than the black suits and grim expressions worn throughout the City. As an IT specialist, George normally dressed casually, but this time he had made an effort, with a smart shirt and trousers instead of jeans. He organised a table in a quiet corner, and having already chatted up the sommelier, he got an excellent bottle of wine. Zoe liked the wine, started to relax, and seemed to blossom into a very attractive woman as they both got a little tipsy and had an excellent lunch. By the time they got to coffee, George had made up his mind, but wanted to know whether it was mutual. Without warning, he leant over and kissed Zoe on the mouth, in full view of people at nearby tables. Again, she surprised him by kissing him back, for real. She said later that was the last thing she had expected him to do, she thought he was playing it cool.

The date became the start of a classic whirlwind romance, except that it was an affair, private and discreet. George would email or phone Zoe 3-6 times a day, maintaining a semi-permanent connection with her on days when he could not see her. As it was a slack time in his job, between projects, he often spent the day with her. They visited exhibitions, went shopping for Christmas presents, visited famous monuments as if they were tourists, explored bars and ancient pubs in the city. The sex was as generous, passionate and happy as George hoped. Looking back, it was Zoe's enthusiasm for life that matched his, that pulled him in, and held him, that brought him alive in a new way, and made him see London in a new light.

Gabriela had always found dark men with black hair and black eyes sexually attractive, so she responded with interest to approaches from men of Indian descent on the dating website. To her surprise, the dates invariably proved difficult.

Ash had lived almost all his life in the United States, and

had a marked American accent, despite looking quintessentially Indian. His wife was a blond American woman who had refused to relocate to London for his 3-year posting abroad, partly because their children's schooling would be disrupted. Ash was alone in his expenses-paid central London flat, and only saw his wife during his periodic visits back to his headquarters office. Not surprisingly, he was on the website looking for a mistress in London. Gabriela was his second date. At her suggestion, they met for lunch in the OXO Tower restaurant near his office, with fantastic views over the Thames. Ash was as attractive as his photo suggested, if a bit overweight, and extremely clever. He clearly found Gabriela attractive, and wanted to see her again. It was the way he set this out that was the problem.

Ash gave Gabriela a detailed account of his demanding work timetable and job responsibilities. He explained when he would be able to fit her in, and for how long at a time. His account told her that he expected meetings to be exclusively for sex at his flat close to his office. He informed her that all appointments with her would be subject to cancellation at very short notice, if anything urgent or important came up at work that day. She had to understand that his job came first, always, but he would do his best not to disappoint her. Ash set out, as clearly and precisely as he could, the terms and conditions he applied to what he apparently took for granted as their agreement to have an affair. Towards the end of lunch, Gabriela realised Ash had never asked, and she had never said, she wanted to see him again. He seemed to think that meeting him for lunch, or at all, implicitly committed her to whatever he proposed and suited him. When she wrote afterwards to say she did not want to take things further, he was surprised and angry.

'Indians do not seem to flirt', she concluded. Gabriela figured that cultures with arranged marriages have a rather dry approach to relationships, with a focus on terms and conditions, contractual obligations, everything negotiated explicitly at the start. She had a similar experience with every Indian man she met, whether they grew up in Britain, India or North America, younger and older, and she finally gave up her fantasy of an affair with one of them.

It is the umpteen small points in a date that can provoke a decision not to take it any further. Married people are much more cautious than are singles in weighing things up. They have less spare time, and far more to lose from mistakes, so many play it ultra-safe in rejecting anyone who raises any doubts whatsoever, rather than taking a chance. Single people have little to lose, and more to gain, so can afford to be more open-minded. Many married people will not make a final decision until after a second date, to be absolutely sure that they feel safe with someone's discretion, and that practical and logistical matters are workable.

Someone who seeks to behave in a familiar, even amorous manner in public places – in the street, on the metro, in cafes and bars – will generally be rejected no matter how attractive they are. This problem arises with single people who use married dating websites, the divorced and separated who are 'between things' and who are not concerned about secrecy. It also arises with married men who travel into the city on business but live elsewhere. Like people on holiday who are far more reckless in foreign countries than they would be in their own neighbourhood, they feel unconstrained, free to do as they like, almost invisible. Behaviour that suggests a careless attitude to discretion and secrecy is an important turn-off for people who live and work in the same place. As Susan points out 'I should not have to *ask* for discretion, it is self-evident in the nature of the website'.

Beyond this, people vary hugely in what is a turn-off, what matters to them personally, what they dislike. Men are usually explicit about preferring a woman to dress well and look good, but style is a matter of taste. Susan again: 'I have this fantastic black leather dress, body tight and very sexy. It suits me so well that strangers in the street compliment me when I am wearing it. But I am very careful about who I wear it for. Some men would regard it as tarty. Which it could be. It depends on how you wear it.'

Amy liked one man, found him really interesting, but was put off by his wearing a shabby grey cardigan under his suit jacket. It made him look old, and cold. She found it off-putting, whereas a modern navy round neck sweater could have been attractive. She felt he was not bothered to dress nicely for her, and that implied he would make little effort more generally.

Another common turn-off is people who change and cancel dates at short notice, due to work obligations. This often happens with men running their own business, who must be responsive to clients' demands, but also with professional people who are at their clients' beck and call. Late changes due to business meetings being re-arranged can be hugely disruptive to the other party, who may have made special arrangements for the date to be feasible. In the nature of things, neither party will be telling the other about the minutiae of their arrangements, and their cover-up excuses, so that changes to meetings (especially late changes) can be far more disruptive than it may appear.

For women, dressing up for a date is a major part of the fun, so late changes spoil it. People often want dates to be 'special' in some way, so that being treated as lowest priority, squeezed in between business meetings can feel insulting. Women who are repeatedly late for dates, thus squeezing the time available, and keeping their man waiting, are a big turn-off. Many women like little gifts from time to time, and will also expect to give small gifts. Men who never offer a gift, even at Christmas or on Saint Valentine's day, or offer a gift that is derisory, may well be quietly dumped. Men who can clearly afford substantial gifts or other treats but refuse to offer one, ever, are also a turn-off.

The outer edge

When he first wrote to her on the website, Kate thought Benedict sounded too good to be true, and she said so. His photo showed a handsome, fit, and cheerful man in a swimsuit. As a company director, he travelled a good deal around Europe and was often in London. He said he had had two previous affairs ('successfully' as he put it) and was keen to meet for lunch at the earliest opportunity. They met in a restaurant that was fashionable and busy in the evenings but was almost empty at lunchtime, so they were able to talk freely without worrying about being overheard. To Kate's astonishment, Benedict was everything he claimed to be, and more. Elegant, attractive, extremely clever, and great company, with wide interests. He had spent twenty years in the army, rising quickly into managerial roles. He was now working his way up the corporate management ladder, aiming for a CEO post in the near future. He talked freely about his two previous affairs, which he presented as being sex affairs, very simply, with women who, for different reasons, had been willing to try anything. To Kate's surprise, both had been single, one aged 20, tall, beautiful and not yet married, the other aged 48, freshly divorced, and determined to sample everything sexual that had been denied her while she was married. He described them both as 'adventurous', and briefly mentioned the threesomes, partner-swapping, and kinky interests of each of them. It then emerged that he had been using another website entirely, one that specialised in hook-ups focused purely on sex. He had only recently joined a married dating website because there was less competition. As the lunch ended, he offered to show Kate around some of the exciting places he knew in London.

The first place was just a few doors away from the restaurant, ostensibly an ordinary cafe and shop, but with a hidden basement full of sex toys, fetish-wear, books and pictures to match. One handout was a leaflet with a map showing other London shops selling similar stuff. Benedict then took Kate on a guided tour of half a dozen other shops, some selling sexy lingerie and sex toys, which she had been vaguely aware of but had never browsed in before, others with the hidden basement down a treacherously steep flight of stairs, sufficient to deter the unwary casual tourist. Down in these 'dungeons' the more advanced sex toys and paraphernalia were on sale. These included a variety of metal objects, some rather sharp, whose function was unclear to Kate, and she hesitated to ask, in case she was told enthusiastically.

Fetish-wear was widely on display, some of it very fetching, most of it designed for women.

The tour ended with a glass of champagne in a bar, with Benedict trying to gauge her reactions to what she had seen. Even after a drink, Kate decided this was a step too far for her. Benedict was fabulous, and very likeable, no doubt about that. But the tour had unsettled her. So much kinky equipment she could barely make sense of, plus the fact that he clearly knew these shops very well, frequented them regularly, presumably as a customer. In addition, he was exceptionally fit, visibly so, and would thus be far stronger than her. There was no indication he was interested in anything other than consensual activities, but trusting a complete stranger seemed too much to ask for in this case. She decided to decline this opportunity to explore the outer edge.

Oliver thought Scarlett sounded like exactly his sort of woman, tall, blonde, with blue eyes and an hourglass figure. So he readily agreed to complicated arrangements for meeting one evening, at an address in a suburb unfamiliar to him. He assumed he was picking her up from her home, and they would go out for a drink. When he got to the house, it appeared a party was in progress, with lots of people and a bouncer guarding the front door. He explained he had come to meet Scarlett, and was given entry.

It was not an ordinary party, but a swinging house party. Men and women were in various states of undress in all the rooms, engaged in sexual activity in pairs, in small groups, or sometimes just watching. He was told that as a newcomer, he was allowed to stay dressed and just observe this time, if he did not want to join in. If he returned to attend any future party, he would be expected to perform. When he finally met her, Scarlett seemed disappointed that he did not want to join the action, and went off to have a good time again.

After an hour at the party, Oliver decided he was unlikely to take up swinging. There appeared to be some element of 'pot luck' about pairings, and he preferred to have a lot more control over his choice of partner. The very public nature of the sexual activity encouraged competitive rivalry in performance, especially among the young men, he thought. But what he found most disconcerting was the pursuit of orgasmic sex in an impersonal context. Sex became a spectator sport, a competition, almost a porn show, divorced from any relationship or social context. He could see how this might appeal to libidinous young men but decided it was not for him. He preferred to stay private, know his partner, and have some sort of a relationship.

What went wrong?

Robert openly offered a photo on the website, which was unusual. He looked stunningly handsome, and cheerful, so Samantha did everything she could to attract his attention, and get a date when he was next in the city. Robert agreed quite readily, even without a preliminary photo. He had met several women, and found photos to be so unreliable as to be pointless. He ran his own business, which involved lots of risky decisions about people and investments, so he was used to judging people, on paper and in person, and was used to hiring and firing people. He knew that you have to meet someone face to face to take a view about them.

They agreed to meet for a drink in the bar of the Criterion, an old restaurant in the centre of London with a beautiful gold mosaic ceiling and an old fashioned style. Samantha thought it would be fairly quiet at 5.30 pm. It was a blisteringly hot day in July, and the bar felt cool as she came in, smiling with anticipation, in a brilliant blue silk dress. Robert was there already, waiting for her. For once, the photo was truthful, and he was also really nice. He had had a good day talking to investors, so they had several margaritas. It seemed obvious he found her attractive, so the conversation was relaxed and cheerful. He talked a lot about his business which was so unique that people came to him, and he never advertised. After a couple of hours, it seemed clear they would be meeting again, after he returned from an imminent summer holiday with his family.

Several weeks later, there was still no word from him. Finally Samantha wrote, hoping they could make another date? Robert apologised, but an accident left him immobilised at home. Another long silence. Samantha wrote again. This time, Robert said he had now met someone locally, unconnected with the website, which was far more convenient for him, so he would not be seeing her again. His parting words were 'But don't think for a minute that I did not fancy you!' Even the most promising first dates can still go nowhere, and it can take a long time to establish this.

The date went well, you thought. You both got on fine, had a pleasant time. You cheerfully expect to meet again, but next day are astounded to find the other party politely declining. Understanding rejection, and coping with it, is the hardest part of dating. Because you have met already, the rejection feels far more personal than the usual fade-out of email messages. The first reaction to any rejection is to read it as a sexual rejection, and in many cases this is at least part of it. He or she did not fancy you. But quite often, other factors come first, and take priority, including purely practical matters of time and place, or personal style and tastes. They are not necessarily things that you can sort out or change, so there is no point in mentioning them. Most adults over 30 are sufficiently stuck in their ways that it is pointless hoping anyone would change their habits.

Women seem to tolerate rejection with greater equanimity than men. Possibly this is because women have a lifetime of being chosen, or not chosen, by men, so are used to it. Men seem to find rejection more difficult to cope with, or accept. Men who are successful and wealthy seem to have the greatest difficulty, especially if they found a woman attractive. Their response is typically: 'This cannot happen to me! This is unfair! It must be her fault!' and they proceed to tell the woman where she went wrong, how she misled them.

Saffron thought Victor sounded like the ideal married boyfriend in his profile description. As a professional running his own consultancy business, he had some control over his time. He kept a flat in central London which he used during the week, while his family lived in a house well outside the city. In the discussion of possible restaurant venues for the first (blind) date, he mentioned several fashionable up-market places, implying he had a certain style and sophistication. He made it clear he had enough money not to work full-time, to keep two homes, to eat out regularly in stylish places. There was a certain relaxed cheerfulness about his messages that led her to expect the best. He finally chose an Italian restaurant she did not know but was convenient for them both.

The date itself was not too bad. The restaurant turned out to be a really ugly basement place, looking like a gentleman's lavatory with white tiled walls. But ten minutes after Saffron arrived, the electric lights blew, so they were sitting in pitch black darkness. Waiters brought candles for every table, plus some extra, so it began to look cosy, even if it was a bit difficult to read the menus. The food was brilliant, and Victor chose a nice wine. He looked older than he claimed, and was dressed more shabbily than she had been led to expect, but he was pleasant company. He complimented her on how nice she looked, which always helped. After the awkwardness caused by the lights going off, and the sudden darkness, they gradually relaxed, and she was soon laughing at the crazy stories he told of his experiences as a consultant, and clients' ridiculous behaviour. By the time, they were leaving, it looked very much as if they would be meeting again.

Then it all went wrong. In the street, he slipped his arm around her waist, and suggested they go for a little walk, hinting that maybe they might make their way to his apartment in due course? Saffron had never indicated that she was free for the afternoon, or would be so daring on a first date anyway, and she was close enough to her office to be embarrassed about possibly being seen in public with him, especially as Victor had already started touching her in a familiar way. When she demurred, he became aggressive, insisting she stay with him, not spoil the day. She explained that she had to return to her office. He said he would follow her, to check exactly where she worked. He was clearly serious about this, and Saffron got frightened, told him she would find the nearest policeman to ask for help. Victor got angry and stormed off in the opposite direction.

Within an hour, she received a vitriolic message from him, complaining about her dishonesty, saying he always knew she was just a tease, protesting at the fact that she had not paid half the restaurant bill, and that she was a complete cheat, since she did not want to go to his flat for sex. He had written in a rage, and said exactly what he thought. She sent a short emollient reply, even though it would make no difference.

Some men complain even at the stage of exploratory introductory messages, long before any meeting, berating women who say they are not interested. Some men later demand detailed feed-back on any date, so they can improve their future performance with other women.

From his profile and early messages, Harry promised to be an energetic, clever man and his photo looked good. Yet Jade barely recognised him when they met. He was far thinner, and therefore looked a lot older and tired – or maybe just stressed? Far from having a wild streak, he seemed to play it safe, in his choice of restaurant and his choice of food. He did make an effort, and arrived with a small gift of scent, nicely wrapped, for their first date. But Jade felt she had to make all the running in making the date a success. She had steered him away from a dull pizza and pasta place to a restaurant serving excellent Spanish food in the same street. She worked hard to get him to relax and enjoy the date, and had dressed specially nicely. She would have been happy to see Harry again, but already had other first dates lined up that were more promising, so she decided it was kinder not to extend the liaison and then turn him down after further dates. He was clearly upset. He complained that her profile had not been sufficiently specific about what she was seeking, so as to save him the wasted effort of meeting her. He insisted it was her fault entirely.

Singles dating is competitive. Married dating is even more ruthless and competitive. Most of the time it is women who have the final choice. This is hard for men to accept.

Success or failure? After the first date

Basic courtesy requires both parties to write thanking the other for the date, and clarifying whether or not they would like to take things forward. Married daters who got on fine during the date often ruin things afterwards because each waits for the other person to write first. Some people take the view that there is no point in writing a 'Thanks, but no thanks' note, but total silence is considered rude. Some men solve the problem by making it clear at the very end of a date, when parting, whether they do or don't want to meet again. Women sometimes like to reflect and decide afterwards, rather than during the date itself, partly because it is less embarrassing to say No by email or text, especially if it is courteously worded.

Even if both sides want to meet again, there is often a tricky further phase of negotiation to go through, possibly on a second date. How often do they want to meet? Where and how? How quickly or slowly will things proceed to sexual intimacy. The most elegant relationship develops naturally over a few more dates, and this is the usual pattern for fuller relationships that start with a social element. However people whose sole interest is in sexual encounters often make this clear early on, and take it for granted that the second date will include a hotel room, and maybe nothing else. So even if they get on brilliantly, and find each other attractive, there may be fundamental differences. Married daters often forget that seduction continues long after the first date. Nothing is fixed in stone.

8

Logistics

An affair is costly – in time, money and effort. Novices delude themselves that an affair can be simple and easy and somehow 'free'. H Cameron Barnes' book *Affair* offers plenty of practical advice on how to conduct an affair, written by a man for other men. He advises people to give serious thought to the practical aspects well before they embark on anything. How will you make the time to meet someone? Where will you meet? How will you ensure your new activities (or absences) look normal to your family and others, and do not arouse suspicion? What will you do to ensure privacy and secrecy? Barnes advises people to clear space in their lives, and agree rules of communication with a lover, to avoid mishaps. However he fudges the financial cost of seeing a lover, pretending that somehow it will cost nothing more than a few cups of coffee, a walk in the park, and the occasional bottle of sparkling wine (Spanish Cava, or Champagne if you really want to impress). Wisely, he insists that lovers should never ever meet in their respective marital homes, even if that appears to be the easy solution. So someone has to pay for hotel rooms, as well as the social activities attached to seeing someone – drinks, lunches or dinners out, and maybe the odd show, film, art exhibition, or other entertainment for those with a fuller relationship.

Whether a married affair is centred on sex, or is a broader affectionate boyfriend-girlfriend relationship, it will entail costs, in time, money, effort and planning. Failure to deal with the logistics explains why so many people who join dating websites get nowhere at all. To start with, there are search costs, requiring time and effort. Websites appear to offer infinite choice, but searching for and courting several potential partners in the hope of seducing at least one person you like (and who likes you) takes significant time and effort. Attractive lovers simply do not fall into your lap at the press of a button.

Some dating websites for married people invite users to state up-front the times when they are able to meet. In practice, this is a fundamental selection criterion. With singles dating, evening and weekend dates are the norm, as most people have jobs. For married people, there is much greater variation, including weekdays, daytimes, in school hours and term-time only, with trips either feasible or impossible. Websites that rely on unmodified software packages for singles dating leave it to users to mention this themselves in their profiles, forcing users to sift through profiles looking for this information, which may not be given.

Lawrence had been married three times, but had never used internet dating. Although he had plenty of experience with women, and had dated lots of women in between his several marriages, he found internet dating daunting. In particular, he disliked having to record his height, as he felt slightly short at 5'6". At 65, his age also counted against him, although he felt, and did indeed look 50. All the women seemed to be looking for men six feet tall and aged 40-50 years. Initially, he sent only virtual kisses to the women he fancied on the website. No-one replied except one, so he pursued her enthusiastically. Christina agreed fairly quickly to meet him for dinner.

To Lawrence's amazement, Christina arrived on time and looking exactly as she said, tall and slim in a lovely figure-hugging dress, with a shock of curly black hair. So slim, in fact, that he could not resist a quick grope of her waist during dinner, just to check the figure was real and not due to a tight restraining corset. All he felt was soft flesh, and Christina shot him an alarmed and puzzled look at his groping. She seemed far more interested in his expertise in wine than his height, so he found himself relaxing and enjoying her company over a very good bottle of Zinfandel. He had come straight from a business meeting where he had successfully negotiated a contract with a new client for his software firm, so he was in a good mood anyway. Two hours later, it was clear they would be meeting again. The cheerful conversation ranged over diverse topics, and he found himself chatting away easily about all aspects of his life.

When they met again for lunch, Lawrence started to discuss the practicalities of where and when they might get intimate. Where seemed easy, as he had a small studio flat in central London that was used mainly for business purposes, but did have a pull-down bed, which could be used if the piles of files and boxes were cleared away. Christina seemed a bit doubtful about this as 'hardly romantic!' But the killer ended up being the question of time. He preferred to meet in the evenings, and could also find time at weekends, even for trips in one of his classic cars. Christina could only do weekdays, and evenings would always be more difficult than daytime. None of this had been clear from their profiles.

Undeterred, Lawrence said he could make time during the day, as it was his own business, so he could control his timetable. Over the next six weeks, dates were repeatedly arranged, then postponed or cancelled, in response to changes in his business meetings and the handholding demanded by a new client installing a crucial bit of software. In practice, Lawrence did not have as much autonomy in his timetable as he thought. Christina got fed up, and they finally agreed that their timetables were not compatible enough for it to work. It seemed to be the only impediment, but in the end it was crucial.

Geography can also prevent some people ever meeting. This feeds the myth that the one person you were unable to meet was your perfect partner, the fantasy made reality. By never meeting, the erotic image of this person remains intact, you can never be disappointed, and can continue to believe that there is a special person out there, someone you just missed.

Dominic lives in Portsmouth, on the coast, but he widened his website search to all the south of England. His search eventually focused on Jacqueline, who sounded like his type of woman from the style of her profile and emails. Unfortunately, she lived out in the country near Reading, but worked in central London. At first, Dominic was sure he could find time to meet her on one of his occasional business trips to London. In practice, after three months of cheerful correspondence it proved impossible to find a mutually convenient date and time for them to meet in London or elsewhere. The longer it took to fix a date, the more Dominic became convinced Jacqueline would be his ideal woman, and the clearer it became that even if they ever managed an initial meeting, regular meetings would be effectively impossible.

First impressions count. First dates need to create a good impression, a pleasant memory.

Guy was an oil trader, working long hours because the market had become truly global, and increasingly volatile. He found it difficult to find time even to use the dating website he had joined, as he dared not access it in his open-plan office with colleagues around. So he was delighted to make contact with Tamara, a South American who preferred to switch immediately to using private email addresses. He suggested meeting for lunch, as drinks after work would always be tricky given activity late in the day in the American markets. He also knew exactly where to take her, a buzzy Latin-Brazilian style restaurant and bar that he passed every day on his walk between Waterloo railway station and his office. Every evening he gazed in wistfully at the bright lights, the laughing couples in sexy clothes, hearing the strong Latin beats that suck you into their rhythm, and wished he could be in there entertaining a girlfriend himself. So now he would, even if it was a lunchtime date. Tamara said she would be wearing a sexy red dress, so she was clearly entering into the spirit of things. It didn't quite work out as he imagined.

It took Guy far longer to walk over to the restaurant than he realised, so he arrived 15 minutes late. Tamara was already waiting for him in the bar with a drink. However the place was otherwise empty and in darkness. The electrics had fused during the morning, so the kitchen was entirely out of action, there were no lights, and customers were being regretfully turned away. The bar had huge windows overlooking the Thames river, so was light enough to be open. He suggested they transfer to another place along the river that he had once seen, so off they went. Once installed at a table, it became clear it was a poor choice for a date. The place was popular with families and teenagers having a day out, and a large family group installed themselves at an adjacent table, with several noisy small children. Fortunately, the food and drinks were fine, so they began to relax and flirt a little. Then disaster struck again: Tamara lost a contact lens. Desperate to find it, she spent a good ten minutes searching every surface until she eventually located it, in her lap. What might have been an agreeable date, leading to another meeting, was spoilt by a succession of hiccups, with two poor choices of venue being crucial.

Jason had a fixed routine for first dates, one he stuck to because it was reliable, impressed all the women he met, and suited his circumstances. He invited new women to lunch in the bar on the 42nd floor, at the very top of Tower 42 in the City of London. The views over the City were impressive, even in cloudy weather, and provided a topic for conversation at the beginning. For security reasons, it was necessary to book in advance, with names, and staff were punctilious about ensuring that people were matched up correctly to the reserved table. This ensured a smooth meet-up, whereas it was always a bit stressful trying to meet a stranger in ordinary bars and pubs, especially at busy times. If he did not get on with the lady, it was still a pleasant short break. If he did like her, tables were sufficiently private for discussion of arrangements for meeting again. Best of all, it was not a place where he might bump into colleagues or friends who might intrude on the date. Jason found lunch was always good for a first date because it could be kept to a short one hour, if necessary, but afforded enough time to talk to someone properly, without the noise often found in busy bars and hard-edge restaurants in the evenings. By standardising the venue for first dates, he could focus more easily on the lady he was meeting, and differences between the women became more sharply defined. It worked for him, so he stuck to his routine.

Age and affluence also affect the choice between a short initial meeting, for coffee or a drink, versus a longer lunch or dinner. Young people with limited social skills and people with restricted budgets tend to go for the shorter date, which seems more informal. Many people with limited social skills find a one or two hour 'formal lunch' (or dinner) a bit daunting. Unused to eating in formal restaurants, they find menus and waiters intimidating, and are too anxious about doing the right thing to be able to relax and focus on the person they are meeting. Occasionally, people talk about the type of date they enjoy in their profiles, and this can be a helpful clue to their lifestyle and culture.

Adam claimed to be a successful professional wanting to meet a woman 'who enjoys the finer things in life', so Leila assumed he would like to meet for lunch in a good restaurant. She suggested several in his area that had received good reviews, with brief descriptions of their style of food. Adam's reply was: 'Is this about lunch, or is it about me?!' Leila read this to mean that he had grossly overstated what he was used to, would never be comfortable eating in a proper restaurant, and probably could not afford it anyway.

Damian liked the sound of Penny's profile and suggested they meet up some day. She agreed, and they started discussing where to meet. It became apparent that she never went to proper restaurants, being more accustomed to informal wine bars, pubs, and All Bar One style places catering to young people with loud music. She took it for granted that people relied heavily on mobile phones to meet up with others, or even to identify a blind date in a public place. Even so, Damian might have given it a try, until he talked to her on her mobile, and concluded that Penny's lack of polish meant they would never hit it off.

Big cities such as London offer a much wider range of cafes, bars and restaurants to meet in than do small towns – everything from 'greasy spoon' transport cafes to Michelin-starred restaurants, with plenty of options in between. There is also the widest range of hotels, of all grades and styles. The choice of venue exposes the social gradient of an affair. Negotiations over venues can provide an indirect way of checking out someone's financial status, when they have left this vague in their profile. Some married men invite the woman to suggest venues she would be happy with, from which they make the final choice. Women will suggest a wide variety of places, simply to find what 'level' he prefers, or suggest places at the level they would be happy in, and could explain their presence in if seen by someone they know.

Some expensive four-star and five-star hotels offer 'day rates', if requested, for rooms vacated before 6pm. Usually, rooms are available between the usual noon check-in time and the 6pm cut-off. Sometimes, the room can be used in the morning as well as the afternoon – the idea being that they are used for business meetings or interviews that need to be completely private. Day rates can be half the normal overnight room rates, but are never advertised, and depend on hotel occupancy levels. If the hotel is almost full, day rates may not be offered, or only at a higher price, while the price can fall dramatically in low season. There are also internet websites that specialise in last-minute hotel bookings that are normally available at very low prices, in order to fill rooms, many of them in cheaper hotels.

Roland's decision to embark on an affair (instead of fantasising about it) was triggered by noticing a stylish new hotel being built in his run-down part of the city. He had invested his savings in what he hoped would eventually be a successful and profitable business. To save money while he was building up the business, he had taken an office in a shabby and run-down area away from the city centre, where rents were low. The new hotel promised to be modern and trendy, with a good bar and restaurant. Local papers suggested prices would be kept low in the first year of operation, to attract a new clientele. Roland joined a website, and after a focused search, met a series of women. All his first dates were in stylish restaurants in the fashionable part of the city, which he was sure helped him to attract more interesting women.

For subsequent dates, he persuaded two women to come to his own part of the city, near his office, where he had found a few trendy bars and restaurants. In due course, a passionate affair developed with one of them, Joanna, using his new local hotel's day rates for afternoon trysts, after lunch in the hotel restaurant, where the day's menu proved to be excellent value. Despite being a bit short of cash, Roland's attention to local options and new developments produced romantic and elegant dates in a brand new and modern hotel, overcoming his area's limitations, all very conveniently close to his office as well. This became invaluable one day when an urgent business call required him to cut short his date to return to the office quickly.

Money

For women, the hidden financial costs of an affair include the never-ending costs of looking good all the time – regular visits to the hairdresser, make-up, clothes that are sexier than standard office wear or other workwear, perfume, and possibly some additional outlay on sexy lingerie and high heels, basques and stockings. Men too may need to spend some money on sprucing up their clothes, and buying more cheerful attire, but the principal cost is likely to be the 'visible' costs of hotel rooms, meals out, drinks in bars and pubs.

In his book *Affair*, Cameron Barnes implies that visible costs will normally be shared, and so do some dating websites. This may be common in singles dating in Britain, but it is wishful thinking for married dating. In practice, entertainment costs fall to the man. This is just one of the fundamental differences between singles dating and dating for married people, where women are outnumbered by men. In addition, women with jobs will often be earning rather less than the men they meet, and many are full-time homemakers with no earnings at all. Any spare money that women have is usually spent on looking good, which costs women at least twice as much as it costs men.[52]

In the world of married dating, the laws of supply and demand dictate that women have plenty of choice, and attractive women never need pay. When women pay, it is for a handsome toy boy or a stud who makes good arm candy, and even that is an impossible luxury for most women. As Carla puts it 'If a man asks me to pay half the restaurant bill, I will pay my share, but there will never be a second date!' Samantha takes a similar view 'Married men think nothing of spending £60,000 on a fancy sports car, as a treat for themselves, but then assume that the girlfriend comes completely free!' Natalia regards it as very rude for a man to ask a woman to contribute to paying the bill – especially on a first date. Later on, a woman might volunteer to pay for some things, but it would still be elegant for the man to refuse any contribution, says Natalia.

Dating conventions vary between countries and cultures. In America, especially in New York, men invariably pay for all the entertainment on dates, and this applies to singles dating as well as affairs. In bigger cities, the costs can mount up. On the other hand, women are expected to be spectacularly well-groomed for a date, and spend a fortune on hairdressers, clothes and manicures. Dress styles can be more relaxed in London and other northern European cities, but Paris and Milan also require chic dressing. In continental Europe, the man is expected to pay for most costs of a date in most countries, in the New York style. 'Going Dutch' and splitting the bill is more common in northern Europe, especially Scandinavian countries, where 'gender equality' policies promote unisex behaviour, even among single dating couples, partly because income differentials are smaller anyway. The French, who are masters of the art of seduction, are clear about the role of money and the importance of generosity. A survey in France found that virtually all (96%) Frenchmen agree that money is necessary to seduce women, and one-quarter agree that offering a weekend abroad 'works every time'.[53] Americans are even more likely to recognise that sexual encounters involve an economic exchange, that one way or another erotic entertainment '…ain't never been free'.[54]

*

It was clear from his profile that Alexander was cheerful, clever, amusing and affluent, but a bit of a rough diamond, who often felt out of place in the city. In his mid-fifties, he looked ten years younger, tall, with the heavy physique of an ex-rugby player. He lived in a small town, with a wife who ignored him mostly, but they stayed together because of their daughter, whom they both adored. The marriage had been platonic for some years, and he and his wife even took separate holidays, claiming this was due to the incompatible timetables of their jobs. Alexander stayed in London two or three nights every week, meeting clients. He had built up his financial services firm from scratch, working assiduously over twenty-five years to achieve a huge client base, but looking after them all took a lot of time. After many years spent alone in the evenings in the city, Alex pined for some congenial company, possibly a mistress, and he had got to the point where he could afford it. He joined a website.

Alex met several attractive women very quickly. As he puts it 'the website delivered'. The only problem was that some of them found evening dates difficult. Isabel could meet him in the evenings, and she was his first choice really, as she was the most fun, sexy and also interesting. They had first met for lunch, and got on brilliantly. She then dragged him into an exhibition of southern Indian bronze sculptures in the Royal Academy of Arts, something so esoteric that he would never have dreamt of going in. To his astonishment, she gave him an informed but pleasingly informal explanation of the whole exhibition, apparently based on travels in India and books she had read. He enjoyed it, and found the bronzes erotic, as she had promised. Alex hoped that Isabel would show him more of London, the sights and activities he never enjoyed in all his years of travelling in for business only. However he objected to her taking it for granted that he paid for everything, and he finally said so. She reminded him that she had mentioned right at the start that she made no money at all from her voluntary work, so she could not afford to 'pay her share', as he demanded. Even so, Alexander was annoyed, so he dropped her and decided to focus on other women from the website. After all, the choice seemed never-ending.

Three months later, Alexander had spent lots more money meeting lots of new women, and realised he had got nowhere. Some looked older or less attractive than the profile implied; a few were obese despite describing themselves as slim; many were simply rather dull; quite a few were not interested in him (which offended him); and several attractive women who had agreed to meet again had always been too busy to see him when he was free. He began to see that he had been lucky with his first few dates, and finally wrote to Isabel again. Her reply was reassuringly charming and positive, but she said she would be away on holiday for a while, so could not see him immediately.

Alex returned to the website, and spent many more hours, off and on, contacting women with attractive profiles, and meeting them. He finally realised that the more attractive women were not interested unless the man claimed to be an amazing stud in bed (and they clearly expected delivery on this) or else was generous and took them to nice places. So it was brilliant sex or money in the end – he had to offer one or the other, especially as he had never been handsome. Six months after he first met her, Isabel appeared to be his best bet after all. He contacted her again, deciding that this time he would be accommodating and agreeable. Unfortunately, by this time, Isabel had met someone else.

Learning to live

When Terence met Alesha he was knocked out by how wonderful she was. At least 15 years younger than him, Alesha was slim, with long glossy black hair, a nice face, and she was always gay, cheerful, and compliant. Seeing her was almost a holiday in itself. However she did like to be taken out to glamorous and expensive bars and restaurants in the centre of the city. After a couple of dates, Terence explained that he 'could not afford' such entertainments on a regular basis. Alesha's response was a turning point for him. She reminded him that he had just described taking his entire family, plus the spouses and fiancés of his two sons and two daughters, to New York for Christmas and New Year, as his gift to them – and also because he had to be in New York anyway for business just before the Christmas break. She pointed out that he was, on his own admission, a multi-millionaire, not surprisingly, as he had worked very hard all his life to build up his business before selling it for a substantial sum. Alesha suggested that he had spent so many years saving money and costs, re-investing any money in his business, that he had forgotten how to play, how to have a good time. Now is the time to start spending a little money on yourself, she suggested.

Of course he had the money, he had simply forgotten how to enjoy it.

Terence thought about this for a while and realised she had been right. After that, he looked forward to his dates with her as special treats for himself. Each time, they went to a different restaurant, trying cuisines from all over the world, always with a specially good wine, followed by an hour in a hotel afterwards. In time, he started to buy Alesha small gifts, a bottle of her favourite perfume, a bracelet, and found he enjoyed doing so. She was always so appreciative.

Men who have grown up with a Puritanical work ethic regard money spent on their families, however lavish, as an 'investment' whereas money spent on having a good time themselves, or spent on their mistress, is 'thrown away', or even a 'guilty secret'. This is especially true in Anglo-Saxon cultures, which tend to be prurient about sex in any form. Southern European culture is rather more hedonistic and Dionysian in its attitude to entertainment and pleasure of all kinds, which are simply enjoyed, without guilt or shame.

Alesha notes that men who have hoarded money all their lives become almost incapable of ever spending it, even when they become multi-millionaires, even after they have sold their business and are contemplating retirement. Parsimony and cost-cutting, even miserliness, have become so pickled into their perspective that they are unable to break the habits of a lifetime, long after parsimony becomes pointless. Some men have to be re-educated in their attitude to money. She notes that someone who is constantly watching the bills is not relaxed and not much fun

Marilyn has a different perspective. 'All the men I ever met who were generous, with small gifts and nice treats, were not especially wealthy, but they had very few lovers in their lifetime, and they treated them well. All the men who were stingy, even miserly, were cynical men who had a long string of mistresses over many years, and no longer accorded special value to any of them, because they regarded them all as temporary, to be replaced sooner or later.'

*

Rachel once dated a married man who was clearly in love with her, although he refused to admit it because he was too cynical to 'believe in love'. When her employer sent her to Chicago to represent the firm at a trade fair, Anthony decided to go to Chicago himself, so they could enjoy a long weekend together seeing the city, which he knew well. Anthony intended the weekend to be an idyllic and romantic holiday, the only time they had ever spent longer than a few hours together. In practice, it served to alienate Rachel.

Anthony insisted on going shopping, but he only bought things for himself. In one store, he was persuaded to buy himself a fashionable modern watch, but did not offer Rachel the matching woman's version. He took her to Victoria's Secret, to show her the sexy lingerie on offer, but did not buy her any. In one store, they came across the fur showroom, and saw a lovely jacket that suited Rachel perfectly. Anthony admired her in it, said it would be a good buy, as it was on sale at half price, but did not do so. Rachel found Anthony's stinginess so insulting that she dumped him soon afterwards. Although he was not affluent, Rachel's husband had always been generous to her, offering her anything she liked as a gift. She saw Tony's lack of generosity as a fundamental statement of his inability to ever admit that he loved her.

Keeping in touch

Unless a passionate love affair develops, most people have limited contact with their lover between meetings. Married people do not have the time or privacy, usually, for regular correspondence. Some like to send messages at odd times, to remind their lover they are thinking of them. Some never make contact until making arrangements for the next date.

Frequency of contact is very much a matter of personal taste and time.

All married couples have to sort out how they will communicate with each other, and technological tribalism affects this. People regard their own style of communication as 'normal' and can be difficult about adapting to other people's style. Mobile phone users and Blackberry users tend to assume that everyone else will fit in with their preferences. It is easy to forget that others may have different styles and habits. Some people prefer to write 'letters' sent by email; others prefer to chat on the phone; some like texting. Some people prefer to restrict communication to the bare minimum required for fixing meetings and venues, while others enjoy flirting between dates. Blackberry and mobile phone users commonly overlook the fact that landline phones do not have the same facilities as mobiles. Most landline phones still do not display the caller's number (so you have no idea who is calling you); do not list missed calls and their numbers; do not make it easy to recall a missed caller; and do not accept text messages, only voicemail. Some mobile phone users refuse to use voicemail, expecting phones to be permanently switched on. Others have mobiles switched off for long periods, and rely heavily on voicemail and texts.

Andrew had been out of touch with Marisol for over twelve months. He had explained that he would be travelling constantly to the Far East for the duration of an important building project. Given time differences while he was away, and given jet lag when he returned, it was not really feasible to see her while this project continued. Once it was over, he was determined to continue seeing her, as they had an exceptional sexual relationship. At the end of the project, which took rather longer than expected, Andrew called Marisol to say he was back for good this time, and wanted to meet up again. He called from his mobile to her office landline, and left a message asking her to get in touch. Puzzled at her silence after a few weeks, he concluded that she had found someone new, and was rather upset. What he overlooked was that he had changed his mobile number many months previously, after it was stolen, so Marisol did not have the new number. Her landline phone did not record callers' numbers, and he had forgotten to leave his number in his phone message. Marisol had wanted to see him again, had tried everything to contact him, and had failed.

Ingrid was a librarian, something she preferred to conceal from the men she dated. She was aware of the stereotypes of librarians and accountants as exceptionally boring and dull people. As she was lively and attractive, she did not want to ruin her image. However she had to say she often worked in libraries, because she was unable to use a mobile phone at all during the working day. All major libraries prohibit the use of mobiles, which must be switched off on entry, just like cinemas. Email worked far better for Ingrid, as she could access it more readily. Ingrid found that mobile phone users and email users formed two separate communication tribes. Men who insisted on using text and phone messages often had to be ruled out, no matter how attractive, purely because of the communication difficulties, especially as last-minute arrangements did not work for her.

Communication is generally more intermittent and disjointed than it might be in singles dating. Some married people treat weekends as family time, so they never log on to collect emails, nor use their office mobile phones at weekends. Others are more likely to use the internet, and a private mobile, at the weekend than during office hours, if they have no privacy at work. People who go away for the weekend may have no fully private access to email or mobile devices in these periods, so last minute changes of plan cannot ever be made over weekends. On weekdays, someone may spend whole days in meetings which prevent any access to private email and private phone use.

Trips

Many of the profiles posted by men on dating websites talk about how nice it would be to have a companion for their frequent business trips in Europe and North America, or more rarely, the Far East. This is just one of the many clues that men's fantasies and aspirations are based on the classic affair involving a married man and a single woman who is free and willing to fit in with his timetable because she has no family life of her own. By and large, only a single woman will have the freedom to flit off abroad with her lover, at a time and place of his choosing. Married women are almost never able to explain such an absence, even assuming they have no job constraints preventing sudden trips. Even single women can have difficulties doing a trip, if their job does not give them the freedom to flit off at short notice on a timetable determined by someone else. In practice, the fantasy of an agreeable travel companion is most likely to be fulfilled by a mistress who is being paid a monthly stipend for her time and availability, and she will expect all costs of any trips to be fully covered by her lover. Even they will need advance warning. Married men forget that women have lives too, even if these remain barely visible to their lover.

Too often, people assume that anyone they meet automatically favours the same approach to communication and timetable, and the same style of dates, as they do. But the great diversity of people on dating websites makes this unlikely, especially in big cities. An affair involves moving outside your comfort zone, and this may apply to the practical arrangements as well as to who you meet.

Lucas guessed that Valentina was probably out of his reach, financially, but he still wanted to give it a try. She suggested several restaurants to meet for their first blind date, and Lawrence chose one of them, a tapas bar-restaurant, hoping it would be the cheapest option. This worked up to a point, as they shared several small dishes and a bottle of wine. However it was a very stylish place and Valentina chose some expensive dishes of foie gras and prawns, so it still worked out an expensive lunch overall. Lucas felt the investment in a classy first date was worthwhile – the staff had ensured a smooth meet-up at the table, it had been a most agreeable lunch, and Valentina was as attractive and classy as her profile suggested. At the end of lunch, Lucas complimented her on the excellent suggestion, and asked if they might meet somewhere a bit less expensive next time? Valentina took the hint, and took some trouble to find pleasant but more bohemian and cheaper places to meet on subsequent dates. In fact, she got so enthusiastic about it that she discovered some extraordinary bars close to his office that he had been unaware of that provided an entertainment in themselves, with the added advantage that none of his colleagues would ever be found there. When he expressed surprise at her ability to discover such venues, Valentina said that she could be flexible and adventurous – for the right man. Given the diversity of people using the websites, it is not surprising that affairs take many shapes and forms.

9

The Secret Garden

'I didn't know what to expect', says Charles, about the beginning of his first affair, some two years previously. She was a married woman within his social circle of expatriates living in Thailand. Apparently, she had done it before, so he went along with her suggestions on how to proceed. To his astonishment, her husband was aware of her sexual adventures (or so she said) so she didn't conceal anything. She would invite Charles to pick her up at home for an evening out together (including some time in a discreet hotel). This openness became too much for him, eventually. He wondered whether she discussed him with her husband? The affair petered out swiftly, partly due to this contrast – conflict even – between his need for discretion and her openness. He still didn't know what to expect when he decided to subscribe to a dating website a few years later.

Most people do have a template for an affair, whether they realise it or not. Mostly, this comes from films, books, stories recounted by friends (who say they are describing another friend's adventures), or media stories about the affairs of politicians, film stars and other celebrities. Media stories sometimes include heavily embroidered 'kiss and tell' accounts by the spurned mistress – such as secretary Faria Alam's account of her brief affair with the England football manager Sven Goran Erickson, in a media frenzy that was all the more bizarre because Erickson never married his long-standing live-in lover Nancy Dell'Olio, so all parties were single and free to choose whom they liked.

Most media stories concern the classic case of a wealthy and successful married man having an affair with a younger single woman, typically poorer and ambitious, who is delighted to share his glamorous lifestyle. *Lady Chatterly's Lover* is unusual for depicting a wealthy married heroine and her unmarried, sexually uninhibited poorer lover. But literature and films are generally unkind to married women who have affairs. *Madame Bovary* is destroyed by her fantasies and aspirations to luxurious living as much as by her affairs, and *Anna Karenina* also ends badly, throwing herself under a train. In literature and films, married men frequently start affairs with attractive younger single women who seem to find them irresistible, whereas married women rarely do, and affairs end badly if they do. Like the trophy wife, the mistress is a mark of status and success for men, and women are slow to catch up.[55]

The models we select from books and films reflect our fantasy of the 'perfect partner'. Fantasies of the ideal beloved seem to be a permanent companion, updated and enriched by life's experiences. To judge by Indian films, the fantasy perfect partner is someone who bursts into song and dance at every turn in life. Naturally, the perfect partner is attractive, but this is a variable feast. Younger people's fantasy is likely to focus on physical features and looks, such as long blond hair, tall with long legs, big breasts or a muscled body. Older people usually have developed more specific and social images of their perfect partner, such as someone who shares a taste for classical music, golf, wine, travel, skiing, or sexy lingerie.

You might think that one universal feature of the fantasy that is re-awakened by an affair, or the prospect of an affair, is enthusiasm for sex, as illustrated by Erica Jong's zipless fuck in *Fear of Flying*. Actually, not so! As Tony Giddens points out in his book on intimacy in the modern world, the perfect partner can be a soul-mate who wants us for ourself alone, without regard to the practical demands of family life, child-rearing needs and careers – a 'pure and free' choice, a meeting of minds and personalities as much as bodies.

Thus, affairs come in all colours, shapes and sizes. There is diversity rather than uniformity. Married people who use the internet for affairs find their expectations and blueprints conflicting rather then being in harmony. Hence the need for negotiation from the start. One party may try to, or succeed, in imposing their template, or preferences. But generally, affairs are unpredictable for both sides.

Russell chose Sienna because her profile description came close to his perfect partner, his ideal woman's looks. But he became even more enthusiastic after she responded wittily to his opening message. They switched quickly to private email addresses, leading to a correspondence lasting several months. They wrote to each other on weekdays, during work hours, recounting events from their lives, responding to each other's amused or acerbic commentary, in a light-hearted banter that got both of them laughing throughout the day.

The flow of messages was interrupted by their respective summer holidays with their families, then resumed with amusing accounts of holiday catastrophes and high points. Russell illustrated his stories with photos of events and venues. Sienna said she had bought him a present to give to him when they met, finally. A meeting in a half-way spot between their two towns was agreed, then cancelled. Another lunch date was fixed, then cancelled again at short notice. Sienna pressed him for a definite date. Russell then admitted that, after a long heart-to-heart over a drink with a male friend one evening, he had decided he did not want to go that far, so could they please stay friends and write to each other, as before? The fantasy lover and girlfriend he had hoped to meet some day had become so fixed in his mind that he was terrified that the reality might not match it. The fantasy was made real by writing to her, by the correspondence which brought him alive throughout his dull working week. But he did not want any reality testing!

There are websites that specialise in this sort of fantasy romance and cyber sex. There are major advantages. You get all the psychological and emotional excitement of an affair without any of the practical problems and risks. Half the work is done by your own imagination and long-standing fantasies of the perfect lover. Any photos exchanged can be of people with perfect bodies, as young and sexy as you like. Even the profiles can be of invented persona who are more fun than the reality of your own quiet life. Fantasy affairs appear to be common in the USA and other countries where distances between cities pose bigger logistical problems for meetings than in the closely built up areas of western Europe.

Such affairs appeal to certain types of people, those with a vivid imagination and good writing skills. They sometimes become 'real' in their emotional consequences, with proposals of marriage, divorce proceedings and claims of polygamy or multiple affairs, as described by Aharon Ben-Ze'ev in *Love Online: Emotions on the Internet* and other books on internet communities.[56]

Well before the first date, Jack was clear about what he wanted from a lover. As Emma put it 'From the start, I knew what the script was', and it suited her to go along with it. 'It became a challenge to fit the role of mistress to perfection. To play the part so well he could not tell it was all playacting. I wanted to embody this fantasy of the perfect lover, especially as his formula was such a cliché that you could write it from trashy films.'

The fantasy mistress wears sexy lingerie – black generally, also black or pink lace, fussy cream confections, sometimes scarlet red or emerald green, basques and bustiers, low-cut bras and matching panties, often in silk, always with lots of lace or see-through bits. She might occasionally wear a black leather dress, especially if it is skin-tight or has revealing cutouts. She looks the part. She is always ready for sex, eager for it. She happily agrees to sexual encounters in unconventional, slightly public places where there is a danger of being seen – maybe on the back row of the cinema, in a car on a lay-by on a motorway, in a field on a summer's day when people are walking about.

The idea is that she is so keen that she cannot wait to get back to the bedroom, she wants it now! Sex is 'spontaneous', meaning, in practice, whenever the man wants it. And she is always appreciative. No matter how well or poorly the man performs, she displays satisfaction with the encounter, volubly so at times. There will be a variety of positions and sexual variations, limited only by the couple's imagination and fitness. The script comes from porn films, and nowadays men begin to think this is what everyday sex should be like. Women feel pressurised into performing the role, especially in the early stages of an affair, when everyone is on best behaviour.

There is an equivalent fantasy male lover, but this seems to vary greatly between women, some liking a man who is dominant in the bedroom, others not, some liking men who are well-endowed, others not, although being tall and handsome seem to be common features. The good sense of humour (GSOH) that features so often in website profiles, and in what women say they like, is attractive mainly to smooth over the awkwardness of meeting strangers rather than for any role in the bedroom.

After a year, Emma got bored with playing up to Jack's fantasy. She had proved to herself that she could embody the perfect mistress, and be adored for it. Gradually, she started making her own demands, was less complaisant and amenable. After she realised that Jack was rigid and inflexible in his behaviour, unwilling to adapt, she dumped him, in a suitably elegant fashion.

To her astonishment, his reaction was an extended childish tantrum, anger that his favourite toy had been taken away from him, repeated demands for her to return to their normal relationship. He told her she was the sexiest woman he had ever met, lusted after her only, could desire no-one else, thought of her constantly. Emma had turned the fantasy mistress into a living reality for him, and after she left him Jack reverted to his fantasy mistress, who lived on in his imagination. The affair had been light-hearted, smooth and easy while they acted out the perfect affair. Emma's introduction of some reality prompted chaotic upheavals and exposed strong emotional undercurrents.

'He asked for sex, but in reality he wanted unconditional love and admiration for him as a sexual and professional person' recalls Emma. 'He thought it was sophisticated to be cynical, and love was taboo, so the affair was just a game we played. He was unable to say he loved me, or anyone, not even his children, and certainly not his wife. He berated his son for finally marrying a long-standing girlfriend, arguing that his infatuation would not last one year of normal married life. He needed attachment to a regular lover, although he refused absolutely to offer any commitment. At the end, he seemed totally confused as to what it was he wanted, or needed, or offered. But his selfishness was exposed as soon as I started making demands of my own.'

Sex may be the everyday currency of an affair, but it is not necessarily the heart of the matter, even in situations where someone insists it is not about love and affection at all.

The classic sexual 'fling' happens at a wedding, a party, a professional or trade conference, a work event held away from home, a business trip abroad – events where social inhibitions and constraints are weakened, due to drinking a lot of alcohol, a party atmosphere in the evenings, or just from being in a hotel, away from the social constraints of home, in an unfamiliar environment with lots of strangers, some of whom you find attractive.

Andrew has had a long series of flings, partly because his work situation gives him opportunities, and he plans to go on doing so for as long as he is able to attract a partner. As a judge, he travels to courts around Britain, staying overnight where necessary. His work brings him into contact with a constantly changing audience of lawyers, litigants, witnesses, court officials and others involved in the cases he hears. Sitting as a judge, he is in a position of authority and power, making him extremely attractive and sexy to many of the women he deals with, especially as he is tall and handsome, reinforced by elegant dark suits. At the end of the day's proceedings, opportunities arise to seduce the lawyers and other women he encounters, and there is always the convenience of his hotel room close by.

Over the years, he has had agreeable encounters with a series of women, many much younger than him, some of whom he can barely remember. Charming and elegant in his manners, he has perfected his routines over the years. Drinks and dinner usually preface the seduction, and he is careful never to prejudice his work role in any way. If the lady does not take up his offer, nothing is lost, as dining with agreeable company is preferable to dining alone. He cannot imagine having an extended affair with the same person – not because he refuses the idea, but because it seems unworkable given his chaotic work timetable and travels. He once met a woman he liked hugely, and would have liked to see regularly, but four months after first meeting her, he had still not managed to arrange a second date, so he stopped sending the emails and making the phone calls that kept them in touch. He has become a habitual one-night-stand man by force of circumstance.

For Piers, a series of flings is the ideal, a lifestyle choice. After a long drawn out and costly divorce from his second wife of 25 years, he is determined to remain single to enjoy his new freedom, a city centre flat, and all that London and a large social circle can offer. As a hedge fund manager, his timetable can be unpredictable anyway. Depending on the markets, he might work very late, night after night, or else take things easy, with free time during the day. Some weeks, he is inclined to go out and celebrate on a lavish scale; other weeks he is too discouraged or despondent to see anyone.

When he wants female company, he trawls the dating websites for single or married women who sound attractive and fun for an evening together, tries to talk to them immediately (using MSN or the phone) and sets up an immediate date, starting with a drink somewhere classy. He has become adept at sifting through, and deciphering, profile descriptions, so mostly he meets someone who suits him, and has a great night of it. From time to time, his date turns out to be seriously fat rather than slim as advertised, or in other ways not congenial, so he finds an elegant way of cutting the date short after drinks. He enjoys the variety of women he meets, and the challenge of seducing a woman on the first date. He does not always succeed. As Piers admits, his chaotic private life is a close parallel to his work life: high adrenalin, high risk, high turnover, some really big wins, some losses.

Work pressures characterise another arrangement, the long

drawn out extended affair. Flint had been married before, and knew only too well that an initially passionate and intense relationship could fade to calm friendship over time. He was not dismayed when his second marriage, to someone who really understood him and his consultancy work, cooled into an almost sexless but affectionate companionship. This time he had a son, and he adored the boy, who was clever and cuddly, imaginative and playful, everything he could wish for in a child. He did not want to disrupt his son's life with a divorce. More important, he was certain that his wife would get custody, as she gave up her demanding full-time consultancy job to become a full-time mother when his son was born. So he would end up seeing his son far less, or not at all, if his ex-wife moved away, for example.

He headed a team working intensive, hectic long hours, sometimes working long into the night and at weekends until a particular deal was finalised, followed by short gaps before the next project started up. His main pastime at weekends, and in the evenings, had become his son, who provided never-ending entertainment. But he did miss female company and sex, so he joined a married website. After several disappointing meets, he settled for Elizabeth who, like his wife, was a bit older but seemed to understand him and his work situation. After a couple of exploratory lunches in classy central London restaurants, they agreed that future lunch dates would include a hotel room for 'afters', which he organised. He had the money, but time was always the main constraint. In practice, he only saw Elizabeth once every four months, at best. Summer holidays could impose even longer gaps between their dates.

Flint had originally intended seeing his mistress in the gaps between projects when he could afford to take long lunches. But the completion of deals, and timing of any gaps, was hard to predict. By the time he knew which week offered some free time, Elizabeth already had conflicting commitments. On one unfortunate date, he checked emails and messages on his Blackberry as they were leaving the restaurant, as usual, and discovered that he really did have to shoot back to the office immediately to deal with something important. Elizabeth teased him about his priorities, but she understood, and was always happy to see him when he did have time. Despite the haphazard timetable of their meetings, there was a real rapport between them whenever they met, which made the long gaps seem unimportant – which surprised him every time.

Erotic playmates

Florence has always found it easy to attract men, especially older men. In her mid-30s, with long wavy red hair, pale skin and emerald green eyes, her pre-Raphaelite looks always get her noticed, and she dresses in romantic flowery dresses to emphasise the look. Married for ten years to a husband who adores her, she has two perfect children who look like her. Her reasons for using the dating websites is not a lack of sex at home, quite the contrary. However she never gets enough.

'One good orgasm is never enough', says Florence. 'I feel good enough to go on and have three or four more. That happened quite often at the beginning with my husband. Then the orgasms got even better, and easier, after my son was born. It just gets better and better now, so I don't want to stop. But his sex drive is starting to fade now. Instead of sex every night, it is only four or five times a week, and he gets tired after just the one orgasm and can't do it over and over, like he used to. But my boyfriend is OK, because he's only 22. He can keep going for ages, and then still comes back for more, again and again, after he's had a short rest. Also, Orlando is beautiful, and has a fantastic firm, muscled body, really fit. I have no idea whether we would get on if we were to spend a whole day together, but he is gorgeous in bed. And he is wonderful to look at. I used to go for older men, as it is so easy to get them interested, They can be OK the first couple of times, when it is all new. But then they slip back to just once, which is no good for me. So I stick to young men now, under 25 mostly. They are greedy for it, and they have the body.'

Oriana is a nurse who is quite open in her profile about wanting energetic sex, and lots of it. In her early 30s, married for 15 years already, her sex life at home is no longer enough for her. She only started having orgasms after her first child was born, and is now determined to make up for lost time. Through the websites she can meet men her age, or much younger, for the kind of sex she dreamed of when young. Her current lover is Santiago, a Spaniard who keeps her entertained as well. But above all the affair is about exuberant sex, as often as she can make time to see him. 'And the best thing is, if I get bored with him, there is no problem at all about replacing him with another guy, just as vigorous, just as keen. London is full of these students who know how to have a good time'

Even married dating websites are full of young men. There are also many young women with strong libidos and a desire for fulfilling sexual relationships. Some of them married young, and are looking for new excitement. Others find their sexuality blossoms after 30, or after they have a child, and find it necessary to supplement their existing sex life at home, either with a regular lover or with a series of casual hook-ups, depending on circumstances, typically with men younger than themselves.

The regular girlfriend

Most people seek more than sporadic meetings with their lover. Depending on circumstances and opportunities, they meet once every 2-4 weeks on average (or more rarely, every week), for dates that may involve pure sex, a social date (a drink after work, lunch or dinner, maybe a show), or some combination of the two. They keep in touch between dates, passing on new jokes or funny stories they heard, telling about incidents in their work life, describing leisure activities planned or just completed, films recommended, and so on. Total silence between meetings is rare, and such relationships rarely survive long. Most people feel the need to maintain some contact between dates, and this facilitates organising the next one, as both sides know about planned absences due to work trips or family holidays.

Lance worked in a large hospital that was full of gossip about who was (or might be) sleeping with whom, and how it affected internal office politics. As a fairly senior manager, he was concerned to avoid such gossip tainting his work, especially as he had contacts with virtually all parts of the establishment. However the gossip also made him feel it was normal to have a mistress or girlfriend as well as an active sex life with his wife. He was clear that any girlfriend would have to come from well outside his work environment, so he joined a website, choosing contacts carefully so as to exclude women with any connection to medicine or healthcare services. Eventually, he met Kitty, a teacher he got on well with.

After a long series of social dates for lunch and drinks after work, they finally became lovers. Lance proceeded cautiously because he wanted to be absolutely sure there were no hidden dangers that might affect his professional and managerial position as well as his marriage. He found it reassuring that, early on, Kitty provided her email address at work, and was clearly happy in her own marriage apart from the fact that it had become celibate some years previously. Kitty described it as a 'contented platonic relationship'. He delayed giving her details of his own job and home life until he was confident there would be no unwelcome repercussions. Having taken so many precautions, he was hoping desperately that the sex, when it finally happened, would be worthwhile. Fortunately it was. Kitty was very fit and had never had children, so she was supple, energetic and 'as tight as a virgin'.

They met regularly for over seven years – sometimes just for lunch, sometimes he took a half-day off work for an afternoon tryst in a hotel. He found her a sympathetic friend to talk through several upheavals in his professional and family life, including a major change of job, his wife's sudden death from a heart attack, and the transition to being a one-parent household. He in turn provided helpful advice on several practical and financial problems she confronted in her home life. They kept in touch between meetings, in long letter-style emails that would have read as letters between friends if anyone else had come across them, with nothing remotely indicative of their sexual relationship (in sharp contrast to people who insist on flirtatious and sexy messages between dates). He always referred to her as his (anonymous) girlfriend when forced to join office gossip sessions, making it clear she worked in a totally unrelated field.

The relationship even survived his courtship of a divorcee with a young daughter who eventually became his second wife. The affair ran in parallel to his family life, complementing and supplementing it. He regarded the lunch dates and hotel trysts as 'me time', a private luxury which he could afford (in time and money, but also emotionally), which added a welcome extra dimension to his life. Between his wife's death and his remarriage, the affair became his most significant relationship, temporarily.

The permanent lover

Claire was shopping for a lover again. She had been happily married all her life to a much older man who eventually became her best friend, after the marriage stopped being sexual. Eventually, she acquired a lover of her own age, Alex, and had been very much in love with him. He too was in a sexless marriage, and as they lived in the same area, had similar backgrounds and lifestyles, the relationship had been smooth and unproblematic. The affair lasted eight years, and was an important emotional support to her in the period after her husband suddenly died, leaving her alone. Claire continued seeing Alex for a while after she was widowed, but somehow things had changed, the delicate balance had been upset.

Alex gently made it clear that he was not interested in getting a divorce in order to marry Claire. He was just as contented at home as she had been. Claire also realised that in all sorts of ways Alex had suited her because he was so different from her husband, but was not someone she wanted to live with. Addressing these questions tainted the relationship. The affair had always been a glorious secret garden of romantic trysts and sexual excitement. Somehow this spirit had been spoilt by the inevitable indirect and tentative conversations during her husband's brief illness, about how they might react, or not, to the fact that Claire would be free to remarry again.

Claire did remarry, as quickly as she could, because she was not the kind of woman to live alone long-term. She had always been married, and liked the emotional, social and financial security of a permanent relationship. Her new husband was younger than her, in his forties, and was far more lively and energetic than her husband had ever been. He was still actively involved in his business, and went away regularly on long business trips in places of no interest to Claire. After an initial period of sexual exploration and intimacy, their relationship had quickly settled down to a semi-platonic relationship, a close and loving friendship in which sex was unimportant. Although this marriage was so different from her first, Claire found herself looking for a permanent lover again. Given her husband's regular business trips, she had more freedom than previously. In other ways, her expectations for a replacement lover were fixed by the long-standing and happy affair she had enjoyed for so long with Alex.

To her surprise, many of the men she met through a dating website for married people were either puzzled by, or hostile to, her decision to maintain two parallel relationships after her husband's death, one comfortable and secure, the other romantic, sexual and exciting. Everyone seemed to think she should have chosen a new husband who was both friend and lover. Claire liked the separation that made each relationship more pure and intense of its kind. She had chosen a husband for his qualities as a live-in partner: comfortable, reliable, loyal, kind, easy to live with, considerate. In contrast, she wanted a lover who would always be exciting because meetings would be rare. You always dress up for your lover, time is short, so it remains fresh and 'new'.

Looking for a new wife

In contrast, some people really are looking for a new spouse, including some who have not yet dumped the current spouse, and are using married dating websites as an exploratory interim measure.

Randall is not strictly-speaking handsome, with a shaven, almost bald head at 54, but he has such a fantastic smile that he becomes beautiful, looking like the shaven tennis-player Andre Agassi, and almost as fit as him. Women are often persuaded to meet him by the photo, with his smile that lights up the world. Randall is aware that it is his best feature, and makes full use of it, at work and socially. A hugely successful man, he built up his business from nothing and is now enjoying substantial profits from it. He plans to sell the business in the next 2-4 years, which will make him a multi-millionaire. He is looking ahead to the day he retires and leaves London to enjoy a life of balmy weather and permanent leisure in the south of France or southern Spain. He is already exploring ideas for some new activity that will keep him lively in retirement, such as speculative investments in property or a new small business. But crucially, he wants a new wife also for this last stage in his life. Like almost all men, he expects she will be younger than him, attractive, keen on sex, and willing to fit in with his plans. He has been exploring the possibilities for some time, dating single as well as married women from websites.

Randall's first wife lives in their large home in the country, where her passion is developing the gardens and park. Their children have independent lives and rarely come to stay. During the week, he lives in his elegant flat in central London and manages his business, with numerous business-related dinners and other social engagements in the evenings. At weekends, he goes home to his country house and wife, or else enjoys short breaks in other European cities: Paris, Venice and Barcelona are the favourites. Randall has all the advantages of a marriageable single man living in a big city and has never been short of girlfriends and lovers, whom he sees on weekday evenings or takes with him on his weekends away. Adopting continental European values, he says that he will never leave his wife, that marriage is about children and property, so divorce never makes sense. He insists he would never embarrass his wife with his serial affairs, which he keeps well out of sight in his bachelor flat. Implicitly, he holds out the possibility of marriage, if the right person comes along.

At one time, he thought he had maybe found a good match in Suzie, a 33 year old secretary working in one of his client firms, a sparkling girl who was still single. She was clearly in love with him, and was palpably desperate to marry soon and have children. But he refused to contemplate divorcing his wife unless he was certain he had found a worthwhile and secure alternative. Divorce meant giving his wife a substantial share of his extensive assets, possibly half. He would do it only if he was certain that the payoff would be worth the trouble and expense. So he suggested that he and Suzie should live together first, to see if it worked. He bought a house, invited Suzie to decorate it as she liked, rented out his bachelor flat, informed his wife, and stopped going home at weekends. In effect, he took a second wife 'on approval' in a trial marriage. Suzie threw herself into the role of perfect wife, feeling sure that marriage was just around the corner, and hugely enjoying a standard of living well above her previous life as a singleton in an expensive city.

A year later, Randall sat Suzie down for a talk, and explained that it was 'not working out' (for him anyway). He had had this talk innumerable times with his employees who failed to deliver. He would take them out to lunch in a soothingly expensive restaurant, ask them how things were going, discuss the difficulties that invariably emerged, and suggest it was time for them to move on and look for another job, as things were not really working out. His employees always took the hint and found another job quickly. But firing a mistress proved to be a little more difficult. Suzie burst into tears, demanded to know exactly what was wrong, insisted she could put things right with his help, refused the invitation to move on. In the end, he offered to buy outright a flat in central London for her so she had a new home of her own to go to, and he supplied furnishings and fittings from the house he would now sell.

The gift of a new home of her own sweetened the shock of the split-up so considerably that Suzie agreed to move out. Randall presented the flat not as a pay-off for Suzie's sexual and domestic services for one year, but as a gift that would improve her chances in the competitive London marriage market. Which it did. Within one year, Suzie had met and married someone else, and Randall breathed a sigh of relief that there had been no ugly legal dispute about broken promises. On closer acquaintance, he had found the young woman too shallow for his highly educated and cultured tastes. Intellectually, she was too boring for him to contemplate as a permanent partner, even though she had been a perfectly compliant sexual partner and competent housekeeper.

Randall returned to his bachelor flat, went home at weekends again, and renewed his website subscriptions.

Falling in love

The essence of an affair is that it is short-lived, leads nowhere, is a place apart from normal life. For a time, people recapture the excitement of dating and mating when they were younger, recapture some of the intensity of feelings involved in meeting someone new, engaging with the unknown. The challenge of seduction, and risk of failure are part of the excitement. Sex becomes the reward at the end, a reward that is doubly valuable for those in celibate marriages.

There is always the danger that you meet someone who feels even more 'right' for you than your existing partner. In a sense, website users cannot win. On the one hand, there is the risk of meeting people you do not like, with whom you have little in common, or who make a blind date an unpleasant experience. On the other hand, there is the risk that you meet someone who fits you like a glove, seems to be your fantasy perfect partner made real, is such good company that every date flies past without you being aware of the time. Some relationships develop quickly, apparently without effort. Within weeks, one party finds they are 'falling in love', or developing an obsession with their lover. They communicate constantly with their lover, are upset by long absences, seek information about every detail of their life and work, with spells of euphoria at being so lucky to meet such a wonderful person.

Bernard knew he needed a girlfriend and lover long before he did anything about finding one. His wife Jill complained of always being tired and virtually never left home. Over time, her activities had become increasingly circumscribed. They stopped going out together, and their quiet home life was only livened up by one of their children visiting and by their holidays, always on cruises. Bernard's leisure activities revolved around men friends – golf at the weekends, drinks after work. He desperately needed female company, and wanted a sex life again. Unfortunately, he was too busy with running his business to have any spare time for other pursuits. After several years, he finally joined a dating website for married people. He found it difficult to attract anyone's attention, given the intense competition, and when he did finally meet women, he found them dull, even sad at times. Many women seemed to be unhappy in their marriages, or in their lives. But he never gave up looking, even though his search was sporadic at best.

After four years, Lady Luck smiled on him. Allegra had suggested lunch rather than dinner, and breaking up his working day did not suit him greatly, but he agreed. The woman who turned up was cheerfulness personified, happy and relaxed, drinking champagne, laughing immediately at all his jokes, creating a party atmosphere almost instantly. She looked lovely too, wearing a brightly coloured dress and arriving in a cloud of perfume. He felt as if he were on holiday, and lunch sped by so fast he almost forgot to ask for another date. To his astonishment, she liked him too, and agreed happily. After another two dates, he was becoming besotted with her, and felt Allegra had transformed his narrowly work-focused life. An afternoon spent in bed in a hotel felt like a magical and special time, and the obsession intensified. He would write or phone her three or four times a day, started plotting short trips away, and wondered where it would all lead to. After a few months, he started to be irritated by his wife's constant tiredness, comparing her unfavourably with his lively mistress. But he was happier than he had ever been, and to his surprise his business was also doing better than usual, despite his guilt at the hours snatched away from his desk.

Suddenly all his dreams of a new life with Allegra came crashing down. Allegra said her husband had become suspicious; as she didn't want any trouble, she was breaking it off. Nothing he said could persuade her to continue. She refused to answer his phone calls or reply to messages. He was heartbroken, devastated, but powerless to put things right. The misery lasted many months, but the memory of what he had lost pained him for years afterwards. Trying to get over it, he returned to the websites, but compared his new dates unfavourably with the ideal woman he had found, and then lost.

Masters and slaves

In an affair, people can explore aspects of themselves, and

interests, that might be tricky or even dangerous in a permanent relationship. The bounded nature of the affair, the fact that it is separate from your normal life, offers freedom to experiment.

Lennox had always worked in the creative arts and advertising where visual images and story-telling feature strongly. But he was surprised at his eager, excited response to everything he saw in a kinky sex club he visited one evening in New York. He had been posted to New York for two years at least and had plenty of spare time on his own in the evenings to explore. After starting with jazz clubs, he moved on to clubs specialising in fetish wear and BDSM (bondage-domination-sadism-masochism). Living on his own, away from his wife and two daughters, he was free to date, and after a boozy party at work one evening, he started seeing Angelina, an attractive younger American divorcee. Somewhat tentatively, he took her to one of the BDSM clubs, and to his delight she found a lot of what she saw sexually exciting.

In bed that night, the sex had a new dimension, and the next day she went off to buy a leather dress with indecent cut-outs, plus a leather jock-strap for him. It developed quickly from there, with books and the club nights providing ideas for new games to play, new roles, and the costumes to suit. Very soon, they were living together and developing a 24/7 master/slave relationship. As her Master, Lennox made all decisions for her, and for them jointly. As his Slave, Angelina was not allowed to look at him unless he spoke to her, and had to obey any request instantly. At the same time, he had to keep her happy, and she made her sexual desires clear to him, including threesomes and other experiments. In time, she learnt to accept beatings from him. These took place publicly in their preferred club, with the number of strokes of the cane being agreed between them before each club session. Over time, the number of strokes steadily increased.

If Angelina could not bear it, and used their secret signal, he stopped – but she was ashamed at having failed to honour their agreement. The caning was immediately followed by vigorous sex, which was spectacular. In time, they explored a widening range of sexual activities within the Master-Slave relationship that became an all-consuming feature of their private life together. Lennox was embarrassed to realise how exciting he found it to be an absolute Master, dominating his lover in every detail of her life, demanding her total submission to him in a role-playing game that had no boundaries.

Then, suddenly, a family crisis meant Lennox was forced to return early to London, before his project was completed. He resumed life at home with his wife and daughters. It took him a while to re-adapt to ordinary family life again, to come down from his constant high and the intensity of his relationship with Angelina. Lennox had loved Angelina more than any other women he had known, but he concluded it was fortunate that his intense New York affair had been time-limited. It could not have continued indefinitely, and had revealed (and possibly reinforced) dominant aspects of his personality that he had been unaware of.

How long will it last?

Affairs can last a few days, or may continue for ten years. They are full of contradictions, and can follow unpredictable paths. Some lovers meet regularly once a fortnight, or even weekly;

others meet once every 3-4 months. Some insist on flirty emails and texts between dates, others are content with silence, or letter-style chatty emails. Affairs started for superficial reasons may develop into enduring relationships, while love affairs can hit the rocks of reality within months. Men almost never marry their mistresses, even if they become free to do so. Men whose affairs result in a divorce may remarry, but they rarely marry the mistress, who is chosen for her attributes as a mistress, not a wife, which is a different role. Affairs display amazing diversity, but the common element is that they end, sooner or later, sometimes suddenly. Every date may be the last.

10

Bad Behaviour

Many people give up looking for a lover quickly, before they find a partner. They discover that trying to meet someone in the normal course of their everyday life is difficult, at best, even hazardous. Someone at work may visibly like you, and enjoy flirting with you, but still be shocked at the suggestion of changing a friendship into something more intimate. There is always the possibility that they may make a public fuss. Laws forbidding sexual harassment in the workplace now make it even more tricky to make a pass at someone you meet through work, including clients and customers or people in another firm. Even where the proposal is made indirectly, out of work hours, over a drink in a place of entertainment, employers may regard the action as sufficiently discrediting to the firm, or your position, to fire you instantly.

The problem of social and political correctness is more acute in Anglo-Saxon cultures than in continental European cultures. In most continental European countries, it is expected that workplaces can have an agreeable element of erotic tension, people may find colleagues sexually attractive, you may be approached by colleagues, acquaintances and even strangers expressing sexual attraction, and that all competent adults are used to this and know how to deal with it elegantly. Saying No is easy, and can be done without being offended, or causing offence. Anglo-Saxon culture is more prudish about ever admitting that sexual attraction is commonplace between adults, that it can often be mutual, and is the ultimate compliment. Anglo-Saxon culture also treats a short, casual sexual encounter as morally laden and reprehensible rather than innocently pleasurable.

Natasha discovered that she was much more likely to meet men to her taste when she made her own selection and approaches than when she responded to approaches from men on the website. She also discovered that some men registered their profile on the site, then sat back to 'see what happens', just like many women. One such, Holden, turned out to be so perfect a match it was like meeting a soul-mate. He invited her to lunch at Quaglino's, an old and fashionable London restaurant that was busy in the evenings but almost empty at lunchtime. It turned out he often used it for the final goodbye lunch or dinner with any of his staff who were leaving the firm. She arrived first, so went off to the ladies to primp her hair. He was waiting at the bar when she returned, and offered her a glass of champagne.

Holden was exactly as he described himself: 50s, tall and slim, smartly dressed, grey hair, relaxed and cheerful. He was also handsome, intelligent, and successful with a business he had built up from nothing into a large firm employing substantial numbers. He had reached the point in his life when he could step back a little, reap the rewards of long years of hard work, afford some time for himself. A newspaper article about the website caught his eye; he thought he would give it a try.

Having made no previous approaches to anyone, Natasha was his first date, and he was clearly very taken with her. Lunch lasted three hours, with a long succession of glasses of champagne, fabulous dishes, and an easy conversation that felt as if it could go on forever. They talked about everything and anything, comfortable with each other and with the quiet restaurant. After lunch, they returned to the bar, and sat chatting over glasses of Amaro. It was obvious they would be meeting again, after Holden returned from a family holiday planned to start very soon. Natasha was so excited at meeting someone she liked, and found so easy to be with, that she could hardly wait for Holden to get back. He wrote soon after he returned from holiday, with apologies, to say he had decided 'to be content with what I have', was coming off the website, and would not be seeing her again.

Paradoxically, meeting someone you like quickly and easily, can lead people to run away faster. All doubts and questions are resolved so early on. You confront reality and your choices with full information. The decision is just as likely to be No as Yes, especially after a family holiday, which can remind you of why you need something more, or else prove that things are not so bad after all.

Know thyself?

Josephine had been using married dating websites for some time, generally for casual encounters, although she sometimes saw someone for a few months at a time, if they were really good in bed. She saw herself as pretty experienced, especially at sifting out the timewasters, and men who were really looking for a pen-pal. As a rule, she moved pretty quickly to a first date, usually for a drink after work, and then expected to have a hotel date soon after that. Since there were always vastly more men than women on the websites, she found she was rarely turned down, as she took some trouble with her appearance. Several men she met had been a lot younger than her, and were appreciative, albeit a bit rough at the edges in their manners.

When she met Ralph, she found him rather quiet, perhaps due to this being his first such date, and a bit shy, but he was an attractive man, and she was happy to give him a full introduction to the married dating scene. For their second date, they agreed to meet at a small countryside hotel outside the town where neither would be recognised. Josephine wore sexy black underwear with red satin details and a nice dress. They met in the hotel bar for a drink and a sandwich, then went up to the room. They got kissing, and she started undressing to show off her sexy lingerie, and get Ralph excited. Then they were kissing again, and she started to unbutton his shirt, very slowly. Suddenly he stopped her, exclaimed 'I can't do this! I just can't do it!', grabbed his jacket and ran from the room. Josephine hung around for a short while, in case Ralph came back, then finally left, discovering that he departed so precipitously that she was left paying the hotel bill.

Dating websites make an affair look as easy as shopping on the internet: say what you want, and you can have it. The focus on sifting through profiles, making your choice, and contacting people means that some users never get round to thinking through why they are there, and whether they are sure they want to go down this road. For some, the fantasy is more than enough; the reality is a step too far. Others only think things through properly when they are faced with the concrete possibility of meeting someone, and they decide their family life is too important to endanger it this way. Some people do not have the mental toughness required for an affair, and only discover this by trying to start one.

Josephine's experience was extreme, but people can and do quit at the last minute. Mostly, people drop out at an earlier stage. Some men cancel first dates the day beforehand, or even on the day itself, by sending a belated email or text message or leaving an abrupt voicemail message. Some people simply don't show up on the day. When arrangements for meeting are left vague, as to which day of the week, the exact time or the venue, this is generally an indication that someone is not sure of going through with it after all. People who do want to meet, definitely, make precise and firm arrangements that are not open to misunderstanding and confusion.

Tourists

From time to time journalists turn up on websites, doing 'research for a novel' or collecting material for a magazine feature article on internet dating. Like tourists, they are curious enough to look at everything, but do not generally taste the food in case they get a bug. The resulting articles serve to advertise the websites, but the need to create a 'good story' often means that reality takes second place. In December 2008, Lucy Kellaway informed readers of her *Financial Times* column that she had picked up 247 boyfriends in the space of a month, many of them newly idle bankers affected by the credit crunch. However her friend did even better, picking up 295 boyfriends in just one week. They worked hard, obviously, but it is unlikely they actually dated them all, or even any.

*

Jeremy's profile advertised that he travelled around the country on business, so was not restricted as to area. Like many men, he was 'prepared to travel for the right person'. Celestine sounded brilliant, mid-30s compared to his 49, and very pretty. They chatted amiably for a while on the site. She lived in Manchester, while he was in London, and in the past he often had business meetings in Manchester. Just when he would have welcomed it, there were none. Finally, he took the day off work to make the three-hour trip on the train to meet Celestine. She had provided clear instructions for a pub she liked that served food at lunchtime as well as cocktails and the usual beers. He took a taxi to the address, to avoid wasting time through getting lost. He arrived early, so he waited. And waited. And waited. Finally, he ate lunch. Several times he wandered round the pub to make absolutely sure there was no young woman responding to Celestine's description, but there were no young women at all that lunchtime. He took the train home, and three hours later found a message from Celestine saying she was sorry, she had given him the wrong pub name. The one she liked was on the same street, but further down. Jeremy could not decide whether she was incompetent or dishonest, as she could clearly have gone over to his pub, the one she named, at least once in all that time to find him. But by this time he no longer had any desire to meet her.

Roman was very definite about only meeting women who lived in and around London. However he knew he was not a prize catch – late fifties, grey hair, a little extra weight round the middle. So he tried to be realistic, approaching women aged mid-40s and older. One of them, Barbara, agreed to meet him for lunch one day, but she could not come in to the city centre. He agreed to travel out to the outer edge of

London where she lived, which was easy enough on the tube. She said she would pick him up in her blue Mercedes, and they could go to a nice gastropub nearby. He took the train to the agreed station, which took a good hour, and stood outside in a visible spot. He waited. And waited. Finally he got her on her mobile. Barbara said she was running late, and would arrive shortly. A patient man, he waited. Another call to find out where she was. This time she said she was caught in traffic, would arrive soon. Finally, a blue Mercedes drove up and stopped in front of him. He opened the passenger door to see an attractive brunette in her mid-40s looking up at him, checking his name? Before he could get in the car, she exclaimed 'Oh No! You are not at all what I expected! Not at all!' and drove off. Roger was shocked at the bad manners, but also angry. He resented being rejected so quickly, purely on his appearance.

Bad manners

Some people really are keen on getting dates, but then spoil things by their bad manners. Georgina found herself sitting in a bar waiting for over half an hour for her first date with William. She got a drink, and played with it a long time in case he did finally show up. He finally arrived 40 minutes late, offering no excuse, explanation or apology. After they chatted for a while, she asked him the reason. William said he assumed she would be half an hour late, and he did not want to appear 'too eager'. William turned out to be handsome, interesting, and amusing company, so they had a pleasant hour or so chatting over drinks. But his rudeness in arriving late for a first date soured Georgina's view of him, and she decided not to see him again, even though he was keen.

*

What counts as bad manners varies a lot between people, and between cultures. But the general rule is that you cannot take any chances when you are meeting someone you do not yet know well. Strangers are in no position to make assumptions about the other party before actually meeting them. In the western world, etiquette dictates that a man should arrive first for a date, certainly before the woman, because a woman sitting alone in a bar can attract unwelcome attention from other men, especially if she is attractive. In most cultures it is rude to keep someone waiting.

Julian had a habit of being late when he was meeting Maggie, She did not know whether he was also late for business appointments, but he was typically late when meeting her, always offering the excuse that he had been delayed by a client. On one occasion, she saw him arrive half an hour late for a lunch date, then walk back out of the restaurant to stand outside taking a call on his mobile for another 10 minutes. One day, Julian said he would make it up to her, and take her to a place he had heard of, 'the most romantic hotel in London'. Looking it up on the internet, it did indeed sound fabulous, a mixture of modern and antique style, very Italian. They agreed to meet in the bar there. She bought sexy new lingerie for the occasion.

On the day, Maggie found the hotel impossible to find and, unusually, arrived late herself. There was no sign of Julian in the bar, as she expected, so she got a drink. After a while, she called his mobile to check his timetable. It turned out that Julian had arrived early, looked around, decided that he did not like the hotel after all, 'too kitsch' he said, and because she was not there waiting for him as usual, decided she was not coming

and had gone back to work without even leaving her a
message. He had refused to wait at all for her, in part because
he did not want to sit in the bar he disliked. Despite the idea
that this was supposed to be a special date, he had effectively
changed his mind because he found the hotel too fancy. For
Maggie, this was the final straw, and she refused to see Julian
again, even though she rather liked him.

Debbie was overjoyed when she was approached by a man
who was both attractive and wealthy, to judge by the cars he
said he owned. For a first date, Hamilton invited her to dinner
at one of the most expensive and stylish restaurants in
London, somewhere she had read about but never expected to
go to. She did her hair with extra care, and wore her most
glamorous dress (a sequinned number) with high heels. Her
divorce would be finalised within a month, so she had decided
to start dating again. Living at home with a small child, on a
restricted income, it was a long time since she had been taken
out in style. At first she had had no luck on the website, but
finally this seemed to be it. Hamilton said he owned several
businesses, but he seemed to have plenty of free time. Over
dinner, it emerged that Hamilton was staying teetotal for one
month while training hard for a major sporting event that he
hoped to win. He insisted she should drink whatever she liked,
all the same. So she had champagne, and ended up drinking
the entire bottle, after several cocktails at the start of the
evening. Debbie did her best to charm the pants off
Hamilton, who was even nicer than she had dared hope, and
they had a good evening together.

As they were leaving, Hamilton said he would get her a taxi
home as they lived at opposite ends of the city. Then he
realised just how drunk and unsteady on her feet Debbie was,

and thought maybe he should take her home himself, to be on the safe side. As he walked her to his car parked nearby, she seemed to get even more unsteady in the cold night air and her impossibly high heels. When they reached his Porsche, Debbie suddenly leant over it and vomited violently into the gutter. She then felt very faint and weak. At this point, an empty taxi drove by. Hamilton hailed it, got Debbie in, and paid the driver enough to take her home whatever the address. He wiped the vomit off the bonnet of his car as soon as he could, and decided never to see Debbie again.

More bad manners

Desmond fancied himself as a great catch. He was in his mid-fifties, but not fat. He dressed well. He had a senior position with a head-hunter firm, so he was used to being in a position of power vis a vis the many applicants for plum jobs, which were usually a big step up, in status and salary, for the people he interviewed. He generally met them in elegant restaurants and bars in the centre of town, so he regarded himself as a *bon viveur*. The first time he tried a dating website Desmond had the good fortune to meet an attractive younger woman, who was just finding her feet again after her divorce from a much older husband. She adored him, that was obvious. Best of all, she lived on his side of the city, not too far from his own home, so he found it very convenient to drop in to see her when he wanted, in the early evening and sometimes at weekends. But now he was back on the dating websites, looking again.

Once again he got lucky, and his third date was with Juliette, a gorgeous blond, dyed blond, but blond nonetheless, and she had a very good figure. She was new to the whole enterprise, and seemed nervous, so he gave her some idea of how things worked. As a head-hunter, he was used to being in the driving seat for interviews, and he found himself slipping into his usual role here too, quizzing Juliette on what she did, what she was looking for, what experience she had so far. When she proved reluctant to provide details of her job, he told her that head-hunters had ways of finding out – for example he could find out what people earned, even if they were reluctant to tell him their current salary. Juliette remonstrated that this was not a job interview! Desmond was treating her as if she had applied for the post of his mistress?!

He relaxed a little then, and explained that he was still seeing his current mistress, but had decided the time had come to replace her. She had become far too attached to him, had become demanding, interfering in his life. She kept sending him text messages, phoned him at inconvenient times, and wanted to see him every day. Desmond had woken up to the fact that she might conceivably try to embarrass him at home. So he was looking for a replacement now, and he would dump her as soon as he found one. He reassured his gorgeous blonde date, Juliette, that she need not worry, the other woman would be out of the picture as soon as they got together for real! He could not understand why she found his offer unappealing, and refused a second date. Juliette concluded that if he was so insensitive towards his current lover, he would be equally selfish and calculating with her too.

Men who have had a long string of lovers can become blasé and insensitive to a degree that is shocking to newcomers, who are still feeling their way cautiously.

Olivia was not terribly keen on meeting Christofer. But he was persistent and persuasive, so they met for lunch one day in one of the many classic French restaurants in London's Soho. At first sight, her heart sank, as he looked far older than he claimed, and he appeared stiff, ill at ease. She worked hard to get him to relax, and within ten minutes got him laughing. Christofer was clearly surprised at her being as attractive and stylishly dressed as her profile promised, and kept telling her she was beautiful, which cheered her up. She quickly found a neutral topic to talk and joke about, which gradually revealed details of Christofer's work and Olivia's travel experiences. Although Christofer chose a watery wine, the food was excellent, and a sense of camaraderie developed as they shared the first dish to arrive at the table. They had a good time, and she found she liked him a lot. After he relaxed, he became witty and charming, and was a gracious host. Christofer was openly keen to meet again. It emerged he had only recently joined the website, so he had been nervous, not knowing what to expect, and was relieved it was such a success. 'It was the best time I've had in a long time' he concluded.

They started to meet regularly, in principle, although work timetables and holidays entailed long gaps between dates. They met for lunch, visited art exhibitions, met for a drink after work. Olivia thought she was really lucky to have met someone she got on so well with. Christofer kept telling Olivia she was his ideal woman, clever as well as beautiful. In the long gaps between dates, he kept in touch, saying he could not wait to see her again. He rented a flat in central London for weekdays, as he worked long hours and his family home was a good distance away. Eventually one day, they finished up in his flat for a glass of champagne, and fell into bed. Christofer was a fantastic lover, playful, imaginative, enthusiastic and energetic. They agreed to meet again, soon. Once again incompatible timetables meant that a date could only be fixed two months ahead.

Then suddenly, all communication ceased. As their agreed date approached, Olivia wrote to check they were still meeting? No reply. She tried again, with no response. Olivia might have given up then, except that Christofer had found a gold bracelet of hers left behind in his flat, so he knew she needed to retrieve her property, whatever happened. Early on, he had given her his business card as well as his private mobile number, making it clear he was a senior manager in a national corporation. Reluctantly, she decided to write to him on his business email, with a suitably brief and cautious message about retrieving her property. Again no reply. Starting to feel desperate, she left messages on his mobile and work telephone numbers, repeatedly. Still no response. She wondered whether Christofer had a serious accident, or illness, but thought that in such a case someone else in his office would be dealing with his messages, or else his mailbox would have become full in his absence. Finally, she decided to use his corporation's central telephone number to reach him, to say it was fine if he did not want to see her any more, but she absolutely must retrieve her property please. She assumed she would probably be put through to a secretary or colleague covering for him in his absence, which would at least allow her to find out what had happened to him.

To her astonishment, she was put straight through to Christofer, who agreed to return her bracelet. He agreed instantly to the date and time she requested, asking her to drop by his flat to collect it. But on the day agreed, there was no answer to his doorbell. She rang and knocked for ten minutes before he opened the door, wordlessly, looking angry. Olivia said she had come to collect her property. Christofer handed it to her. Then invited her to come in. By this time she was too upset to be able to speak, and left quickly.

One week later, Christofer wrote to apologise for his 'rude and boorish behaviour', claiming that he had been incredibly busy with work. Olivia pointed out that did not excuse his rudeness and contempt. To her astonishment, he wrote again two months later, after he returned from his summer holiday, admitting that he had behaved very badly previously, but saying he would love to see her again, all the same. Again, Olivia reminded him that work pressures could not excuse his failure to spend two minutes cancelling the date he had fixed, and refusing to respond to any of the telephone messages and emails to both private and work addresses that she had sent over a period of three weeks. She was shocked to discover that there had never been any excuse preventing Christofer from responding. He had simply not bothered to reply. She accepted that his job took precedence. But she could not accept four weeks of contempt, from a man who said she was his ideal woman and had been wildly enthusiastic about her.

11

Ethics

In the ladies' restroom of a fashionable Mayfair restaurant two women are talking quietly as they reapply lipstick and primp their hair. Both are in their fifties, dressed in expensive silk dresses, with large diamond rings on their hands, oozing money and confidence. But they are being secretive, instead of talking in the usual self-assertive voices of the wives of successful men. One looks angry, positively fuming with rage.

'He's done it before. It's not the first time.'
'How awful for you!'
'I know the signs now. I don't say anything of course.'
'Do you have any idea who it is?'
'Oh yes – I think I know who it is this time.' And then with some bitterness she adds 'We met them a short while ago, soon after they moved into Hampstead. I could tell he was rather taken with her, ever so courteous, refilling her glass and so on.'
'Why don't you confront him then?'
'What's the point? If not her, then it'll be someone else. Sooner or later. He can be charming, you know, when he's minded to bother. They all fall for him. He takes me for

granted, part of the furniture, and anyway I refuse to let it
bother me....'

And they sail out of the room, putting brightly professional
public smiles on their faces for the world at large.

For most people, the main cost of an affair is psychological: the need to maintain secrecy, which can become a
permanent, constant source of worry. For some, anxiety about
the risks prevents them getting anywhere with their fantasies
and plans, and they quickly give up. For those who make it
through their first affair 'successfully' (as they see it) without
visible problems, and later progress to further liaisons, the
ability to compartmentalise their lives becomes second nature.
A certain mental toughness is required, is essential. Libertines
also develop a raft of techniques and procedures to keep them
out of trouble.

Married dating has a certain morality. The first rule is
'never in your own backyard', where you are most exposed to
gossip, and most likely to be found out, as illustrated above.
This is one reason for the success of the websites: they allow
everyone to reach well beyond their own social circle, safely,
and without repercussions. The second reason is that married
dating websites permit more honesty: both parties are in the
same position, so do not need to lie to each other about their
home lives, which makes everything more relaxed. Both
parties are on the same level, and are equally committed to
secrecy and discretion.

People who allow their spouse to discover an affair are
sometimes doing it 'accidentally on purpose' to provoke
discussion of problems in the relationship. For such people
the affair is just one weapon to use in an overt or covert
marital war, or just one symptom of problems in the relation-

ship. These cases often end up in counselling sessions – with expensive private therapists in the USA, or with charitable organisations such as Relate in Britain. Julia Coles's book *After the Affair* discusses the relationship problems that trigger the affairs that lead couples into Relate counselling, and suggests how couples can rebuild trust after such an affair is over. Typically, these relationships are characterised by friction and arguments. Spouses usually know when the relationship is not working well.

People in happy marriages take a variety of practical steps to ensure that an affair remains sufficiently out of sight that it does not interfere with everyday life. Timothy bought a second, separate mobile phone which he used exclusively for contacting his lover. It was normally left in a drawer at work, and turned off when he was not expecting any calls. When this phone rang, he knew who was calling, and could decide whether it was safe to answer or not. Within his own office at work, he normally had privacy, but people often came in for meetings. In contrast, Michael was happy to give out his main mobile number. He never found it difficult to deal with unexpected private calls, and if necessary would elegantly postpone the call, saying he would call back at a later time.

Most people start a separate email account for communicating with their lover. Hotmail, Yahoo and some other service providers offer free email accounts, which can easily be set up and discarded as necessary. Because the email address has only one purpose, there is no need to log in every day, and there is no risk of messages being seen by someone else. A separate email address also offers anonymity, if wanted, by allowing you to use a different 'stage name'. You can even invent a different persona for the address – if you can remember it! The disadvantage is that it can be tricky explaining why you are logged into what is obviously 'someone else's account' when you are on-line at home.

Rod was ultra careful about revealing his identity because he was concerned about the possibility of blackmail. He started a new email address under the name Tim Small, and used this to write to several women he met through a dating website. After a while, his demanding nature led him to fall out with all the women except one, Lily, who seemed miraculously to blend into his every mood, and sail through his temper tantrums while having a good time with him anyway. He continued seeing her for well over a year, when it became more convenient to switch to his normal email address. So he told Lily, with some embarrassment, that his real name was Roderick Lamontagne. The fact that he had effectively been lying about his name for over a year did not go down well. At first, Lily joked that she had always thought Tim Small was a tiny name for such a big personality. But she then started to wonder what other falsehoods he had told her, and started to quiz Rod about all aspects of his life. Soon after, they broke up, apparently on some other pretext, but possibly due in part to the lack of trust that had been revealed by the issue of false names and identities – and for so long!

In sharp contrast, there are many people who switch easily and quickly to using their work email address for corresponding with their lover or girl/boyfriend. Some people exchange business cards at the end of the first date, if they plan to see each other again. They may be disinclined to talk much about their family life, which remains private, but they make no effort to conceal their professional identity. In extreme cases, men even invite women to meet them at their office.

*

Raj was immensely proud of his fabulous suite of offices on the top two floors of a lovely modern building in central London. 'Come up to see my views' he would say smilingly to new women he fancied. As the boss and sole owner of his business, he was unafraid of anyone trying to embarrass him, and he was confident of his ability to deal with anyone who might get silly ideas. He liked the fact that women were invariably impressed by his stunning offices and his relaxed manner at work. He felt he was a good judge of character, and could easily weed out any doubtful personalities on the websites he used. In fact, he was privately keen for his colleagues and staff to know that he had a whole string of mistresses, who came to meet him at his office, dressed to kill for the evening. It became his private amusement, providing a sharp contrast with his normal daytime role as manager and company director.

In other cases, people can be almost paralysed by paranoia over potential discovery and exposure, to the point that they are unable to meet anyone. A man who chose the unfortunate profile name of 'Tiddles' was a successful lawyer who decided to try a married dating website. He sent off half a dozen approaches to women who sounded attractive. Only one responded, a woman using the profile name of 'Nightingale'. They agreed to meet for lunch, but Tiddles started to worry because the table would be booked in his real name.

It then emerged that Tiddles' worries came from a story posted on some website's chat room, which unquestionably sounded awful. The man had given his full real name to a woman he met for lunch, after chatting most agreeably on-line for a while. The woman used the name for the table reservation to obtain his phone number from the restaurant, then did a thorough internet search on his name, and followed up with phone calls to obtain his home address and telephone number as well as employment details. Clearly, she did a lot of research. She then phoned his wife to inform her about her husband's activities on the dating website. The predictable result was a crisis at home. Tiddles was now trying to ensure he did not get caught in the same way. In practice, he became so anxiety stricken that he felt unable to trust anyone enough to agree to a date.

There are people with all sorts of personal hang-ups on dating websites. On married websites, there are two main stumbling blocks for men. One is escort girls and call girls (amateur and professional) who ask for money to take things further, on the first date if not beforehand. Another version of this is the woman looking for a sugar-daddy, a benefactor who will pay her a regular monthly retainer; in return she will be available to see him whenever he wants, whenever he is in the city and free. The opposite problem is the enraged 'feminist' who seeks to expose and deter men from using the websites, just as there are people who seek to deter curb-crawlers from picking up street prostitutes. Website managers are aware of problems of this nature, but rely heavily on subscribers to identify such users so they can be excluded. Since women are usually offered free membership, they can easily re-join under new names and new profiles. For obvious reasons, these women post attractive profiles, and many of them are indeed exceptionally attractive.

People who are employees generally feel more vulnerable to exposure than people who are self-employed, freelance, or have their own business. This latter group has more freedom and autonomy, greater exposure to risk, more experience in coping with risky negotiations and having to judge the integrity of people they deal with. Business owners are more accustomed to interviewing for new recruits and new staff, and appreciate the immense value of face-to-face meetings compared to CVs and self-presentations on paper. For all these reasons, employers and the self-employed are over-represented on married websites compared to employees, who are more cautious and fearful.

People who regard themselves as famous, or in the public eye in some fashion, feel especially vulnerable to being exposed. Of course, it is easy to exaggerate the risks. As Andy Warhol pointed out, everyone is famous for fifteen minutes. Most people are only famous within a very small social circle, which may constitute their whole world, but is actually invisible to everyone else. A high profile corporate lawyer is unlikely to appear 'famous' to someone working in fashion or the charity sector, and vice versa. Academics may be internationally renowned within their own narrow discipline (such as economics or literature) yet be a nobody to academics in a different discipline (such as architecture or medicine). So long as you avoid meeting anyone who works in the same broad area of business, it is easy to remain low profile. The advantage of internet dating is that you can become a nonentity, if you choose.

The problem is that men, especially, want to boast about their successes and achievements, want to be seen and appreciated for who and what they are, in the round. So they struggle between maintaining a low profile, being a nobody, and parading their achievements and abilities in vast detail. In essence, their problem is 'Can I trust someone enough to enjoy the benefits of their admiration, without the risk of any downside?' Technically, people could boast about their successful career as a judge, or hedge fund manager, or business owner, without revealing their real name. In practice, men need to attach their real names (and egos) to their achievements.

Clifford's public persona was wrapped around a one-hour radio show he broadcast every week. Millions listened to it. The vast majority of the population had never heard of it. Those who did listen had no idea what he looked like, and probably did not care. It was the voice that mattered, and the substance of the programme. He adopted the name Oxford for his private adventures, and remembered to use it when reserving tables for lunch. However when telling stories about his exciting life and achievements, he could not stop himself from quoting his own real name at the centre of the story. A Google search using several spellings of the name quickly identified who he was. Successful, certainly, but not a celebrity. Also, the search did not reveal any details of his private life, apart from proving he was ten years older than he claimed to be.

The advent of Google and other internet search systems, makes a huge difference today to privacy, and strengthens the case for using a separate 'stage name' when in doubt. However it is worth checking that your alternative name does not already belong to a real person, who can be traced through the internet. Even people with low-profile jobs as accountants, librarians and charity workers can end up being identifiable through internet searches, especially if their photos are attached to a media story or company report. Of course, some names yield hundreds of listings. Even odd and exceptional names are rarely unique. Most of the time, you cannot be sure you have identified the right person in a Google search. Internet searches on an individual name can be even more misleading, most or all of the time when it comes to ordinary people with ordinary names.

Sandra thought her prospective date had a very unusual name, so she Googled him to find out what she could in advance. She found a lot of material (including a photo) on a man of that name, who was rather old, wealthy, living in Scotland, and active in local politics and community affairs. When she finally met her date for a drink, he was someone else entirely: early 30s, working hard to make money, and living exclusively in southern England.

The extreme solution to anxieties about blackmail and exposed identities is to provide only one's first name, and refuse ever to divulge the surname. Some people use obviously fictitious surnames, such as Smith or Morris. Others openly use a pseudonym where a full name is necessary, for example, booking a restaurant table under the name Ian Fleming or James Bond. The anonymity of 'first names only' or invented 'player' names, is common on websites focused on purely sexual encounters, just as it is common in the world of commercial sex. You have to decide whether it is something you welcome, can go along with, or cannot tolerate. Users of general dating websites expect to know full names, in line with the idea that relationships go beyond exclusively sexual encounters, and some people apply the same rule on websites for married people.

People who complain to the other party that they are

having problems maintaining secrecy are usually dumped as quickly as possible.

Keith had paid for several lunches, and hotel rooms, on his credit card. One day, he started talking anxiously about being found out by his wife, who might potentially see the items on his monthly card bill. He kept asking Veronica, his lover, if she knew anyone with a flat they might use instead? At one point, he even suggested they might use her flat in London, when her husband was away. Veronica was irritated by these complaints, since she was ignorant of Keith's arrangements at home and could not be responsible for them. She was clear she would never impose on her friends, even if they had a conveniently located apartment, as this would invite gossip, and she would not dream of using her own home. Not surprisingly, Keith soon found that Veronica no longer had the time to see him, as she had changed jobs.

The normal method of ensuring secrecy is to pay all bills, however large, in cash. This leaves no trace at all. Experienced married daters remember to carry sufficient funds to cover predictable expenses, plus some extra. For obvious reasons, they discard all receipts, bills and other hard evidence of entertainments. They know that affairs require planning to permit fun and spontaneity.

It is not clear where the idea comes from that internet dating is more dangerous than meeting strangers in bars and clubs, or even in your neighbourhood. Anyone who has read Judith Rossner's book *Looking for Mr Goodbar*, or has seen the film based on it, knows that perfectly nice handsome strangers can turn angry enough to kill the unsuspecting girl they picked up in a bar. Where you first make contact is irrelevant. Ultimately, it is always your responsibility to gauge whether someone is emotionally unstable, or prone to violence. It is much easier to check this out face to face.

'Aren't you afraid who I might be?' asks Francis, a handsome middle aged man in a dark suit who was already at the table, waiting for her. 'Why should I be afraid?' replied Bianca. 'Here we are, sitting in a restaurant, a public place, surrounded by waiters who are waiting to take our orders, who will intervene at the slightest hint of trouble.' As it turned out, Francis was the CEO of a major corporation, happily married with three children, extremely courteous and congenial company. The last man in the world to be a crazy axe murderer.

If anything, dating married people is the safest bet in the world. Married people come with their own Health and Safety Certificate: the spouse and family who testify to their being normal, decent, law-abiding, sane, responsible. Single people, and social loners, are far more likely to have an eccentric perspective on the world, a hang-up about something that other people regard as unimportant, an inability to control their temper, or no disposition to accept the compromises required by relationships.

'One guy was really shocked when I quickly suggested meeting for lunch', says Sally. 'He approached me first, but he thought that my suggesting lunch was rather 'fast' behaviour for a woman, or rather a lady! Some people think meeting someone, for a drink or lunch, involves more risks than chatting on-line or chatting on the phone. I never understood that. It's the other way round. You have no idea who you are writing to on-line. They can claim to be anybody and anything.

Even the photos can be misleading – years out of date, so fuzzy you see nothing, or just false. Whereas in a face-to-face meeting, you can take a view, check out the half-truths, gauge their character and honesty. And you learn far more about someone, much faster, than on-line. Meeting someone is just a quicker way to find out whether you want to know them at all. After all, what is the worst that can happen? Two possibilities. One, he doesn't show up. It happens. It can happen to anyone. That is why I will never meet anyone outside, it has to be indoors, out of the rain and wind. Two, he is ugly, or dishonest, or rude. I can cope with any of those for the one or two hours of a lunch,' says Sally. 'And if the place itself is nice, then you have a nice time anyway. It can be a pleasant or interesting interlude even if the date is a disappointment and you will not meet again.'

People who have a fixed script, and like to stick to it, tend to be novices who are nervous and insecure, so prefer to take things step by step. People who are happy to move straight to meeting people are a distinct group. Some have had affairs in the past, so are more relaxed about everything anyway. But most can loosely be described as cosmopolitans. They travel a lot on business, or have done so in the past, especially outside Europe. They are used to meeting complete strangers and having to do business with them, including people from other cultures, different social classes or occupations. They have learnt that written communication can be misleading, potentially misunderstood, and that you have to meet people face-to-face to be sure of understanding them. They may own their own business, and be used to interviewing new recruits, hiring and firing staff. Some have lived in other countries, particularly in countries beyond the comforting similarities of western European or Anglo-Saxon culture (North America, Britain and Australia). Some have attended boarding schools, so are used to getting along with strangers at close quarters. A few are wealthy people for whom the cost of a lunch or dinner in a restaurant is too trivial to think about, whereas time is always at a premium.

For a first date, especially, it is important to meet in a public place where there are other people. At the same time, discretion requires that you are never too visible. Finally, venues must be chosen so that they can be explained if you should be seen by someone you know. The last thing you want is a sociable and gossipy neighbour exclaiming that they saw you in X place last week with an attractive stranger! The requirement of poor visibility suggests that it may be unwise to meet in very public places, such as main squares, railway stations or metro stations, where there are large numbers of people passing through who may see and notice someone without necessarily stopping to chat. Meeting indoors, in bars, cafes or restaurants also means that if one party is late, the other can sit in comfort, with a drink and a newspaper, while waiting for them. Late arrivals are amazingly common for dates of all kinds.

Maddox works in the Canary Wharf business district of London, so he decided he would only meet someone who did not work in that area, to be absolutely safe from gossip, especially as the area has a restricted choice of bars and restaurants. He agreed to meet Camilla, a promising-sounding woman working in the City of London, a short metro ride away. Having agreed on the restaurant, he suggested that they meet outside at a given time, so they could walk in together, which seemed more elegant. However Camilla insisted on meeting at the table, saying she found that a more elegant and smoother meet-up. Reluctantly, Maddox agreed, but then felt he had to arrive first, as this is standard etiquette for a date.

On the day itself, it was pouring with rain, so he began to think Camilla's plan was the better one, after all, as he would not be obliged to stand outside in the wet, waiting for her. Just as he was walking out of his office, he bumped into a senior manager who stopped him to ask about his strategy for a forthcoming important negotiation. Maddox ended up having an extremely useful informal discussion which lasted a good 20 minutes. By the time he finally got to the restaurant he was half an hour late, but in high spirits as a result of his chance meeting in the office. Camilla had been sitting waiting for him for half an hour, with a glass of champagne to soothe her nerves. A delay that could have ruined the date finally did not matter, largely due to her insistence on meeting at the table instead of in the rain outside.

People invent all sorts of devices to help them to compart-mentalise, to create mental barriers between their affairs and their normal life, between their spouse (or long-term partner) and their lovers.

By her mid-thirties, Martha was already a regular user of dating websites for married people, because she did not get enough sex at home. A very attractive blonde, slim, petite woman, she worked in marketing and travelled around the country quite a bit, visiting clients. This provided her with an ideal cover for any dates she made. Over time, she had developed fixed routines that worked for her. She would proceed as quickly as possible to a first date, to check whether she found a man physically attractive or not. She also wanted to be clear about whether she trusted him. If she liked the man, she would then meet him one more time, just for sex, and would never see him again. She felt this guarded against her getting emotionally involved with anyone else.

Knowing it was a one-off encounter made her feel less inhibited, socially and sexually. It was also nice and tidy: everyone knew where they stood. Most men agreed to her conditions, because men rarely say No to free sex. However she noted that a lot of men, generally the nicer, more intelligent men were not interested. They preferred an ongoing relationship with one person, not a string of one-offs. Apart from anything else, a series of flings entails a permanent search for partners.

Martha's approach differs little from that of men who seek a never-ending stream of short-term flings. They too regard these encounters as ephemeral, so there is no long-term attachment, and hence the affairs do not really matter. In terms of ethics, they do not count, are irrelevant to the main, permanent relationship.

Another way married people avoid too much emotional attachments is the 'safety in numbers' strategy. Here, relationships are ongoing, but with several people rather than one only. Two seems to be the minimum number, but some men and women see three partners periodically. This approach works well in cases where meetings are few and far between in any case (due to problems of distance, or work pressures), rather than regular weekly or fortnightly dates. The safety in numbers strategy does lessen the risk of becoming attached to one person, due to familiarity and habituation. However it does not eliminate the risk of one party falling in love, which seems to be due to intensely personal responses and positive interactions rather than purely situational factors.

Libertines who have had a series of affairs, and may be seeing several partners concurrently, invariably use condoms. People who are completely new to this game rarely get round to thinking of condoms, and forget to buy them.

Women's magazines commonly advise readers that it is important to 'know someone's sexual history' before sleeping with them. This is rubbish, of course. Too often, not using condoms is treated as a statement of trust and emotional commitment to a person. This too is ridiculous. Whether or not someone has any disease that can be sexually transmitted is a question of fact that has nothing to do with their sexual history, nor their feelings for you. AIDS and Hepatitis C can be transmitted by blood transfusions, infected needles, and other accidental processes. Carriers of disease can be totally unaware they have been infected, and have no symptoms of any kind.[57] No-one can be completely certain of being disease-free unless they have the relevant tests.

Heidi was in her fifties when she had to have loads of tests to try to pin down the cause of a medical problem. To her aston-ishment, doctors told her she was HIV positive (although this had nothing to do with her medical problem). She insisted this was simply impossible! She was a virgin when she married, and she had never had sex with anyone other than her husband, although she admitted that sex had become a rare event. Doctors insisted nonetheless that she was HIV positive, and wanted to test her husband, as her main contact. He too was found to be HIV positive. Gradually, the story came out. Several years earlier, her husband had gone to Kenya on a sales trip, and spent one week there. One evening, he decided to treat himself to the excitement and novelty of sex with a black woman, especially as there were several very attractive young women hanging around in the hotel bar. He did not use a condom, having no experience of them. He was unaware that some reports estimate around half of all workers in the sex industry in Kenya to be HIV positive. He contracted the virus, and later passed it on to his wife Heidi, who was naturally oblivious of his Kenyan adventure.

Chlamydia has few or no troublesome symptoms, so people can easily be unaware of having picked it up. Because it can cause infertility, and is concentrated among young people, it is especially dangerous for those who plan to have children. Other sexually-transmitted diseases that are often the focus of media scares, such as herpes, are easily treated, and are not dangerous despite being painful. You cannot rely on pain being the key indicator of diseases that can be sexually transmitted and that are dangerous.

The only way to know with certainty that you are free of any Sexually Transmitted Diseases (STDs) is to have all the relevant tests. This involves giving blood and urine samples, which are sent away for testing. In Britain, the tests are offered free of charge and anonymously in NHS Sexual Health Clinics, which are often located in discreet small establishments, outside and away from hospitals. Customers can use an alternative name in order to remain private, but they are usually asked to identify their correct local NHS health trust (via their home address postcode) for centre funding purposes. Results are usually given within a week or so, over the phone, and counselling is available if needed. As a result of tests and treatment being free in Britain, at such clinics or through local doctors, STD infection rates in Britain are one-tenth of the levels found in the USA, for example.[58]

In Europe, the vast majority of the population is free of STDs, which are concentrated in particular groups. For example, AIDS is concentrated among gay men and African heterosexuals in Britain. Some take the view that people using dating websites are automatically putting themselves at risk unless they use condoms every time. In big cities in North America, couples who decide to become 'exclusive' often insist that both parties first have the complete set of tests for STDs, with the written test results read by both, before they stop using condoms.

Obviously, the best course is never to tell anyone else about the affair. Once you tell anyone, even your best friend, it is no longer a secret within your control. Even if they are sworn to secrecy, there is always the possibility they will blurt something out, unthinkingly, when they are drunk, or if they get the idea they are speaking to someone who 'already knows about it'. This is the hardest rule to stick to. For some men and women, one of the extra delights of an affair is the enjoyment of telling close friends, effectively boasting about one's amorous exploits, and the fact that you can still attract a lover. Failing to maintain perpetual secrecy can cause the downfall of many otherwise successful and discreet lovers. As the saying goes: You can fool all the people some of the time, and some of the people all of the time, but it is hard to fool all the people all of the time.

Fraser had successfully concealed his affair with Teresa, a divorcee within his social circle, for many years. Thankfully, she too was not inclined to talk about it to anyone, not even her girlfriends, which was hard. He visited her at home on and off over a period of ten years, until both his sons had left home and become independent. He then decided that he had done his duty to his family, and was now going to quit his celibate marriage and live his own life again. Fraser moved out of the family home to a small bachelor flat, and started what he hoped would be an amicable (if costly) parting of ways with his wife. He split up with his long-standing mistress, and threw himself into his new life as a single man, free to date women as he liked, free to come and go as he wanted, not answerable to anyone any more.

One evening, after dinner with a male friend, they sat talking over a final drink, and Fraser told him about his long-running affair with Teresa, a mutual acquaintance. Two weeks later, the story had gone through several embellishments, and finally reached his wife, who was enraged to discover she had been deceived for ten years of her marriage. What had started out as a broadly amicable divorce became so soured that it dragged on for years, with his wife assuming that Fraser was a liar about every aspect of his finances, as well as about his sexual adventures during the marriage.

Whether you let slip some revealing fact, or someone else claims to have seen you in a place where you should not have been, with the wrong person, the usual advice is to deny it, always, consistently, persistently, for ever. Denials are simple enough to remember. Any admission of something going on will be met by demands for more and more information, until every detail comes out. So the best advice is to never tell, ever. Even if found out.

Risk can never be completely eliminated, in any part of life. People who do not have sufficient mental toughness and agility to cope with the inevitable risks should not go down this road. However there is a whole raft of basic precautions that create a 'fire wall' providing a large degree of security.

12

Endings

Grace had been seeing Gabriel for six months when he was obliged to go to Houston on a long business trip. Despite not knowing very much about each other's lives, they had developed a strong rapport, in and out of bed. Without being fully aware of it, Grace had fallen in love with Gabriel, who was close to being her ideal man. Gabriel was a big, tall and dark man, immensely clever, invariably good-humoured and energetic, an alpha-male on every level who was very successful in his business, and hugely attractive to women. Grace hoped he would return from the Houston trip with a gift for her, as this might indicate that he was more attached to her than his breezy cheerfulness ever admitted. She was encouraged by his writing to her regularly while he was away, describing his experiences. Then Gabriel's final email said he was returning to London. He would be jet-lagged and weary, he said '…but keep the week free because I can't wait to see you. I shall phone you as soon as I land to fix when we can meet'. That was the last time Grace ever heard from him.

Sudden silence can happen at any time. Mostly, the married lovers never discover why. As illustrated by the story of

Christofer and Olivia in Chapter 10, sudden silence can simply be due to a man getting busy at work, on some new project or major deal that matters far more than the business of keeping in touch with a mistress, no matter how enthusiastic he said he was. In that case, Olivia had a reason to pursue the matter, due to the lost property she needed to retrieve. Hence she discovered that there was in fact no good reason at all for Chris' silence, the failure to explain. Some people do bother to explain, at the time, or months later, when they finally re-appear. All sorts of events can precipitate a sudden silence, such as – his wife had a serious accident; there were problems with the children; he had a heart attack and was in hospital and then at home convalescing for months; problems at work or in the marriage; death of a close relative and organising a funeral; or simply general work pressures. Men often do not bother to say they will be out of touch for a while, especially if the event is sudden and unforeseen, or if it concerns work and business. Women can also be carelessly forgetful. It is almost invariably incorrect to assume, as people often do, that it was something to do with them, some failure or rudeness on their part – in other words, 'my fault, in some way'.

Fergus was a dream date as far as Valentina was concerned. Putting aside the full head of white hair (not black as stated in his profile), he was good-looking, had a trim figure and elegant manners, was smartly dressed in a navy blazer, and open about how wealthy he was. He had chosen a very nice restaurant for a first date, and was charming throughout. Fortunately, he seemed to like her just as much, apparently greatly relieved she did not turn up in jeans and trainers but wearing a beautiful silk dress that showed off her figure with pearls. He was definitely old school, and she had chosen the right outfit.

A couple of weeks later, Fergus invited her to lunch again, in Hakkasan, a fashionable Chinese restaurant decorated like an opium den, in a dark basement. The food here was spectacular, and the atmosphere exciting. They had a lovely time again, and this time Fergus started to hint at making a hotel booking for their next date? He also started to talk about his taste for sexy lingerie: basques and bustiers, traditional black stockings with a seam at the back worn with high heels. Valentina was happy to go along with this, especially as Fergus was offering to pay for the special lingerie. To get things started, he checked her size, and ordered some seamed black stockings. Valentina said she preferred to buy basques herself, to get the right fit, and bought an expensive French black lace number. Fergus said he couldn't wait to see her in all her glory, and he would book somewhere special. That was the last time she heard from him.

Being new to the website, Valentina was hurt and baffled. She tried once again to get in touch with Fergus, but had no reply. Clearly, she would not see him again. But there was no indication as to why? It was hard to see that it was something she had said or done. However no explanation was forthcoming.

In most cases, the parting of ways is a gradual process with each party making less and less effort to meet up, or even to chat on-line or by email – the classic fadeout.

Mike's first affair was with a woman he met by chance in a bar one evening. It lasted a year, and cheered him up greatly during his weekly business trips to London. Over the years, he had got fed up with the loneliness of his hotel room and evenings alone in central London, when everyone around him seemed to be having a good time with their friends and he had no-one to talk to. He felt he needed a girlfriend in town, and signed up to a married dating website as this seemed more honest than using singles dating websites. Mike worked out fairly quickly that men outnumbered women by at least seven to one. So he knew he would have to make an effort.

In practice, it was easier than he expected, and he met several attractive women fairly quickly. He decided to continue seeing two of them, Amaya and Larissa, in the hope that at least one of them might be free to see him on the evenings he was in town. Over a period of six months, he discovered that even with two girlfriends, he was routinely unable to get a date on the particular days or evenings he was free. Sometimes both women had other engagements booked weeks in advance, so neither was free on the evenings he wanted company. Sometimes, both accepted his offer of a date, and he had to cancel one of them by saying he was forced to work late after all. On several occasions, he was forced to cancel a date anyway. He would fix up to see Larissa (or Amaya) for dinner, then find that an important client insisted on seeing him in the evening as this was his only free time, so his dinner date had to be cancelled at short notice. A few times, he had fixed a lunch date with one of his girlfriends, only to realise that his morning meetings were running so late he would never make it, with another last minute cancellation of the date. Added to this, he was away for weeks at a time seeing clients in his New York and Los Angeles offices, and away again for his own holidays in the southern hemisphere during the winter, so contact was regularly broken, and had to be re-established on his return. What started out as looking easy and convenient, ended up being far more tricky than he realised. He got on well with both Larissa and Amaya, in part because he was playful, amusing company and a generous boyfriend. But the long gaps between dates, and the numerous cancelled dates, meant that both women started drifting away, seeing other men who were in town more often, or travelled less. What started out as enthusiastic friendships were gradually eroded over the months, until Mike was spending evenings in London on his own, as usual, as before. Mike found it easy to get girlfriends, but he had great difficulty in keeping them, due to his unpredictable timetable and work constraints.

In many cases, the fade-out happens more quickly, at the start of a relationship.

After 20 years of hard work building up his business, Theo had sold it to a larger company wanting to expand. He needed only to work out the remaining two years, then he would be a free man again, and wealthy enough to enjoy life to the fullest. Looking ahead to the good times coming, he subscribed to a dating website to find a girlfriend. His search focused on women in the town where he lived, plus London, which he visited regularly on business. Possibly because he openly advertised his new-found affluence, he had no difficulty getting attractive-sounding women to meet him. At 50, he was neither young nor old, and just average-looking, 'nothing special' as he put it modestly in his profile. He concentrated on women in their forties, who seemed to be numerous.

His first date was in London, with Kathleen, a stunning redhead with a fantastic figure, which felt unbelievably lucky to him. He had invited her to 'choose somewhere expensive' for lunch, so they met on the terrace at Le Pont de la Tour, with lovely views of Tower Bridge. They had champagne and they got on brilliantly. So much so that when they left the restaurant, walking back over Tower Bridge, he was walking with his arm round Kathleen's waist, and found he had an erection that refused to go away. They agreed to meet again very soon, and fixed a second date two weeks away.

Unfortunately, Theo found he had to be in Brussels for a meeting with the takeover firm bosses on the day he had planned to meet Kathleen. It was not something he could re-arrange for his convenience. The date was cancelled, to his chagrin. Kathleen was sympathetic, and they fixed another date for a Monday a few weeks ahead, when Theo could be sure of being free for the day. They chose a nice restaurant, and he booked a room in a small hotel nearby, just in case things progressed in that direction after lunch. Kathleen arrived at the restaurant a little early, eager with anticipation, and was offered a glass of champagne while she waited at their reserved table. After half an hour, she asked the Maitre D' to check Theo's whereabouts on whatever telephone number he had used for the table reservation. He returned with bad news: Theo apologised but he could not make it. His wife had a car accident over the weekend and was in hospital. Apparently, Theo had left a last-minute message to this effect for Kathleen, but she had been unable to collect any messages due to a morning appointment, and anyway she had been convinced that Theo would never cancel a date at short notice twice running. Initially, Kathleen was upset and put out. Later, she fully accepted that the cancellation had been inevitable. But it became clear to them both that in practice Theo did not have the time control and autonomy that he had advertised, and that further dates might also be subject to cancellation or postponement. Reluctantly, Theo decided he probably had to focus on women in his home town area rather than London, even if this was more risky, and he never saw Kathleen again, to his great regret.

When relationships are terminated abruptly, it may help if the reason is made clear.

Luciano had been seeing his new girlfriend Anastasia almost every week for two months, in part due to a lull in his projects that gave him some spare time, but also because he was determined to enjoy the adventure while it lasted. Even over the Christmas break, when they were separated, he sent regular messages to keep in touch while he was away on holiday with his family. Then, just when he was due to return to work, he heard his father was taken ill, and he left for Italy. In the event, his father died, so Luciano stayed on for the funeral, and to sort out financial affairs for his mother. The trip prompted a period of reflection, as he reviewed his childhood and youth, family events and relationships, how his own family life differed from the family he grew up in, the family his parents had created. When he finally returned home, he was a changed man. He decided he would devote more time and effort to his wife and children, to ensuring their family life was warm and strong. Without any regret, he told Anastasia he would no longer see her, he was not that kind of man any more. His family life was more important to him, and he would not endanger it in any way at all.

The most common cause of an affair being terminated is any hint that a spouse has become suspicious. This is also the easiest excuse to give if lovers want to end a relationship without going into the real reasons.

*

Nigel had taken every precaution to ensure his wife was kept ignorant of his affair with Bridget. He had chosen someone who lived a good way away from his home town, so there could never be embarrassing accidental encounters. Nigel would meet Bridget in a spot half-way between their respective towns, in the same small hotel he had found. The relationship was superficial, light-hearted, and centred on sex. It worked, because they both had effectively celibate marriages, yet did not want to disturb things. Then one evening, when he arrived home after seeing Bridget, his wife commented that he smelt of a woman's perfume. The next day, he wrote to Bridget saying he would not be seeing her any more. He even stayed off the dating website for three months, before he finally returned to look for a replacement.

Sometimes, affairs start and end for the same reason, which changes, or is resolved in some fashion. For Frederick, using a dating service was closely tied up with the success and failure of his business. At first, he saw the affair as a gift to himself, a reward for the three years of hard work he had put into developing the product his company would be selling, and leading it to the take-off point where he became mega-rich within months. He knew that he would finally be signing contracts with three major clients within the next month, and after that his firm would no longer need to advertise. He wanted a girlfriend to celebrate his success, and to help him unwind from the stress and disappointments of the last three years. Jasmine was the second woman he met, and he thought she was ideal – cheerful, sexy, attractive, expensive-looking, real arm-candy. She lived on the opposite side of town to his office, but she was happy to come over to his area, and she even introduced him to a string of sexy bars and nice restaurants that he had never known existed in the vicinity. At least he had identified a fabulous hotel, brand new and very elegant in a bohemian way, with a good bar and restaurant, and low prices in its first year of operation, until it got established. For three months, they met periodically, for drinks, lunch or dinner, sometimes with a few hours in the hotel bedroom for dessert. Jasmine was great fun, and Frederick was happier than he had been for years. The only trouble was that after three months, he had to admit that sales had not taken off as expected. In fact he was in exactly the same position as he had been six months before, with success just around the corner, tantalisingly close, but still no big contracts signed quite yet. For a while, he continued the affair as a consolation prize, an interim reward. Then he finally admitted that the celebration was premature, that he just had to get back to the hard slog again. Reluctantly, he bid Jasmine goodbye.

The end of an affair is clear-cut when there is a clash over something that seems to matter. This was how an otherwise idyllic affair between Soraya and Nelson ended. She had good looks, and he was wealthy. They got on exceptionally well because they shared intellectual and cultural interests, and could talk easily about a huge range of things. Soraya found Nelson a rather dull lover, with fixed routines, but that did not matter too much in the wider picture. He took her to top-end restaurants, and she provided intelligent and glamorous arm-candy for some of his business meetings and cocktail parties. Nelson told her repeatedly that he loved her, that he wished he was married to her instead of his wife. He kept trying to persuade her to go away with him for a weekend together – something Soraya regarded as impossible, however attractive the idea was. Then they suddenly fell out over a necklace that

Soraya asked Nelson to buy for her.

The necklace was unusual, something she had seen in an antique shop, that suited her especially well, and was a rare find. She knew Nelson could easily afford it – it was a trifle for him. Indeed, he had been talking at length about investing in antique furniture for his London flat, and maybe also a holiday flat in Venice that he fancied buying. Since he was in shopping spree mode, she asked if he might buy her the necklace? At first, Nelson agreed, and went to see it. Then suddenly he went sour on the idea, telling her that he was 'not in the habit of showering expensive gifts on his girlfriends – apart from lunch and dinner', and that she had better drop such ideas if she wanted to continue the relationship.

Soraya was dismayed by Nelson's domineering and con-temptuous tone, such a contrast to the affectionate lover she had enjoyed until then, and was feisty enough to rebel at this attitude. She was enraged at being treated as just one in a string of girlfriends, in marked contrast to everything Nelson had said so far. She also objected to him behaving as if he was in control, made the rules, simply because he was wealthy. Worst of all, she disliked miserliness in a multi-millionaire. Both her father and her husband had always been generous to a fault, and she was used to receiving gifts of anything she liked. She found she was unable to respect a wealthy man who was openly stingy, and condescendingly rude with it. With no regrets, she walked away from the relationship.

Tania was a novice when she met Karl through a website, and fell for him on their first date. He was a big, tall man, somewhat overweight, but this pleased Tania. She hated thin men (or women), thinking they looked as if they had no appetite for life. Karl certainly did. He liked good food, wines and classic cars, and knew how to enjoy himself. He was clever, successful, self-assured, charming, elegant in his person and his manners, and a fantastic lover. Very quickly, she developed an obsession with Karl, even though he had made it clear from the start that he was looking for an essentially sexual relationship. With a wife safely tucked away in a small town, he felt free to do as he liked in London on weekdays and the occasional Saturday when he drove in to put in some overtime work at the office. At first, Karl enjoyed Tania's open admiration verging on adoration. It had been a long time since that had happened to him. His first mistress was a Frenchwoman he met at a business-related dinner, and it had been an exclusively sexual affair. She pursued him until he gave in, surprised and flattered at being courted by a woman. The affair had lasted three years, until she returned to Paris. Afterwards, he felt a big gap in his life, so he turned to a website, and met Tania. He liked her, but her obviously intense feelings for him were inconvenient. Eventually, he decided he had to drop her, but he was intelligent and considerate enough to do it gradually.

He told Tania he had been offered an attractive position in Hong Kong, and would be leaving London. As he expected, she was very upset. Over the next three months Karl replaced their weekly trysts with ad hoc and unpredictable meetings, some of them for lunch only, some of them cancelled at short notice. He stopped calling her regularly, and took a long time to reply to her emails. He talked constantly about his preparations for leaving his home in England and new arrangements in Hong Kong. There was a final hotel tryst with Tania, with fond farewells, and he was gone. For several months, Tania continued to write to him, hoping he might reply, but she finally gave up, and Karl breathed more easily again. He had bcen worried that Tania could potentially cause trouble, as she knew enough about him to track down his home address. Once she was persuaded he had gone abroad, this became unlikely.

Being a man, Sean never ever admitted he had fallen in love with Roxanne. He prided himself on being too worldly-wise, too cynical, too sophisticated to do 'falling in love' nonsense. So yes, his men friends knew he had been seeing Roxanne exclusively for three years, and thought the world of her, but he insisted this was only because he had an amazing libido, needed a good mistress, and she was the most sexy woman he had ever known. Occasionally, he did things that suggested it went further than that, such as the time when he flew out to New York to spend a long weekend with her, when she was out there alone on a business trip. He spent four days and nights showing her the sights and taking her out for dinner and shows. He had always wanted them to go away for the weekend together, but that had proved impossible, so this was his only chance to have a few days alone together. Roxanne, however, was not in love with Sean, and the weekend in New York was not a great success as far as she was concerned. In any event, she decided to drop Sean soon afterwards.

She told him she had lost the sexual buzz with him, somehow it had vanished. She still liked him, of course, so maybe they could be just friends? Unable to admit that he felt anything for her, Sean proudly said that he too had got bored with the affair. But he kept in touch for the next 18 months. For a long time, he would have lunch every few weeks with Roxanne, hoping that after a bottle of wine and a nice meal she would fall into bed with him, as in the old days. After this failed to revive her desire for him, he saw her less frequently, but made greater efforts to seduce her when they did meet, explaining that he did not have any new girlfriend because he 'still lusted after her, constantly'. The third and final phase consisted of periodic emails chatting as if nothing had really changed between them, and wondering whether she wanted to get back together again? Roxanne was relieved when the emails finally stopped, and was surprised that it could take so long to finally extinguish an affair. Paradoxically, every meeting after the split simply confirmed her view that she was right to drop Sean, that the affair had been lop-sided, arranged for his advantage, and that he had failed to fully appreciate her when he had the chance. But at least there were no ugly repercussions from the break-up.

Affairs are fragile flowers, contingent and ephemeral, conditional on so many other aspects of two people's lives. Even the most enthusiastically successful pairing can be abruptly terminated by one party, for unrelated reasons within his or her life. Even the most whirlwind love affair and happy partnership can come to a sudden halt, due to practical problems, a change of attitude on one side, a small quarrel that is not easily resolved when two people meet very seldom anyway, or a difference of perspective or style that matters a lot to one person but not to the other. Awareness of this existential fragility allows people to believe, quite honestly, that an affair 'does not matter', to regard it as unimportant, within the wider picture of their lives, almost irrespective of how happy it makes them. It is only when someone is consciously looking for love, for an alternative spouse, as some are, that the affair matters. And then it can be soul-destroying when it goes wrong and ends.

13

The Floating World

The hidden world of married dating is more exciting, diverse, and risky than singles dating. It is much smaller too, so in some sense it must be more selective. This is reflected in the types of people who join the dance, however briefly.

Given the constant turnover of people on the websites, it is hard to define who the players are. Whenever a newspaper, magazine article, or a late night TV show discusses affairs and mentions any of the websites, there is a flood of new enquiries and subscribers from that particular audience, social group, or leisure interest group. In one month, there might be a wave of new users in the 20-40 age group, or from people who read men's magazines. Another time, there may be a spate of new subscriptions from older men, or people in financial services, or people who travel on business. The principal market is always men. Overall, male players are concentrated in the upper echelons of the professions and business, including City bankers, corporate lawyers, consultants, accountants, finance professionals, entrepreneurs running their own business, company directors, executives, hedge fund managers, and IT specialists. There are fewer people in administrative and support jobs that have more rigid work hours and fixed office locations. For the same reason, doctors and hospital workers are infrequent users of these websites. Perhaps more surprisingly, professionals in education also seem rare, perhaps because the work culture does not attract risk-takers, even if professors and college lecturers have some time flexibility. Alternatively, academics are intellectuals whose main interest is in ideas rather than more physical and social entertainments.[59] Overall, most subscribers work in the private sector.

There is a clear preponderance, even over-representation, of self-employed men.[60] Somewhere between one-third and one-half of male subscribers are business owners and managers of various kinds, including small builders, plumbers and electricians, as well as men running much larger, high-turnover businesses and corporations. This is probably because these groups have more control over their time and work patterns, enjoy more autonomy, and are accustomed to making risky decisions. Perhaps, too, they are more adventurous: entrepreneurs are not generally homebodies. There is a sprinkling of people from the creative professions – photographers, writers, musicians, and people in advertising. But most men will be wearing a suit and tie during the week, and look extremely conservative. As one man puts it in his profile 'You may have met me, and thought I wouldn't…but I would'.

Finding the time to play can be the biggest problem for these workaholic men, some of whom are driven to succeed, achieve, and climb ever higher. As one admitted sadly when bowing out of a proposed affair, 'I find I have the personality and the purse, but unfortunately not the time'. He had just set up a new business (his third) and realised it demanded more of his time and attention than he anticipated.

And the women? They are far more diverse, since there are no subscription fees to limit access to the websites, which also means that women can drop in and out as they please . Housewives, secretaries, nurses, teachers – all the usual female occupations feature – along with women in professional and business jobs. Women's key advantage over men is that many work part-time or not at all, so that they have a degree of time autonomy and control that is rare among ordinary male employees. However women generally have far less money to spend, and most of them clearly expect that their lover will be solvent enough to cover any costs.[61] Women of all ages between 20 and 70 join the websites, and all ethnic groups are represented, as for men. Most of the women look very attractive, unlike the men.

Narcissism

All love affairs involve an element of narcissism. People seek a flattering reflection of themselves in the eyes and admiration of the other person. This is why so many website profiles consist of preening self-satisfaction. Many of the men and women in these affairs are acting out an image of themselves: the debonair man-about-town, the model mistress, the wild romantic, the sexual athlete, the serene beauty, the sophisticated libertine who knows all the games and all the lines. This is part of the reason why call girls and escort girls are not a complete substitute, even when they might be the more practical choice. As described in the popular memoirs of *Belle de Jour*, and more recently by Cheryl Summerton, they provide more professional, skilful sex games, are available on demand at a time and place of your choice, and are generally young and very attractive. Most have regular clients who become real friends, and they report that the girlfriend experience is the most requested style of date.[62] But call girls create an illusion. Website affairs pretend to be reality, and sometimes are.

Erotic power: dance to my tune.

One thread running through introductory correspondence and subsequent negotiations over dates, meetings, timetables, venues and activities is the question of who is in control. Men are accustomed to being in the driving seat in courtship, the initiators in sexual encounters, so they take it for granted they control the process in this context as well. In fact women are in control, simply because supply and demand gives them the upper hand here. Men outnumber women by at least 10 to 1, in terms of sheer numbers of subscribers. But given men's high standards for women's physical attractiveness, and nowadays their expectation of intelligence, education, and social status as well, or the manners, style and polish that go with them, relatively few women qualify as seriously attractive. So really attractive women are in short supply, and it is these women who can afford to pick and choose in this mating market. Women can also set the rules of the married-dating game.

Men never want to recognise this reversal of the usual power relations, as it contradicts the idea that the subscription is a special treat for themselves, the gift of a mail-order mistress, or an agreeable girl-friend, instantly available, constantly at their beck and call. Men do not really accept this reversal that removes their control of relationships, and leaves them without the final choice over who they see. This is a key stumbling block for very successful older men, who are used to being in charge and in control. Age is a factor here too:

younger men are more often brash and arrogant, fail to check sex ratios on the websites, and have fewer years of experience in relationships with women. However older men who married very young can be in a similar position, with relatively narrow experience of dating and mating rituals, so they are clumsy at seduction and courtship, or fail to pick up signals from the women they meet.

One reason why men do not make enough effort to please is that websites routinely imply that there are as many women subscribers as men (by including 'ghosts' and invented profiles), and that men are knocking on an open door. Some say so directly, saying they allow men to meet sexually available women 'with minimal effort'. But most sexually active and potentially available women are still choosy as to whom they actually meet, and who they bed. Dating websites are not brothels (even prostitutes choose, and reject, customers!). Some married male users appear to think that paying a website subscription entitles them to success with a sexually attractive woman of their choice, which is far from the truth. Membership fees only give them access to the website, offering the opportunity to court and attract women.

The transparent mating markets of the websites expose what we might call each person's erotic power, something quite separate from how wealthy and successful they are, something that transcends their education, social status, or the degree of authority they have at work – all the things that men rely on most to prove that they are winners, successful alpha-males. Some of the men and women on the websites have erotic power, and some don't. It is more than sexual attractiveness alone, a fuzzy combination of appearing youthful, beauty, fitness, personality, elegance, charm, style and manner, maybe a nice voice, a sexy walk or way of laughing.[63]

A high score on one factor alone is rarely enough. Men often comment that a stunningly beautiful girl can lose everything by a grating voice and accent, ugly and vulgar clothing, or by being unable to sustain a proper conversation. Wealth and success at work do not automatically produce erotic power – quite the contrary, most workaholics and businessmen have none at all, no matter how self-confident they are. The French actress Catherine Deneuve and the American singer Tina Turner still had it at over 60, looking far younger than their age implies. Youth typically makes someone sexually attractive, but this can dissipate quickly in their 20s if they do not acquire good grooming and essential social skills. Beauty confers erotic power, but tastes differ a lot in this area, especially among older people, whose tastes have been refined over time. Among older and successful players, elegance, personality, style and good manners seem to matter more than among younger people, as they do not want to be seen in public with someone so visibly different from themselves that it prompts questions about the relationship and attracts unwelcome attention.

Education seems to matter because it shapes conversation, and how readily people can talk about a wide range of topics. One man rejected an attractive younger woman because she had no idea where Niagara Falls was located. Another man was greatly attracted to a woman who knew that people in northern Nigeria speak Hausa and Fulani. Given the preponderance of intelligent, successful and cosmopolitan men on the websites, an education and being well-informed are important for women also.

The normal power balance that favours men in most contexts, and especially in the workplace and in marriage markets, is reversed to favour women in married dating where erotic power becomes salient. Even if there were equal numbers of male and female subscribers, attractive, sexy and glamorous women are in short supply, and are in great demand. Men need to offer their financial and status advantages just to attract and keep a woman. Men can be slow to learn that they have to work hard to please, and keep, a sexually attractive lover – including offering gifts, trips, and anything else she likes. If they refuse, there are a dozen alternative men like them that she can consider instead, all bombarding her with approaches on the websites.

One particular bugbear among men is that women can potentially have two (or more) lovers, quite easily, overlapping to some extent, since all affairs are so hidden and discreet anyway. A certain bitter resentment at women's erotic power seems to lie behind some of the snide criticisms, sour jealousy, and domineering attitudes expressed by male players, and sometimes displayed up front in the profiles they post on websites. Men complain that women 'exploit' men, that women 'take advantage of men' – as if men never do this themselves! Another bugbear is that the most sexually attractive women can ask for money or gifts while they are the lover of an older or sexually unattractive man (or indeed a sexual non-performer). His money is necessary to balance his lack of erotic power. Men routinely try to frame this as a 'moral' issue, to stigmatise such women, in order to sidestep the realities of the negotiation that is present (usually implicit rather than overt) in all mating markets. As one self-aware man ruefully admitted, he could well afford the money his date had asked for, but it forced him to recognise that he did not have the 'pulling power' to get the woman (who was 20 years younger and an extremely attractive blonde) into bed without the extra incentive.

Social status is a factor: the richer and more powerful the man is, from his occupation or business, the harder it is for him to accept that actually it is the woman, younger and more physically attractive (usually), who can do as she likes, and present him with a 'take it or leave it' offer. Men who own and run their own business, are used to being The Boss and giving orders to their employees and subcontractors (however courteously), probably have the greatest difficulty with the power reversal that characterises this particular mating market. Business owners most keenly recognise and resist women's independence, freedom of action, and bargaining power, and resent their own loss of control, domination, right to make all key decisions. They believe that 'he who pays the piper calls the tune'. In married dating, it is attractive women who call the tune, and men typically end up spending quite a lot of money, more than they initially anticipate, in consequence.

Many men, especially men over 45, are not particularly good lovers (no matter what their spouses led them to believe), so generosity with money and entertainment has to be their strong card. Men often think that a strong libido and desire for regular sex proves they are good lovers. This is simply not true. In practice, it is generally men who exercise regularly in a gym (or who engage in whole-body sports such as gymnastics or skiing) who are guaranteed to have the stamina and flexibility to perform well in bed. Regular exercise in a single sport, such as running, rarely offers the whole-body fitness and suppleness that is required, something dancers and yoga practitioners often have. Long years spent in office politics and management are not generally conducive to the imaginative playfulness and *joie de vivre* that are attractive in a lover. Although men are most overtly concerned with establishing 'sexual chemistry' at the start of a liaison, women are most likely to report that the men are poor lovers, can even be hopeless in bed. As men get older, their performance in the bedroom fades over time, leading wives to lose interest in 'all that nonsense'. One reason for marriages becoming platonic is that the husband's libido remains lively, but his performance does not.

The challenge of social diversity

The social diversity of the dating websites creates different challenges for users. All of them claim to be 'upscale', as Americans put it, and attract managerial and professional people. This is generally the case, simply because such people have greater sovereignty over their time, and the financial means to cover the expenses of an affair. But websites are open to anyone who pays the subscriptions and does not infringe the basic rules. Dating websites are open mating markets, and you can meet absolutely anyone at all. This is one reason they appeal to men who did not attend university but are nevertheless successful entrepreneurs and businessmen, wealthy enough to afford an affair in great style with a glamorous woman. Total openness is the only way websites can pull in women, who may be housewives with no earnings, attractive but impecunious young women, and sexually attractive (and sexually active) women in low-paying occupations who could not possibly afford the costs of an affair, and may even need some financial help to cover the additional costs of sexy lingerie, clothes and hairdresser visits. There is every chance that you might meet someone with a very different social and economic background to yourself. For many people, this social diversity is one of the attractions of the websites.

Selene was astonished to be approached by a 24 year old medical student, unmarried and poor, when she joined a website. In her mid-40s, she had expected to be meeting men of a similar age and class. But Sebastian was handsome, charming, honest, and persistent, so she finally agreed to meet him for coffee one weekend when he was in London. They got on brilliantly, as Sebastian made up in good looks, elegant manners and intelligence for his relative lack of cash. He also turned out to be an amazing lover, who regularly presented her with small, thoughtful gifts. He was always nicely dressed, and complimentary about her frocks and perfume. Although the affair was not at all what she had anticipated, perhaps even because of it, Selene found it all a wonderful 'holiday' away from her usual life. Being with a younger man made her happy and younger too, in outlook and style.

As a journalist, Martin was used to meeting all sorts of people, and was skilled at getting on with anyone he met – he had to be, in order to get his stories. He was thus completely comfortable about seeing Jane, whom he described as a 'lorry driver' but was in fact a deliveries driver with a white van. Compared to him, she was uneducated and brash. But he liked her directness, boldness, vitality, lack of artifice. Jane found him very funny and laughed at all his jokes. They got on enormously well, despite their differences, for the duration of their affair, which petered out after a year. When he returned to the website, Martin was looking for a similar level of novelty, even a challenge.

However not everyone enjoys moving outside their comfort zone. Many people prefer to meet potential partners with similar levels of education, at least, as this makes conversation and communication easier. Even so, misunderstandings are commonplace, both in initial correspondence and even after meeting someone. Appearances can be deceptive. Someone who appears totally English may have grown up in Singapore and Peru in quite different non-European cultures. Someone who seems solidly Welsh may have spent all his working life in Texas, Nigeria and Hong Kong. People who are visibly of African, Caribbean or Indian descent may have lived in Britain since birth and never travelled abroad. Even within Europe, there are big variations in customs, manners, etiquette, assumptions about how relationships should proceed, ideas about what constitutes 'proper behaviour', even how to cross the road. With people from other countries and cultures added into the mix, the potential for clashes over appropriate behaviour is magnified. London is probably the most cosmopolitan city in the world, in terms of the huge number of ethnic groups, cultures, religions, languages and foreign nationalities in the population. So cultural differences exacerbate the socio-economic diversity of website users. People do not necessarily reveal all the details of their disparate backgrounds early on when meeting strangers for the first time. So inevitably, there will be friction, even conflict at times, over taken-for-granted assumptions about what is 'right' or 'fair' or 'reasonable' or 'proper behaviour'. There are no fixed rules and a large measure of tolerance and good humoured negotiation resolves most disagreements.

It follows that social skills can be important in being successful on the websites – both in getting dates at all, and in getting second and subsequent dates. It appears to be a lack of social skills that leads so many men to make initial approaches that are so nominal and half-hearted as to be ridiculous – such as 'Try me!' – or are too routine to be enticing – such as the standard message used by hundreds of men 'Your profile is interesting, you might be interested in mine' or 'I saw your profile and thought you might be interested'. Even more nominal are the 'electronic winks' and 'virtual kisses' with no message at all – sent by men with aphasia, perhaps. Given that men outnumber women, they need to make a serious effort to catch the attention of a woman, and show they have actually read her profile. Men who have obtained a clear view of the sex ratios on websites are aware of this, and are more likely to make an effort to seduce, to please, to court women.

Social skills are important in dealing with the frequent mismatches and misunderstandings that occur given the social diversity of websites. One person thinks a pub is the perfect venue for a first meeting, especially if a major football match will be on big screen TV; another never sets foot in pubs and prefers cocktail bars. One person thinks a walk or picnic in the park is an excellent option for a date; another would never take a chance on being seen in public that way, with no obvious excuse to hand, or thinks of shoes ruined by muddy paths, or dwells on the possibility of rain. One party thinks that once a mutually convenient date for a meeting has been selected, he can leave it to the day itself to fix a venue, while the other party believes that someone who does not firm up details immediately will probably never show up in practice. One person wants to get physical pretty quickly, like now; the other assumes several dates are necessary before going that far. One person analyses profile names and call names in great detail for clues about someone's interests and personality. Others choose profile names almost at random, in a hurry, and have no idea how misleading they may appear. Some people believe that punctuality is polite, with strangers as with friends, and is an essential courtesy in this context, given that everyone is short of time, while some women think it is 'elegant' to turn up 20 minutes late for a date, even for a first date, and some men think it is justifiable to arrive 30 minutes late due to 'being busy at work' or even 'not wanting to look desperate'. Some people assume that the costs of dates are invariably shared, as they were when they were students. Others assume that New York dating rules apply, so the man pays for everything, always, while the lady must be glamorously well-dressed and well-groomed for every date. Some people assume that clarity and honesty are standard on dating websites, while others take it for granted that people write anything to attract attention and interest, so there can be a large gap between what profiles claim and the reality. One person thinks kissing in the street is fine, at any age. Another regards any physical intimacy in public places as vulgar, or else sees kissing in the street as reckless madness for married people, even in big cities. Some people take it for granted that everyone provides their real name, talks openly about their circumstances at home, and are relaxed about mentioning the names of their spouses and children. Others refuse to divulge their full name, and would not dream of revealing anything about their home life, nor even about their work life and precise job, seeking almost total anonymity. The list goes on.

Illusions of infinite choice

All dating websites exaggerate the number of subscribers, in the belief that people will choose the one offering the largest choice of potential mates. Some people prefer specialist and selective agencies, but there is a widespread belief that large numbers offer more choice, and that more choice is invariably beneficial, because it ensures you can get exactly what you want, or else offers the best match to suit your tastes. Scientists have been analysing speed dating, and dating website activity, to check these assumptions, with surprising findings.[64]

Several studies have found that people presented with too many options make fewer choices than people presented with smaller lists of options. Too much choice does not work well for most people, who are overwhelmed by the task of selection, and do it badly as a result, or else give up before making any choice. Only people with very well-defined preferences find it easy to wade through large lists of profiles and dating options – to find the blue-haired Latvian cyclist they alone are seeking. Women find the optimum size list is between 20 and 50 men (assuming they are broadly the sort of people they might want to meet at all). Men have a stronger preference for sexual variety, so are inclined to prefer slightly longer lists. But for men and women, memory problems limit people's ability to deal with the selection process when lists reach 100 or longer. In practice, people are equally satisfied with more restricted lists as with longer lists of dating options. It has also been found that excessively long lists of dating options lead people to simplify and routinize their selection strategy so that it crudely rejects high quality options due to minor 'defects' or mis-matches – the Latvian cyclist once had green hair.

Studies of speed dating also show that actual choices do not closely reflect stated preferences, especially for men. Men choose women who are physically attractive, and women choose men who are desirable mates overall. Women are aware that being attractive 'buys' desirable males. Women are more picky than men, who make more offers to lots of women in the hope of getting at least one date. For both men and women, choosiness increases the more they perceive themselves to be attractive.

Generally, when people know they are faced with huge mating markets, they respond by refining and extending their selection criteria, effectively becoming even more choosy. But this in turn makes the selection process more arduous. One of the most common reasons for men abandoning dating websites without having met someone they like is that they found the search process too time-consuming. It involves not only sifting through profiles to identify people that sound suitable, but also extended correspondence with each of them to open communication and attempt to fix dates. Men who become aware of the shortage of women can sometimes lose heart right at the start. Women who are swamped by initial approaches day after day, week after week, can become very superficial, even careless, in their sifting process, and end up rejecting good matches. These patterns are reflected in married website users' comments and profiles.

Daphne says: 'At first I was flattered by all the attention, but I have to admit I could not cope, in the end. About 5-10 approaches every day, almost. I had this idea that I should be polite, and reply to everyone, if only to say No. But it took so much time! And some of the approaches were so minimal, careless, that I started to wonder. Some men clearly had no idea who they had written to, as they started calling me by other women's names, or said we had chatted previously, when we hadn't. So I became blasé and careless rather quickly, unfortunately. I realise now that in the first month I rejected one or two men who would have been ideal – but it got so much I was not really reading the profiles properly, just automatically saying No to everyone, because I couldn't cope.'

Scorpio: I'm looking for someone to change my life. Someone to spend a bit of time with, take to dinner and maybe a drink or two. Converse, laugh, and anything else that comes naturally. I do not fear relationships, neither do I mind a casual acquaintance. Someone who can introduce me to the Arts would be a nice bonus, but not essential. I prefer slim ladies. A pretty face goes a long way. I have travelled the world for years to discover… I also wonder if I'll ever meet a woman on this site, given all the men on here! If you have an ounce (or even a few milligrams) of caring in your heart, maybe you could contact me after I check myself out of the Priory. If not, there is always the Salvation Army… I am not a manic depressive, quite a cheery chap really. I used to be 6'1' before I started to shrink. Muscular torso, and dare I say good looking? No? OK, I won't. All my own hair and teeth, very intelligent but not particularly well read. Sensitive and caring, but manly with it (of course!). GSOH, HSD (I've read the personals)…

The most successful and satisfied website users seem to be those who do not allow themselves to be distracted by the illusion of infinite choice. They decide what their key selection criteria are, and write to the first 6-12 people they identify as suitable, ignoring all others. They then stick with the first person they meet who they get on well with, and where the practical arrangements are convenient, cancelling all forthcoming dates with the other options unseen. This 'satisficing' strategy means that they actually get some dates, and find a lover, instead of spending many months exploring the endless opportunities of the dating websites only to end up with nothing finally.

The Rules *revised*

The Rules' recommendation to let men do all the chasing may work for women on singles dating websites, where the ultimate goal is commitment and marriage, and it may work for some women on married dating websites. But the system is not optimal for attractive and desirable women on married websites. Such women can be inundated with approaches, and waste all their time responding to men who are unsuitable or have made little effort. Most men will sleep with anyone, if they have the chance; men are not choosy for casual flings.

Given this unique mating market where women can pick and choose, women should behave more like men – decide what their criteria are, search the profile lists to find suitable matches and write to the men themselves. The initial approach should be short and tentative, but it must include something that shows the profile has been read. For men as well as women, one of the most irritating turn-offs is a standard initial approach that suggests the writer never bothered to read the profile properly – for example suggesting dinner to someone who stated that they were not free in the evenings. On these websites, an approach from a woman is so exceptional that men take serious notice, treat it as good luck, and generally offer to meet immediately. This gives the opportunity to take a closer look, and decide whether first impressions were fair.

Women who take the initiative themselves say that it works better for meeting the sort of men they are interested in, and gives a higher success rate than responding to approaches from men. It does not eliminate mistakes and mis-matches, but is a shorter and more direct route to getting where you want to be.

Taking the initiative at the selection stage still allows women to follow *The Rules* thereafter, leaving it to men to suggest dates, to chase and court you, if they want to keep you. On the other hand, lack of time is possibly the most common problem for men in senior professional and managerial jobs, and they cannot usually ask their PA to organise lunch or dinner bookings for their affairs – although some men do. So it is often helpful for the woman to make suggestions as to venues and activities, while leaving the man to make the final choice and booking.

Novices versus libertines

Opinion is divided on whether it is a good thing, or not, to be someone's first lover. Some women refuse to meet men who have 'no experience'. Others prefer first-timers. First affairs exhibit all the needs and desires that someone seeks to fulfil in an affair, or else provide the template and pattern for later affairs simply because habits form quickly. So there is some advantage in being the first lover – you can write the rules yourself. If not, find out about someone's previous liaisons, as they may set the unstated pattern for this one too. Someone who 'fell madly in love' the first time round will probably be inclined to do so again. Someone who was fairly instrumental and selfish the first time round will be even more hard-hearted and calculating in subsequent affairs.

No-one controls an affair. Men often make the mistake of transferring their behaviour in the boardroom to the bedroom. It doesn't work, because women with any spirit at all will walk away from a domineering control-freak. In this mating market, women have alternatives. The most general rules for an affair apply to everyone, novice and libertine: clear some free space in your life beforehand; agree communication rules with your new lover; be your best self; stay relaxed and cheerful (even when things go wrong, as they do) as this is about playtime and fun; and never adopt the attitude that this is MY affair, so I should get exactly what I want, all the time – you are not in control and cannot fix the rules unilaterally. An affair is always an adventure, an exploration, so requires an open mind, a willingness to experiment, to move outside your comfort zone. Some people may want to explore the outer edge, but in that case, check out the relevant magazines and websites. Do not assume you can impose your fantasies on members of ordinary dating websites. One regular complaint is that swingers try to recruit partners for threesomes, and extra players for house parties, on ordinary dating websites.

Perhaps most important for all users is to be clear (even honest with themselves?) as to what they do and do not offer, as well as what they are looking for. This means being realistic about how sexually attractive you are, and your competence as a lover. Anyone whose erotic power is limited, must be generous with whatever else they can offer instead, including the attractions of money to spend on entertainments and fun, good company, courtesy and kindness. And remember to smile! The quickest way to look ten years younger and more agreeable company.

A new life

All good things come to an end, sooner or later. Even the happiest affairs peter out, eventually. Some do not last more than three to four months, when important cracks appear in the relationship. One year seems to be a very widely quoted average, after which the novelty has worn off, and one party starts to get bored. Some affairs last three years then tail off due to changes in circumstances on one side or the other. Very exceptionally, affairs last ten years or more, where both parties are in fairly settled circumstances and the practical arrangements are mutually convenient. The most famous of French official royal mistresses, Madame de Pompadour, lasted 20 years, but her relationship switched quickly into that of companion and confidante, mistress of entertainments, and she even arranged alternative sexual liaisons for King Louis XV. Most women do not have anything like her resources and determination, and the need for novelty typically brings a liaison to an end within months.

The need for discretion and secrecy is just as important after an affair has ended as when it is ongoing. If the other party has terminated an affair against your own wishes, it can be hard to continue as normal and conceal your disappointment, anger, even misery, from your own family. Any temptation to confess all, in order to gain absolution, or with the idea that this will restore things to their original status, must be resisted.

As so often happens, Thomas' first affair was with a colleague at work. She was at the same level of management as him, so they attended the same training courses, briefings and annual events. These were always held away from the office, in classy hotels, sometimes abroad, and included some social evenings to develop camaraderie between colleagues in the firm. It was not unknown for affairs to develop at these events, so no-one took much notice of Thomas and Linda's hook-up. Eyebrows were raised when they later opted to share an office back in

London, and they were told to keep it cool and discreet. Otherwise, it was all very easy, and pleasant. They got on really well, worked well as a team when they had to, and had no communication problems since they met at work every day, knew each other's timetables and workloads, had plenty of time to talk. When something came up that forced him to cancel an evening date, Linda already knew about it, so was not upset. Everything seemed so easy, as well as exciting, and the affair lasted three years. It only broke up finally because Linda applied for and got a sideways promotion that did not interest Thomas, so she moved out of the London office.

Thomas decided to make a fresh start, and focus more on his marriage, his wife and two boys. One evening, he decided to make a confession and tell his wife about the playfair, to make it clear, to himself as much as to her, that it was over now, and would not be repeated. In many ways he was pleased it was over, as he was feeling he should devote more time and effort to his family, especially the two boys. So he told his wife. She was devastated. Thomas instantly regretted his confession, but it was too late. She started to ask questions, and became even more shocked to discover it had gone on for three years, without her knowing anything was amiss.

A year later, his wife said she needed to talk to him. She was having an affair herself now, with someone she had met through her job, and she wanted to get divorced and marry the new man. It had started as a tit-for-tat affair, simply to get even with Thomas, but then had developed into a serious relationship – and she now wanted to quit the marriage. Thomas was devastated. Having thrown himself back into family life and family activities, he was even more committed to them all, even more attached to his two sons, even happier than he had been before the affair started. But his wife was determined, and moved out to live with her new man.

A year later, Thomas and his wife were divorced, both living alone while sharing responsibility for the two boys, who lived at both homes in rotation. Her lover had decided he did not want to get married after all – the trial cohabitation had not been a success. It was routine family life, not the exciting illicit affair he had enjoyed previously. He returned to being the confirmed bachelor he had always been, with several girlfriends. Thomas and his wife ended up divorced, but both living alone, with the boys shuttling to and fro between them. As he ruefully admitted, this was the worst possible outcome of his confession, in the end. He wished he had kept his mouth shut.[65] He now saw his marriage as having been the only solid thing in his life, and that playfairs were too ephemeral for anyone to rely on, part of a floating world[66] of fantasy, excitement, and adventure that could sink and vanish within hours, once it was punctured by reality.

Sex may be the central driving motivation, but an affair also creates an emotional space apart, a place free from the power struggles of work life and the routine practical concerns of family life. Men often relish the idea of 'no strings' sex, but it is the wider freedom from social obligations and emotional ties that make the affair a perfect garden of delights, a place for sexual exuberance and playtime without any ensuing obligations. Time spent with a lover is a holiday from day-to-day life. But relationships that may flower gloriously in short bursts of 2-4 hours, or for a few days on a trip in an exotic location, may wilt and die when exposed to the humdrum realities of day-to-day life. It is essential not to confuse tourism with immigration

*

Radford was a rolling stone. He had perfected his technique over the years. In his initial approach he mentioned that he had a flat in an expensive part of central London and worked in Mayfair in 'finance'. He chose his women carefully, looking for enough intelligence and personality to make interesting company as well as good looks. He knew he was not an obvious winner, being overweight and rather thin on top, but he compensated by offering a flashy evening out. His ideal date started with champagne in a classy bar, moving on to dinner and maybe a show or a club, or even his own exclusive club Annabel's if his date looked right. Most of the time, he would meet someone who looked good, dressed right, and was cheerful enough for a spectacular night out, finishing up in bed in his flat. He was happy to spend money on having a good time, but he always told his dates at the start 'You won't get any presents from me'. In any case, Radford's rule was never to see anyone more than once. It was tidier that way. Most of the time, the women he met were keen to see him again, and he was sometimes very tempted himself when he met someone who felt like a perfect fit. But having felt trapped in his marriage, he was determined to stay free in future. The divorce had been ridiculously expensive and manifestly unfair. This was a new life.

There are some people who make a new life from playfairs and flings, for whom the floating world becomes a way of life. They are generally older divorced men (plus a few women), whose children have grown up and left home, in principle at least – ignoring the wastrels who continue to return for parental handouts and a safe haven. They stuck with their wives (or husbands) as long as the children were still at home, and needed parenting. Once the kids have gone, they get a divorce, in as civilised a manner as possible, even if this means giving their spouse half of all their assets. Then they become carefree bachelors, enjoying a succession of girlfriends, or multiple girlfriends and lovers at times, in a return to the hedonism of their youth, prior to marriage, but with the money and the experience to fully enjoy it. They use all the dating websites, for singles as well as for married people, because they are sexually active but intend absolutely to remain non-married for the rest of their life.

This can work extremely well for men. As long as they have enough money to spend lavishly on evenings out, and other entertainments, they can attract women of all ages, including young women who are still enjoying the carefree hedonism of youth. It can work well for older divorced women as well, so long as they keep themselves fit and in good shape, are still sexually attractive and have enough erotic power to win in the fiercely competitive adult dating scene. Alternatively, they need the affluence to attract toy boys.[67]

For this small group of committed hedonists, married dating websites can work better than singles websites because there is no expectation that liaisons will ever be anything more than short-term, whereas singles dating websites are used mostly by women who seek a permanent relationship, ultimately. This elite group of hedonists have forged a new lifestyle that solves the problems created by increased longevity and marriages that have become stale or dull over the decades. Some of them use the married dating websites even before their final divorce leaves them free to re-enter the dating scene with a completely clear conscience. In a sense, their earlier affairs provide the training ground for a new life post-divorce. In modern societies, these affluent older hedonists are making the floating world a permanent lifestyle alternative to the rooted and grounded nature of marriage.

Notes

1   West 2007, page 3. Kremer 1998 reports that two-thirds of American and almost half of British couples divorce.

2   Eurostat figures for 2000 show that within the 1981 marriage cohort, only 8%-9% of Italian and Spanish marriages ended in divorce, compared to almost half of all marriages in the Nordic countries and Britain. France also had historically low divorce rates, but numbers have shot up in recent years.

3   Nye 1999. It is said that when a clumsy English journalist once asked Mitterand during an interview about reports that he had a mistress, Mitterand cut him short with '*Et alors?*' (So what?) meaning 'And what business is it of yours?'

4   Johnson and others 1994; Wellings and others 1994; Chadwick and Heaton 1999; Rouse 2002.

5   Between 1970 and 1997, public opinion in the Netherlands swung from majority acceptance to majority rejection of affairs, from only 26% to 57% rejecting the idea that 'one single sexual adventure on the side cannot damage a good marriage'. See Cas Wooters 2004, page 138.

6   Vaccaro 2003.

7   Malo de Molina 1992.

8   Spira and Bajos 1993; Nye 1999; Mossuz-Lavau 2002.

9   Mossuz-Lavau 2002, page 173

10   One USA study shows that people who have ever had an affair are less likely to be strongly disapproving than those who have never had an affair. However, the vast majority of men and women disapprove of extra-marital affairs, whether they have done it themselves or not; only 1% of those who had never had an affair, and about 5% of those who had, thought it was not wrong at all. See Weiderman 1997, page 171.

11   Green 1974; Thompson 1983.

12   Wellings and others 1994; Stanley 1995; Cameron 2002; Rouse 2002.

13   Laumann and Michael 2001, page 445.

14   Wiederman 1997 claims that sex differences are shrinking among people aged under 40. However all recent surveys continue to show that men are much more likely than women to have affairs.

15   Lafayette De Mente 2006

16   Liu and others 1997.

17   Kontula and Haavio-Mannila 1995, page 112; Haavio-Mannila and others 2000; Zetterburg 2002.

18   However one Swedish sex survey found that people did not differentiate between affairs involving only one, or two, married people, regarding them as equally improper (Zetterberg 2002, page 122).

19   Halper's interviews with over 4000 business executives in the USA found that almost all of them had affairs, but only 3% of those who left their wives did so for their mistresses. Most chose a fresh start. Similarly Lawson (1988, page 287) reports that in Britain less than 10% of those who divorced as a result of an affair married their lover.

20   For example Helen Gurley-Brown 1962; Ron Louis and David Copeland 1998, 2000; Sherman and Tocantins 2004.

21   Brame 2001.

Notes

22   Johnson and others 2001; Copas and others 2002.

23   Kelly 2008.

24   Perel 2007, pages 73-74.

25   A study of 62 societies around the world found that the peak divorce period is 2-4 years after marriage, typically after the first child is born. See Fisher, 1992.

26   A Swedish study noted that even in the 1960s, at least 90% of heterosexual activity was purely recreational, with no interest in reproduction, yet sexual morality focused exclusively on sex for procreation within marriage (Zetterberg 2002, page 78).

27   Western European culture also offers love as the rational for sex. In practice, love as a precondition for sex is just a modern formulation of the moral rules centred on procreation, which require a long-term committed relationship for sexual relations, to safeguard the nurture of any children that ensue. The ambiguous meaning of love also allows it to be the justification for sexual relations pursued purely for pleasure and personal gratification, including affairs.

28   Zetterberg 2002. In France, Elizabeth Badinter notes that Christianity demonised both sex and money, so that prostitution became a double victim of morals. 'In the double lineage of Christianity and Marxism, money is the expression of corruption and the means for the brutal domination of one person by another.' Badinter (2003, page 66)

29   In some societies, it would be inconceivable for a married woman to go out for a meal with another man, or to dance with another man, or even to dance at all in public. In other cultures, wives and husbands readily swap partners at public dances. Cultures differ in what activities are regarded as so erotic they must remain private, or sexy but nonetheless sociable. A Swedish sex survey which asked for views on infidelity also asked whether people could imagine going out dancing with someone other than their spouse, and whether they could accept their spouse going out dancing with another partner (Zetterberg 2002, page 274). The advent of modern contraception laid the ground for an explosion of sexual activity that includes increasing diversity and variation, as well as greater frequency, within both commercial sex and private sexual activities. For example, in the past, anal intercourse remained such a rare minority practice that sex surveys never asked about it (apart from Kinsey, who assumed everyone did everything). Sex surveys in all countries now report a steady increase in the proportion of men and women who choose it, occasionally or regularly, and women who sell sex are now expected to offer it routinely as an option instead of it being a specialist service, priced accordingly, as noted by Belle de Jour, 2005. Today, there is greater scope for spouses and partners to find that their sexual tastes differ, or have diverged over time, so that one partner might pursue their preferences outside the primary relationship, as illustrated by Max Mosley, the President of the Formula One Association, who engaged very discreetly in BDSM sex parties outside his marriage.

30   Badinter 2003.

31   In some cultures, marriage is a contract of variable length anyway. For example, Floor (2008) describes the Persian tradition of the *seegheh*, a wife with a fixed-term contract. This temporary marriage can be set at any length from 24 hours to several years. Customarily, the *seegheh* receives some money to formalise the arrangement, or financial maintenance from her husband, and any children born of the union are of course legitimate. The tradition was revived after the eight year Iran-Iraq war, when many young widows had little chance of remarriage due to the large numbers of young men killed in the war, yet still had sexual and social needs. Given that the average duration of first marriages (supposedly 'permanent') in Britain is around five years, and that around half of first marriages end in divorce in the USA, the fixed-term contract marriage is in practice not dissimilar to modern marriages in duration, but with explicitly negotiated terms and conditions. However the *seegheh* marriage contract appears to be unique to Iran.

32   Nye 1999, page 105.

33   Giovanni 2009.

34   Nye, 1999, page 104; Spira and Bajos, 1993, pages 157-8; Kontula and Haavio-Mannila, 1995, pages 106-7, 171.

35   Jones 2009.

36   Wolfe 1975; Lawson 1988; Griffin 1999; Praver 2006; Arndt 2009

36a   A study by Michael Weiderman (1997) based on the 1994 USA General Social Survey data points out that spouses were not differentiated from other 'regular sex partners' in the data, making it impossible to identify

Notes

celibate marriages and affairs rigorously.

37 Wellings and others 1994, Table 3.5, page 109.

38 Wellings and others 1994, pages 143-5 and Figure 4.1, page 138.

39 Donnelly 1993.

40 Vaccaro 2003.

41 Malo de Molina 1992, page 72.

42 Baumeister, Catanese and Vohs 2001.

43 In Britain, for example, around half of all men accept casual sex, whereas almost all women reject flings as wrong (Wellings and others 1994, page 251). Sex differences in attitudes are also striking in the USA (Laumann and others 1994, page 547).

43a Richters and Rissel 2005, page 15.

44 Kontula and Haavio-Mannila 1995.

44a Buunk 1980.

44b Buunk 1980.

45 Wolfe 1975.

46 Laumann 1994, page 141.

47 Badinter 2003, page 20.

48 Malo de Molina 1992, pages 121-125.

49 Vaccaro, 2003 page 119.

50 Laumann and others 1994, pages 134-141.

51 Twenge and her colleagues (2008) reviewed thirty years of research by psychologists to assess trends in narcissism.

52 Across the EU, young women aged under thirty spend twice as much as men, on average, on clothes and accessories. Obviously, the best dressed spend far more than this. In contrast, young men spend twice as much, on average, on alcohol and tobacco and entertainment. The most socially active will be spending a lot more.

53 Badinter 2003, page 68.

54 The 'principle of least interest' means that men have to offer inducements such as money, entertainment, food, flattery and gifts to persuade a woman into a sexual relationship, conclude Baumeister, Catanese and Vohs (2001, page 270). See also Baumeister and Vohs 2004; Frank 2002, page 185.

55 In *Daring Wives*, Frances Cohen Praver identifies several historical periods and places where men so outnumbered women that wives were able to freely engage in extra-marital affairs; if their existing husband divorced them, they could easily remarry. She says this was the case in Chesapeake, for example, in the early era of America's settlement. However Western literature and films rarely depict libertine wives as successful and happy. And Praver herself, like most other counsellors who write books about wives who have affairs, insists they are essentially unhappy in their marriages and experience emotionally traumatic affairs. See Praver 2006, pages xii, 14.

56 In *Love Online: Emotions on the Internet* Ben-Ze'ev describes people who felt they were so in love with their internet correspondent that they were prepared to marry them despite not yet having met them, and at least one case of an internet libertine who pursued several women romantically, with marriage proposals, despite being already married. Intense online relationships are also described by Monica Whitty, Celia Romm-Livermore and Kristina Setzekom. Constable's study of 'mail-order brides' also reveals several women who felt they had fallen in love after six months' correspondence with their American pen-pal, leading to bitter disillusionment when the prospective fiancé finally came to visit them in China or wherever they lived.

57 It is estimated that half of all HIV infected persons in Britain were heterosexually infected, and that one-quarter are unaware of their infection.

58 Laumann and Michael 2001.

59 Studies of sexless marriages and wives who have affairs reveal an over-representation of husbands in academic jobs. See Wolfe 1975.

60 Self-employed people account for only one-fifth of the male workforce in Britain.

61 Samuel Cameron's analysis of the 1990 British sex survey found that high education and greater wealth increased the chances of having an affair for men, but had no effect for women. People who had affairs

Notes

tend to be sexual experimenters, people with an early sexual debut (in their teens), and people whose work takes them away from home, which creates opportunity. See Cameron 2002. Similar patterns are reported in other studies.

62   Belle De Jour 2005, page 231.

63   This combination of physical and social attractiveness has been labelled 'erotic capitol' by Catherine Hakim 2010, 2011. She shows that it is an important personal asset, for men as well as women, in public life as well as private life. In modern societies, erotic capital has just as large an impact on success as educational qualifications.

64   Todd, Penke, Fasolo and Lenton 2007; Lenton, Fasolo and Todd 2008.

65   A Swedish survey found that men and women who had experienced a divorce are twice as likely to endorse *concealed* affairs. See Zetterberg 2002, page 196.

66   Yoshiwara, to the north of Edo (now Tokyo) was the entertainment and pleasure centre of the city, with restaurants, tea houses, geishas, kabuki theatre, sumo wrestlers, courtesans and prostitutes. It was the centre of the 'floating world' of fleeting pleasures and conspicuous consumption, where the distinctions between classes could be blurred, and a glittering centre of fashion that dictated fashion trends for the rest of Japan. This floating world is depicted in the *ukiyo-e* prints of Utamaru and other artists, showing popular actors and the fabulous costumes of beautiful geishas and courtesans.

67   Audrey Tautou stars in the French film *Hors de Prix (Priceless)* which depicts such a specialised elite mating market in southern France. Wealthy older men and women, typically divorced for many years, hook up with poor, young, attractive men and women who become kept lovers and companions, travelling with their sponsor and enjoying a lavish lifestyle. There are also websites that facilitate more ad hoc link-ups between 'sugar daddies' and young women with high erotic power, as described by Helen Croydon in Sugar Daddy Diaries, 2011. There are equivalent websites for affluent women seeking toyboys.

Further Reading

Ali, Lorraine and Miller, Lisa (2004) 'The secret lives of wives', *Newsweek*, 12 July 2004.

Arndt, Bettina (2009) *The Sex Diaries*, London: Hamlyn.

Atkins, David C, Baucom D H and Jacobson N S (2001) 'Understanding infidelity: correlates in a national random sample', *Journal of Family Psychology*, 15: 735-749.

Badinter, E (2003/2006) *Dead-End Feminism (Fausse Route)*, Cambridge: Polity Press.

Barnes, H Cameron (2005) *Affair! How to Have Your Cake and Eat It*, London: Metro.

Barry K L (1984) *Female Sexual Slavery*, New York: New York University Press.

Barry K L (1995) *Prostitution of Sexuality*, New York: New York University Press.

Baumeister R F and Twenge J M (2002) 'Cultural suppression of female sexuality', *Review of General Psychology*, 6: 166-203.

Baumaister R F and Vohs K D (2004) 'Sexual economics', *Personality and Social Psychology Review*, 8: 339-363.

Baumeister R F, Catanese K R and Vohs K D (2001) 'Is there a gender difference in strength of sex drive? Theoretical views, conceptual distinctions, and a review of relevant evidence', *Personality and Social Psychology Review*, 5: 242-273.

Belle de Jour (2007) *The Intimate Adventures of a London Call Girl*, London: Phoenix.

Ben-Ze'ev Aharon (2004) *Love Online: Emotions on the Internet*, Cambridge: Cambridge University Press.

Blanchflower David and Oswald Andrew, 'Money, sex and happiness', *Scandinavian Journal of Economics*, 2004, vol 106(3), pages 393-415.

Brame Gloria (2001) *Come Hither! A Commonsense Guide to Kinky Sex*, London: Fusion Press.

Brandon, Mark (2008) *Swinging: Games Your Neighbours Play*, London: HarperCollins Friday Books.

Brownmiller S (1977) *Against Our Will: Men, Women and Rape*, Harmondsworth: Penguin.

Buunk B (1980) 'Extramarital sex in the Netherlands: motivations in social and marital context', *Alternative Lifestyles*, 3: 11-39.

Cameron S (2002) 'The economics of partner out trading in sexual markets', *Journal of Bioeconomics*, 4: 195-222.

Chadwick B A and Heaton T B (eds) (1999) *Statistical Handbook on the American Family*, 2nd ed., Phoenix Arizona: Oryx Press.

Chancer L S (1998) *Reconcilable differences: Confronting Beauty, Pornography and the Future of Feminism*, Berkeley CA: University of California Press.

Cole, Julia (1999) *After the affair: How to build trust and love again*, London: Vermilion.

Copas A J et al (2002)'The accuracy of reported sensitive sexual behaviour in Britain: exploring the extent of change 1990-2000. *Sexually Transmitted Infections*, 78 (1): 26-30.

Croydon H (2011) *Sugar Daddy Diaries*, London: Mainstream.

Davis J A and Smith T W (1996) *General Social Surveys 1972-1996: Cumulative Codebook*, Chicago:National Opinion Research Centre.

Donnelly D A (1993) 'Sexually inactive marriages', *The Journal of Sex Research*, 30(2): 171-9.

Druckerman P (2007) *Lust in Translation: The Rules of Infidelity from Tokyo to Tennessee*, New York: Penguin Press.

Further Reading

Dworkin A (1981) *Pornography: Men Possessing Women*, New York: Perigree Books.

Dworkin A (1987) *Intercourse,* London: Secker & Warburg.

Eder, Franz X, Hall L A and Hekma G (eds) (1999) *Sexual Cultures in Europe*, Manchester: Manchester University Press.

Ehrenreich B and Hochschild A (2004) *Global Women: Nannies, Maids and Sex Workers in the New Economy*, New York: Metropolitan/Owl Books.

Ericksen J A with Steffen S A (1999) *Kiss and Tell: Surveying Sex in the Twentieth Century*, Cambridge MA: Harvard University Press.

Fair Ray (1978) 'A theory of extramarital affairs', *Journal of Political Economy*, 86: 45-61.

Faraone C A and McClure L K (2006) *Prostitutes and Courtesans in the Ancient World*, Madison Wis: University of Wisconsin Press.

Fein, Ellen and Schneider Sherrie (2000) *The Complete Book of Rules: Time-Tested Secrets for Capturing the Heart of Mr Right*, HarperCollins.

Fisher Helen (1992) *Anatomy of Love: The Natural History of Monogamy, Adultery and Divorce*, New York: Collins.

Frank Katherine (2002) *G-Strings and Sympathy: Strip Club Regulars and Male Desire*, Durham NC: Duke University Press.

Franck Michel (2006) *Voyage au Bout du Sexe: Trafics et Tourisme Sexues en Asie et Ailleurs*, Quebec: Presses de l'Universite Laval.

Gagnon J and Simon W (1973) *Sexual Conduct: The Social Sources of Human Sexuality*, Chicago: Aldine.

Giddens A (1991) *Intimacy*, Cambridge: Polity Press.

Giovanni Janine de (2009) 'We will teach you to make love again', *Guardian*, 26 March 2009.

Green B L, Lee R R and Lustig N (1974) 'Conscious and unconscious factors in marital infidelity', *Medical Aspects of Human Sexuality*, pp. 87-105.

Griffin V (1999) *The Mistress: Histories, Myths and Interpretations of the 'Other Woman'*, London: Bloomsbury.

Haavio-Mannila E and Rotkirch A (1997) 'Generational and gender differences in sexual life in St Petersburg and urban Finland, pp.133-60 in *Yearbook of Population Research in Finland*, No. 34, Helsinki: the Population Research Institute.

Haavio-Mannila E and Rotkirch A (2000) 'Gender liberalisation and polarisation: comparing sexuality in St Petersburg, Finland and Sweden, *The Finnish Review of East European Studies*, 3-4: 4-25.

Haavio-Mannila E, Rotkirch A and Kuusi E (2001) *Trends in Sexual Life Measured by National Sex Surveys in Finland in 1971, 1992 and 1999, and a Comparison Sex Survey in St Petersburg in 1996*, Working Paper E10 for the Family Federation of Finland, Helsinki: Population Research Institute.

Haavio-Mannila E, Kontula O and Rotkirch A (2002) *Sexual Lifestyles in the Twentieth Century: A Research Study*, Houndmills: Palgrave Macmillan.

Hakim C (2010) 'Erotic capital', *European Sociological Review*, 26 (5): 499-518.

Hakim C (2011) *Honey Money: The Power of Erotic Capital*, London: Allen Lane.

Halper J (1988) *Quiet Desperation: The Truth About Successful Men*, New York NY: Warner Books.

Jankowiak W R (ed) (2008) *Intimacies: Love and Sex Across Cultures*, New York: Columbia University Press.

Johnson A, Wellings K, Field J and Wadsworth J (1994) *Sexual Attitudes and Lifestyles*, London: Penguin Books.

Johnson A. et al (2001) 'Sexual behaviour in Britain: partnerships, practices, and HIV risk behaviours', *Lancet*, 358: 1835-1842.

Jones, Simon (2009) 'Where did my sex kitten go?', *Sunday Times Magazine* , 15 March 2009.

Jong Erica (1973) *Fear of Flying*, New York: Holt, Reinhart and Winston.

Kakabadse A and and Kakabadse N K (2004) *Intimacy: An International Survey of the Sex Lives of People At Work*, Basingstoke: Palgrave Macmillan.

Kelly I (2008) *Casanova*, London: Hodder & Stoughton.

Kirshenbaum Mira, *When Good People Have Affairs: Inside the Hearts and Minds of People in Two Relationships*, New York: St Martin's Press.

Koktvedgaard Zeitzen M (2008) *Polygamy: A Cross-Cultural Analysis*, Oxford and New York: Berg.

Kontula Osmo and Haavio-Mannila Elina (1995) *Sexual Pleasures: Enhancement of Sex Life in Finland, 1971-1992*, Aldershot: Dartmouth.

Kremer P D (1998) *Should You Leave?*, New York: Gollancz.

Further Reading

Lafayette De Mente B (2006) *Sex and the Japanese*, Tokyo: Tuttle Publishing.

Lampard R (2007) 'Couples' places of meeting in late 20th century Britain', *European Sociological Review*, 23: 351-371.

Langley Michelle (2008) *Women's Infidelity: Living in Limbo and Breaking out of Limbo*, from womensinfidelity.com.

Laumann E O, Gagnon J H, Michael R T and Michaels S (1994) *The Social Organisation of Sexuality: Sexual Practices in the United States*, Chicago: University of Chicago.

Laumann E O and Michael R T (eds) (2001) *Sex, Love, and Health in America: Private Choices and Public Policies*, Chicago: University of Chicago Press.

Lawson A (1988) *Adultery: An Analysis of Love and Betrayal*, Oxford: Basil Blackwell.

Lenton A P, Fasolo B and Todd P M (2008) 'Shopping for a mate: expected versus experienced preferences in online mate choice', *IEEE Transactions on Professional Communication*, 51: 169-182.

Liu Dalin, Ng Man Lun, Zhou Li Ping and Haeberle E J (1997) *Sexual Behaviour in Modern China: Report on the Nationwide Survey of 20,000 Men and Women*, New York: Continuum.

Louis R and Copeland D (1998) *How to Succeed with Women*, Prentice-Hall.

Louis R and Copeland D (2000) *How to Succeed with Men*, Prentice-Hall.

Malo de Molina C A (1992) *Los Espanoles y la Sexualidad*, Madrid: Temas de Hoy.

MacKinnon C A (1981) 'Sex and violence', in *Feminism Unmodified*, Cambridge MA: Harvard University Press.

Maykovich M K (1976) 'Attitudes versus behaviour in extramarital sexual relations', *Journal of Marriage and the Family*, 38: 693-699.

Mercurio Jed (2008) *American Adulterer*, London: Jonathan Cape.

Michaels S and Giami A (1999) 'Review: sexual acts and sexual relationships: asking about sex in surveys', *Public Opinion Quarterly*, 63(3): 401-420.

Millet C (2001/2002) *The Sexual Life of Catherine M (La Vie Sexuelle de Catherine M)*, trans. by A Hunter, London: Serpent's Tail.

Mossuz-Lavau J (2002) *La Vie Sexuelle en France*, Paris: Editions La Martiniere.

Mullan B (1984) *The Mating Trade*, London: Routledge.

Muller, Charla (2009) *365 Days: A Memoir of Intimacy*, London: John Blake.

Murdoch G P (1949) *Social Structure*, New York.

Nelson N (1987) 'Selling her kiosk: Kikuyu notions of sexuality and sex for sale in Mathare Valley, Kenya', pages 217-219 in *The Cultural Construction of Sexuality* (ed) P Caplan, London: Routledge.

Neubeck G (ed) (1969) *Extramarital Relations*, Englewood Cliffs NJ: Prentice-Hall.

Nye R A (1999) 'Sex and sexuality in France since 1800', pages 91-113 in *Sexual Cultures in Europe* (eds) F X Eder, L A Hall and G Hekma, Manchester: Manchester University Press.

Pateman Carole (1988) *The Sexual Contract*, Cambridge: Polity Press.

Perel Esther (2007) *Mating in Captivity: Reconciling the Erotic and the Domestic*. London: Hodder & Stoughton.

Posner R A (1992) *Sex and Reason*, Cambridge Mass.: Harvard University Press.

Praver F C (2006) *Daring Wives: Insights into Women's Desires for Extramarital Affairs*, Westport CT and London: Praeger.

Raboch J and Raboch J (1989) 'Changes in the premarital and marital sexual life of Czechoslovak women born between 1911 and 1970', *Journal of Sex and Marital Therapy*, 15: 207-214.

Richters J and Rissel C (2005) *Doing It Down Under: the Sexual Lives of Australians*, Sydney: Allen & Unwin.

Romm-Livermore, Celia and Setzekom, Kristina (eds) (2009) *Social Networking Communities and E-Dating Services: Concepts and Implications*, Hershey PA: Information Science Reference.

Rouse L (2002) *Marital and Sexual Lifestyles in the United States: Attitudes, Behaviours, and Relationships in Social Context*, New York: Haworth Clinical Practice Press.

Saxena S, Carlson D, Billington R, and Orley J (2001) 'The WHO quality of life assessment instrument (WHOQOL-Bref): the importance of its items for cross-cultural research', *Quality of Life Research*, 10: 711-721.

Schnarch David (1998) *Passionate Marriage: Keeping Love and Intimacy Alive in Committed Relationships*. Holt.

Sherman A J and Tocantins N (2004) *The Happy Hook-Up: A Single Girl's Guide to Casual Sex*, Ten Speed Press.

Shrage Laurie (1994) *Moral Dilemmas of Feminism: Prostitution, Adultery and Abortion*, New York: Routledge.

Simon P, Gondonneau J, Mironer L and Dourlen-Rollier A M (1972) *Rapport sur le Comportement Sexuel des Francais*,

Further Reading

Paris: Julliard.

Smith D J (2008) 'Intimacy, infidelity, and masculinity in Southeastern Nigeria', pages 224-244 in *Intimacies* (ed) W R Jankowiak, New York: Columbia University Press.

Spira A and Bajos N (1993) *Les Comportements Sexuels en France*, Paris: La Documentation Francaise.

Staheli L (2007) *Affair-Proof your Marriage: Understanding, Preventing and Surviving an Affair*, New York: HarperCollins.

Stanley L (1995) *Sex Surveyed 1949-1994*, London: Taylor & Francis.

Summerton C (2008) *The Profession of Pleasure*, London: Robert Hale books.

Symonds, Sarah J (2007). *Having an Affair? A Handbook for the Other Woman*, New York: Red brick Press.

Thomas S (2006) *Millions of Women are Waiting to Meet You*, London: Bloomsbury.

Thompson A P (1983) 'Extramarital sex: a review of the research literature', *Journal of Sex Research*, 19: 1-22.

Thorbek S and Pattanaik B (ed) (2002) *Transnational Prostitution: Changing Global Patterns*, London: Zed Books.

Todd P M, Penke L, Fasolo B and Lenton A P (2007) 'Different cognitive processes underlie human mate choices and mate preferences', *Proceedings of the National Academy of Sciences*, 104, No. 38: 15011-15016.

Twenge, J M and others (2008) 'Egos inflating over time: a cross-temporal meta-analysis of the narcissistic personality' *Journal of Personality*, vol 76(4), 875-902.

Vaccaro C M (ed) (2003) *I Comportamenti Sessuale degli Italiani: Falsi Miti e Nuove Normalita*, Milan: FrancoAngeli for Fondazione Pfizer.

Vaillant M (2009) *Les Hommes, L'Amour, La Fidelite*, Paris: Albin Michel.

Widmer E R, Treas J and Newcomb R (1998) 'Attitudes to non-marital sex in 24 countries', 349-58.

Weiderman Michael W (1997) 'Extramarital sex: Prevalence and correlates in a national survey', *Journal of Sex Research*, 34: 167-174.

Weiderman M W and Allgeier E R (1996) 'Expectations and attributions regarding extramarital sex among young married individuals', *Journal of Psychology and Human Sexuality*, 8(3): 21-23.

Weiner-Davis M (2003) *The Sex-Starved Marriage*, London: Simon & Schuster.

Wellings K, Field J, Johnson A and Wadsworth J (1994) *Sexual Behaviour in Britain: A National Survey of Sexual Attitudes and Lifestyles*, London: Penguin Books.

West R (2007) *Marriage, Sexuality, and Gender*, Boulder CO: Paradigm Publishers.

Whitty Monica and Carr A N (2006) *Cyberspace Romance: The Psychology of Online Relationships*, Basingstoke: Palgrave Macmillan.

Whitty M T, Baker A J and Inman J A (2007) *Online Matchmaking*, Basingstoke: Palgrave Macmillan.

Widmer E D, Treas J and Newcomb R (1998), 'Attitudes toward nonmarital sex in 24 countries', *The Journal of Sex Research*, 35: 349-358.

Wolfe Linda (1975) *Playing Around: Women and Extramarital Sex*, New York: William Morrow.

Zelizer Viviana A (2005) *The Purchase of Intimacy*, Princeton: Princeton University Press.

Zetterberg Hans L (2002) *Sexual Life in Sweden*, translated by Graham Fennell, New Brunswick NJ: Transaction Publishers.

Index

Index